the ubiquity of the dragnet—and the near impossibility of evading it. I'll never use Google in the same way again."

—Gretchen Rubin, bestselling author of
Happier at Home and *The Happiness Project*

"Julia Angwin's pathbreaking reporting for *The Wall Street Journal* about online tracking changed the privacy debate. Her new book represents another leap forward: by showing how difficult it was to protect her own privacy and vividly describing the social and personal costs, Angwin offers both a wake-up call and a thoughtful manifesto for reform. This is a meticulously documented and gripping narrative about why privacy matters and what we can do about it."

—Jeffrey Rosen, president and CEO, National Constitution Center,
and author of *The Unwanted Gaze* and *The Naked Crowd*

"*Dragnet Nation* is an impressive picture of the new world of electronic surveillance—from Google to the NSA. Julia Angwin's command of the technology is sure, her writing is clear, and her arguments are compelling. This is an authoritative account of why we should care about privacy and how we can protect ourselves."

—Bruce Schneier, author of *Liars and Outliers:*
Enabling the Trust That Society Needs to Thrive

"*Dragnet Nation* is a fascinating, compelling, and powerful read. Many of us would simply prefer not to know how much others know about us, and yet Julia Angwin opens a door onto that dark world in a way that both raises a new set of public issues and canvasses a range of solutions. We can reclaim our privacy while still enjoying the benefits of many types of surveillance—but only if we take our heads out of the sand and read this book." —Anne-Marie Slaughter, president
and CEO of New America

DRAGNET
NATION

DRAGNET NATION

A QUEST FOR PRIVACY, SECURITY, AND FREEDOM IN A WORLD OF RELENTLESS SURVEILLANCE

JULIA ANGWIN

ST. MARTIN'S GRIFFIN   NEW YORK

DRAGNET NATION. Copyright © 2014, 2015 by Julia Angwin. All rights reserved. Printed in the United States of America. For information, address St. Martin's Press, 175 Fifth Avenue, New York, N.Y. 10010.

www.stmartins.com

Designed by Meryl Sussman Levavi

The Library of Congress has cataloged the Times Books edition as follows:

Angwin, Julia.
    Dragnet nation : a quest for privacy, security, and freedom in a world of relentless surveillance / Julia Angwin. — First edition.
        p. cm.
    Includes bibliographical references and index.
    ISBN 978-0-8050-9807-5 (hardcover)
    ISBN 978-0-8050-9808-2 (e-book)
    1. Privacy, Right of.   2. Electronic surveillance.   3. National security—Moral and ethical aspects.   4. Information technology—Moral and ethical aspects.   5. Civil rights.   I. Title.
    JC596.A54 2014
    323.44'8—dc23

                                                                              2013042041

ISBN 978-1-250-06086-0 (trade paperback)

St. Martin's Griffin books may be purchased for educational, business, or promotional use. For information on bulk purchases, please contact the Macmillan Corporate and Premium Sales Department at 1-800-221-7945, extension 5442, or write to specialmarkets@macmillan.com.

First published by Times Books, an imprint of Henry Holt and Company, LLC

First St. Martin's Griffin Edition: February 2015

10   9   8   7   6   5   4   3   2   1

For my children

CONTENTS

DRAGNET
NATION

1

HACKED

Who is watching you?

This was once a question asked only by kings, presidents, and public figures trying to dodge the paparazzi and criminals trying to evade the law. The rest of us had few occasions to worry about being tracked.

But today the anxious question—"who's watching?"—is relevant to everyone regardless of his or her fame or criminal persuasion. Any of us can be watched at almost any time, whether it is by a Google Street View car taking a picture of our house, or an advertiser following us as we browse the Web, or the National Security Agency logging our phone calls.

Dragnets that scoop up information indiscriminately about everyone in their path used to be rare; police had to set up roadblocks, or retailers had to install and monitor video cameras. But technology has enabled a new era of supercharged dragnets that can gather vast amounts of personal data with little human effort. These dragnets are extending into ever more private corners of the world.

Consider the relationship of Sharon Gill and Bilal Ahmed, close friends who met on a private online social network called PatientsLikeMe.com.

Sharon and Bilal couldn't be more different. Sharon is a forty-two-year-old single mother who lives in a small town in southern Arkansas. She ekes out a living trolling for treasures at yard sales and selling them at a flea market. Bilal Ahmed, thirty-six years old, is a single, Rutgers-educated man who lives in a penthouse in Sydney, Australia. He runs a chain of convenience stores.

Although they have never met in person, they became close friends on a password-protected online forum for patients struggling with mental health issues. Sharon was trying to wean herself from antidepressant medications. Bilal had just lost his mother and was suffering from anxiety and depression.

From their far corners of the world, they were able to cheer each other up in their darkest hours. Sharon turned to Bilal because she felt she couldn't confide in her closest relatives and neighbors. "I live in a small town," Sharon told me. "I don't want to be judged on this mental illness."

But in 2010, Sharon and Bilal were horrified to discover they were being watched on their private social network.

It started with a break-in. On May 7, 2010, PatientsLikeMe noticed unusual activity on the "mood" forum where Sharon and Bilal hung out. A new member of the site, using sophisticated software, was attempting to "scrape," or copy, every single message off PatientsLikeMe's private online "Mood" and "Multiple Sclerosis" forums.

PatientsLikeMe managed to block and identify the intruder: it was the Nielsen Company, the New York media-research firm. Nielsen monitors online "buzz" for its clients, including major drug makers. On May 18, PatientsLikeMe sent a cease-and-desist letter to Nielsen and notified its members of the break-in. (Nielsen later said it would no longer break into private forums. "It's something that we decided is not acceptable," said Dave Hudson, the head of the Nielsen unit involved.)

But there was a twist. PatientsLikeMe used the opportunity to inform members of the fine print they may not have noticed when they signed up. The website was also selling data about its members to pharmaceutical and other companies.

The news was a double betrayal for Sharon and Bilal. Not only had an intruder been monitoring them, but so was the very place that they considered to be a safe space. It was as if someone filmed an Alcoholics Anonymous meeting and AA was mad because that film competed with its own business of videotaping meetings and selling the tapes. "I felt totally violated," Bilal said.

Even worse, none of it was necessarily illegal. Nielsen was operating in a gray area of the law even as it violated the terms of service at Patients-LikeMe, but those terms are not always legally enforceable. And it was entirely legal for PatientsLikeMe to disclose to its members in its fine print that it would sweep up all their information and sell it.

This is the tragic flaw of "privacy" in the digital age. Privacy is often defined as freedom from unauthorized intrusion. But many of the things that *feel* like privacy violations are "authorized" in some fine print somewhere.

And yet, in many ways, we have not yet fully consented to these authorized intrusions. Even if it is legal for companies to scoop up information about people's mental health, is it socially acceptable?

Eavesdropping on Sharon and Bilal's conversations might be socially acceptable if they were drug dealers under court-approved surveillance. But is sweeping up their conversations as part of a huge dragnet to monitor online "buzz" socially acceptable?

Dragnets that indiscriminately sweep up personal data fall squarely into the gray area between what is legal and what is socially acceptable.

✦

We are living in a Dragnet Nation—a world of indiscriminate tracking where institutions are stockpiling data about individuals at an unprecedented pace. The rise of indiscriminate tracking is powered by the same forces that have brought us the technology we love so much—powerful computing on our desktops, laptops, tablets, and smartphones.

Before computers were commonplace, it was expensive and difficult to track individuals. Governments kept records only of occasions, such as birth, marriage, property ownership, and death. Companies kept records when a customer bought something and filled out a warranty card or joined a loyalty club. But technology has made it cheap and easy for institutions of all kinds to keep records about almost every moment of our lives.

Consider just a few facts that have enabled the transformation. Computer processing power has doubled roughly every two years since the 1970s, enabling computers that were once the size of entire rooms to fit into a pants pocket. And recently, the cost to store data has plummeted from $18.95 for one gigabyte in 2005 to $1.68 in 2012. It is expected to cost under a dollar in a few years.

The combination of massive computing power, smaller and smaller devices, and cheap storage has enabled a huge increase in indiscriminate tracking of personal data. The trackers are not all intruders, like Nielsen. The trackers also include many of the institutions that are supposed to be on our side, such as the government and the companies with which we do business.

Of course, the largest of the dragnets appear to be those operated by the U.S. government. In addition to its scooping up vast amounts of foreign communications, the National Security Agency is also scooping up Americans' phone calling records and Internet traffic, according to documents revealed in 2013 by the former NSA contractor Edward Snowden.

But the NSA is not alone (although it may be the most effective) in operating dragnets. Governments around the world—from Afghanistan to Zimbabwe—are snapping up surveillance technology, ranging from "massive intercept" equipment to tools that let them remotely hack into people's phones and computers. Even local and state governments in the United States are snapping up surveillance technology ranging from drones to automated license plate readers that allow them to keep tabs on citizens' movements in ways never before possible. Local police are increasingly tracking people using signals emitted by their cell phones.

Meanwhile, commercial dragnets are blossoming. AT&T and Verizon are selling information about the location of their cell phone customers, albeit without identifying them by name. Mall owners have started using technology to track shoppers based on the signals emitted by the cell phones in their pockets. Retailers such as Whole Foods have used digital signs that are actually facial recognition scanners. Some car dealerships are using a service from Dataium that lets them know which cars you have browsed online, if you have given them your e-mail address, before you arrive on the dealership lot.

Online, hundreds of advertisers and data brokers are watching as you browse the Web. Looking up "blood sugar" could tag you as a possible diabetic by companies that profile people based on their medical condition and then provide drug companies and insurers access to that information. Searching for a bra could trigger an instant bidding war among lingerie advertisers at one of the many online auction houses.

And new tracking technologies are just around the corner: companies are building facial recognition technology into phones and cameras, technology to monitor your location is being embedded into vehicles, wireless "smart" meters that gauge the power usage of your home are being developed, and Google has developed Glass, tiny cameras embedded in eyeglasses that allow people to take photos and videos without lifting a finger.

✦

Skeptics say: What's wrong with all of our data being collected by unseen watchers? Who is being harmed?

Admittedly, it can be difficult to demonstrate personal harm from a data breach. If Sharon or Bilal is denied a job or insurance, they may never know which piece of data caused the denial. People placed on the no-fly list are never informed about the data that contributed to the decision.

But, on a larger scale, the answer is simple: troves of personal data can and will be abused.

Consider one of the oldest and supposedly innocuous dragnets of all: the U.S. Census. The confidentiality of personal information collected by the census is protected by law, and yet census data have been repeatedly abused. During World War I, it was used to locate draft violators. During World War II, the Census Bureau provided the names and addresses of Japanese-American residents to the U.S. Secret Service. The information was used to round up Japanese residents and place them in internment camps. It was not until 2000 that the Census Bureau issued a formal apology for its behavior. And in 2002 and 2003, the Census Bureau provided statistical information about Arab-Americans to the Department of Homeland Security. After bad publicity, it revised its policies to require that top officials approve requests from other agencies for sensitive information such as race, ethnicity, religion, political affiliation, and sexual orientation.

The United States is not alone in abusing population statistics. Australia used population registration data to force the migration of aboriginal people at the turn of the twentieth century. In South Africa, the census was a key instrument of the state's "apartheid" system of racial segregation. During the Rwandan genocide of 1994, Tutsi victims were targeted with the help of ID cards that indicated their ethnicity. During the Holocaust, France, Poland, the Netherlands, Norway, and Germany used population data to locate Jews for extermination.

Personal data are often abused for political reasons. One of the most infamous cases was a program called COINTELPRO run by the Federal Bureau of Investigation in the late 1960s. The FBI's director, J. Edgar Hoover, set up the secret program to spy on "subversives" and then used the information to try to discredit and demoralize them. The FBI went as far as to send Martin Luther King Jr. a tape recording from surveillance of his hotel room that was meant to cause King to get separated from his wife—along with a note that King interpreted as a threat to release the recording unless King committed suicide.

Criminal hackers have also found that using personal data is the best way to breach an institution's defenses. Consider how Chinese hackers penetrated the sophisticated computer security pioneer RSA. The hackers trolled social media websites to obtain information about individual employees. They then sent those employees an e-mail titled "2011 Recruitment Plan." The e-mail looked legitimate enough that one employee retrieved it from the junk mail folder and opened it. That file installed spyware on the individual's machine, and from there the attackers gained remote control of multiple computers in the organization.

In short, they hacked people, not institutions.

Hacking people is not just for criminals. Marketers are following us around the Web in the hopes that they can obtain information that will let them "hack" us into buying their products. The NSA is scooping up all of our phone calls to establish patterns that it believes will let authorities "hack" a terrorist cell.

Here are some of the ways you may be already being hacked:

- You can always be found.
- You can be watched in your own home—or in the bathroom.
- You can no longer keep a secret.
- You can be impersonated.
- You can be trapped in a "hall of mirrors."
- You can be financially manipulated.
- You can be placed in a police lineup.

This is not a comprehensive list. Rather, it is a snapshot in time of real-life events that are happening right now. In the future, we will likely read this list and laugh at all the things I failed to envision.

YOU CAN ALWAYS BE FOUND.

Your name, address, and other identifying details—even the location of your cell phone at any given time—are all stored in various databases that you cannot view or control. Stalkers and rogue employees have consistently found ways to abuse these databases.

In 1999, a deranged man named Liam Youens paid an online data broker called Docusearch to find the social security number, employment information, and home address of a woman he was obsessed with, Amy Boyer. A few days later, Youens drove to Boyer's workplace and fatally shot her as she left work. He then shot and killed himself.

Boyer's family sued the data broker, but the New Hampshire Supreme Court held that while the data broker had a duty to "exercise reasonable care" when selling personal data, it was also true that because information such as a work address "is readily observable by members of the public, the address cannot be private."

Boyer's parents got very little: in 2004, they settled with Docusearch for $85,000, having grown weary of years of legal battles. Docusearch is still in business and its website still advertises services including "reverse phone number search," "license plate # search," "find SSN by name," and "hidden bank account search."

Since then, the price of buying people's addresses has fallen from the nearly $200 that Youens paid to as low as 95 cents for a full report on an individual. Cyber-stalking cases have become so common that they rarely make news.

Consider just one example. In 2010, a Sacramento sheriff's deputy, Chu Vue, was convicted of murder after his brothers shot to death Steve Lo, who was having an affair with Vue's wife. During the trial it came out that Vue had searched law enforcement databases for Lo's name, had asked a colleague to look up Lo's license plate, and had searched for Lo's address using an online phone lookup service. Vue was sentenced to life without parole.

Even the most innocent data—such as airline travel records—can be abused. In 2007, a Commerce Department employee, Benjamin Robinson, was indicted for unlawfully accessing, more than 163 times, the government database that contains international airline travel reservation records. After a breakup with a woman, he accessed her files, as well as those of her young son and husband. He left a message on her answering machine stating that he was going to check the files "to see if there is anything you lied about." He suggested that he might be able to get her deported. In 2009, Robinson pleaded guilty to unlawfully obtaining information from a protected computer, and he was sentenced to three years' probation.

And the day is not far off when real-time tracking will become routine. The United States already embeds radio-frequency identification (RFID) chips that can transmit data over a short range of about ten feet in passports, and schools and employers are starting to embed the chips in ID cards. In 2013, a federal judge in Texas denied a student's challenge to her school's requirement that she wear an RFID-enabled ID card. Some employers have even flirted with the idea of implanting the chips under their employees' skin, which prompted California to outlaw the practice in 2008.

Cell phone tracking has already become routine for police departments. In 2011, my colleague at the *Wall Street Journal* Scott Thurm and I submitted open records requests to the twenty largest state and local police departments in the United States. Eight agencies produced at least summary statistics suggesting that state and local agencies track thousands of cell phones in real time each year. It is as routine as "looking for fingerprint evidence or DNA evidence," said Gregg Rossman, a prosecutor in Broward County, Florida.

Inevitably, phone companies have started selling cell phone location data to a wider audience than just police. In 2013, Verizon said it would sell a new product called Precision Market Insights that would let businesses track cell phone users in particular locations.

One of Verizon's first customers is the Phoenix Suns basketball team, which wants to know where its fans live. Scott Horowitz, a team vice president, said: "This is the information that everyone has wanted that hasn't been available until now."

YOU CAN BE WATCHED IN YOUR OWN HOME—OR IN THE BATHROOM.

In 2009, fifteen-year-old high school student Blake Robbins was confronted by an assistant principal who claimed she had evidence that he was engaging in "improper behavior in his home." It turned out that his school—Harriton High School, in an affluent suburban Philadelphia school district—had installed spying software on the Apple MacBook laptops that it issued to the school's twenty-three hundred students. The school's technicians had activated software on some of the laptops that could snap photos using the webcam, as well as take screen shots of the students' computers. Blake's webcam captured him holding pill-shaped objects. Blake and his family said they were Mike and Ike candies. The assistant principal believed they were drugs.

Blake's family sued the district for violating their son's privacy. The school said the software had been installed to allow technicians to locate the computers in case of theft. However, the school did not notify students of the software's existence, nor did it set up guidelines for when the technical staff could operate the cameras.

An internal investigation revealed that the cameras had been activated on more than forty laptops and captured more than sixty-five thousand images. Some students were photographed thousands of times, including when they were partially undressed and sleeping. A former student, Joshua Levin, said he was "shocked, humiliated, and severely emotionally distressed" when he viewed some of the eight thousand photos and screen shots captured by the camera on his laptop. Levin, Robbins, and one other student sued the school and won monetary settlements. The school board banned the school's use of cameras to surveil students.

We're used to the idea that surveillance cameras are everywhere. It is estimated that there are more than four thousand surveillance cameras installed in lower Manhattan. London is famous for its more than five hundred thousand security cameras.

But as the cameras are getting smaller, they are traveling into our homes and intimate spaces, upending our definitions of public and private. Drones equipped with cameras have become cheap enough that they are becoming a nuisance. In May 2013, a Seattle woman complained on a local blog. A stranger had "set an aerial drone into flight over my yard and beside my house. . . . I initially mistook its noisy buzzing for a weed-whacker on this warm spring day." Her husband approached the man flying the drone, who declared that it was legal for him to fly it and that the drone was equipped with cameras. "We are extremely concerned, as he could very easily be a criminal who plans to break into our house or a peeping-tom," she said.

With all this cool technology, the bad guys are of course setting up their own camera dragnets. In 2013, the journalist Nate Anderson described a robust hacker community that trades tips and techniques for installing spyware on women's webcams. "They operate quite openly online, sharing the best techniques," he wrote. "Calling most of these guys 'hackers' does a real disservice to hackers everywhere; only minimal technical skill is now required."

In 2011, a Santa Ana man named Luis Mijangos was convicted of computer hacking and wiretapping after he was found to have installed malicious software that allowed him to control the webcams of more than one hundred computers. In one case, he gained control of a teenage girl's webcam and obtained naked photographs of her. He used the images to extort further nude images from his victims. During the sentencing, the judge said, "This was nothing short of a sustained effort to terrorize victims." Mijangos was sentenced to six years in prison.

And widespread camera dragnets are right around the corner. The arrival of wearable computers equipped with cameras, such as Google Glass, means that everything is fair game for filming. The *New York Times* columnist Nick Bilton was shocked when he attended a Google conference and saw attendees wearing their Google Glass cameras while using the urinals.

But Google Glass enthusiasts say that wearing cameras on their heads changes their life. "I will never live a day of my life from now on without it (or a competitor)," wrote the blogger Robert Scoble after trying out the glasses for two weeks. "It freaks some people out," he conceded, but he said, "It's new, that will go away once they are in the market."

YOU CAN NO LONGER KEEP A SECRET.

Bobbi Duncan, a twenty-two-year-old lesbian student at the University of Texas, Austin, tried to keep her sexual orientation secret from her family. But Facebook inadvertently outed her when the president of the Queer Chorus on campus added her to the choir's Facebook discussion group. Bobbi didn't know that a friend could add her to a group without her approval and that Facebook would then send a note to her entire list of friends—including her father—announcing that she'd joined.

Two days after receiving the notification that Bobbi had joined the

Queer Chorus, her father wrote on his Facebook page: "To all you queers. Go back to your holes and wait for GOD. Hell awaits you pervert. Good luck singing there."

When informed about the case, Facebook spokesman Andrew Noyes said that the "unfortunate experience reminds us that we must continue our work to empower and educate users about our robust privacy controls." His position seemed to put the blame on the victim for incorrectly flipping Facebook's dials and levers. But there was no dial or lever on Facebook that Bobbi could have set to prevent her being joined to the group without her permission.

"I blame Facebook," Bobbi said. "It shouldn't be somebody else's choice what people see of me."

As more personal data are swept up into various databases, it has become harder for any secrets to be kept—even by professional secret keepers. The most notable example is CIA director David Petraeus, who resigned after an unrelated FBI investigation uncovered e-mails that indicated he was conducting an extramarital affair. In 2012, former CIA analyst John Kiriakou was indicted for passing classified information to journalists, based in part on e-mail evidence. He pleaded guilty and was sentenced to thirty months in prison.

Even minor secrets are difficult to keep. People who download porn movies on their computers have been targeted by so-called copyright trolls who file mass lawsuits that allow them to obtain information about the identities of people who have downloaded copyrighted porn movies from file-sharing networks, with the intent of embarrassing the defendants into paying a quick settlement.

In July 2012, the U.S. Court of Appeals for the Fifth Circuit sanctioned one such plaintiff, an attorney for an adult movie producer, who had sued 670 downloaders based on their computer addresses and sought to obtain their identities without court approval. The court described the attorney's "violations as an attempt to repeat his strategy of suing anonymous Internet users for allegedly downloading pornography illegally, using the powers of the court to find their identity, then shaming or intimidating them into settling for thousands of dollars."

In May 2013, a California judge went even further, declaring that the copyright trolls had used a "nexus of antiquated copyright laws, paralyzing social stigma and unaffordable defense costs" to "plunder the citizenry."

YOU CAN BE IMPERSONATED.

Jaleesa Suell was taken away from her mother and placed in foster care when she was eight years old. She was placed in seven different foster homes before leaving the foster care system. When she turned twenty-one and was nearing graduation from George Washington University, she applied for a credit card. That's when she found out that a family member had stolen her identity, opened up a credit card in her name, and defaulted on the payments.

Without access to credit, Jaleesa couldn't get a car and worried she wouldn't be able to get an apartment after graduation. "I often find myself worried about if I was going to have a place to live the next day or have food, and I've worked so hard to ensure that that won't happen after, you know, I emancipated," she told participants in a workshop on identity theft in 2011. "But now I find myself in that exact situation, just for the simple fact that, like, I don't have a line of credit."

Sadly, foster children like Jaleesa are among the most common victims of the crime known as identity theft. I prefer to call the crime "impersonation," because no one can really steal your identity. Jaleesa is still herself. Someone has simply impersonated her for financial gain.

In response to the rising problem of impersonation among foster children, President Barack Obama signed a law in 2011 that contained a provision requiring the credit-reporting companies to provide foster children with a free credit report annually after they turn sixteen years old for as long as they remain in the system.

But the underlying problem of impersonation continues to rise. Complaints of identity theft increased by nearly one-third in 2012—up to 369 million from 279 million a year earlier—after remaining fairly steady for the previous five years, according to statistics compiled by the Federal Trade Commission.

Credit card fraud used to be the most common complaint, according to Steve Toporoff, the FTC attorney who coordinates the agency's identity protection program. These days, he said, tax fraud is the top complaint. "We also see new forms of fraud, such as medical fraud, in which people use identity information to obtain health treatment," he said. It's harder for people to catch tax and medical fraud, as they do not have access to their files as easily as they do with credit reports.

In 2013, two Florida women were convicted of defrauding the government in a scheme in which they submitted nearly two thousand fraudulent tax returns to the IRS seeking $11 million in refunds. The Department of the Treasury paid out nearly $3.5 million. One of the women, Alci Bonannee, filed many of the fraudulent returns using personal information purchased from a hospital nurse. The hospital, Baptist Health South Florida, stated that 834 patient records had been accessed. An IRS agent, Tony Gonzalez, told a local TV station that "the bad guys that are able to get these social security numbers are buying them from employees that work at these hospitals and these medical centers which are sold up to $150 each."

Identity information is not only being stolen, it is also being lost all the time, for reasons ranging from carelessness to hacking. Public reports of data breaches have been steadily on the rise since 2009, and jumped by a dramatic 43 percent in 2012, according to the Open Security Foundation's DataLossDB website.

And companies are rarely penalized for losing customer data. A test case is playing out as a result of the repeated hacks of the Wyndham hotel chain. In 2008, hackers broke into the computer network of the Wyndham hotel in Phoenix. Through that network, the hackers gained access to the credit card accounts of more than five hundred thousand customers at all forty-one Wyndham hotels and transferred the information to Russia. The hackers allegedly racked up more than $10.6 million in fraudulent charges.

But even after that breach, Wyndham failed to secure its computer network. The following year, it was hacked twice, losing another fifty thousand and sixty-nine thousand customer credit cards, respectively. In 2012, the Federal Trade Commission sued Wyndham, alleging that its failure to secure its network was deceptive and unfair to customers.

Wyndham fought back. It claimed the FTC was unfairly penalizing the company for being the victim of a crime. It called the FTC's case "the Internet equivalent of punishing the local furniture store because it was robbed and its files raided." The FTC responded in a legal filing that "a more accurate analogy would be that Wyndham was a local furniture store that left copies of its customers' credit and debit card information lying on the counter, failed to lock the doors of the store at night, and was shocked to find in the morning that someone had stolen the information."

YOU CAN BE TRAPPED IN A "HALL OF MIRRORS."

Companies that monitor people's Web-surfing behavior say their actions are innocuous: they only want to show ads for shoes to people who have recently looked at shoes, or to show political news to people who prefer political news. I call this type of mass customization a "hall of mirrors."

Sometimes the hall of mirrors is helpful. I don't particularly mind seeing an ad that reminds me to purchase a product I was just looking at. But the hall of mirrors can also veer into disturbing territory.

Consider this: searching for a traditionally black-sounding name such as "Trevon Jones" is 25 percent more likely to generate ads suggesting an arrest record—such as "Trevon Jones Arrested?"—than a search for a traditionally white-sounding name like "Kristen Sparrow," according to a January 2013 study by Harvard professor Latanya Sweeney. Sweeney found this advertising disparity even for names in which people with the white-sounding name did have a criminal record and people with the black-sounding name did not have a criminal record.

Data about people's Web-surfing behavior is also increasingly used to provide so-called customized content. For instance, Google uses information from past searches and browsing habits to provide different search results to different people—even when they conduct identical search requests. Sometimes those extrapolations can be useful, such as when Google suggests a restaurant near where you live instead of across the country. But sometimes they are intrusive.

In the months leading up to the November 2012 presidential election, Google took its guesses into the political realm in a controversial way. Searchers who looked up Barack Obama saw news about the president threaded into their future searches on other topics. Searchers who looked up Mitt Romney did not see news about the Republican presidential candidate included in subsequent searches.

Google said that the disparity was simply the result of the mathematical formula it was using to predict users' queries. Google's technologists viewed their effort as helping us figure out the answer to our needs before we know we have those needs. But it is worth noting that if a newspaper did the same thing—inserted Obama news into articles about toothpaste for certain readers—it would be roundly called out as biased and intrusive. Similarly, a newspaper would be called out if it placed only gay ads in the papers of subscribers it deemed to be gay, or diabetes treatment ads in the papers of subscribers it guessed had the disease.

Does technology immunize Google from something that would not otherwise be socially acceptable? Or is Martin Abrams, a leading privacy expert, right to call this type of behavior restrictive "boxing," where "my vision of what is possible is limited by the box" in which I am placed?

YOU CAN BE FINANCIALLY MANIPULATED.

As companies gather more digital data about potential customers, they have the ability to use that information to charge different prices to different users or steer different users to different offers.

Ryan Calo, a law professor at the University of Washington, calls this the "mass production of bias," in which companies use personal data to exploit people's vulnerability. For example, companies can chip away at consumers' willpower until they finally give in to making a purchase. Or a computer algorithm can set prices for each individual at exactly the price that is the most he or she is willing to pay for a given product or service.

The credit card companies have started using some of these techniques. In 2010, my colleagues at the *Wall Street Journal* and I discovered that Capital One was showing different credit cards (with different rates) to different website visitors, based on its guesses about their income and geographic location. The result was that when Thomas Burney, a Colorado building contractor, visited Capital One's website, he was greeted with offers for a card for people with excellent credit, the "Capital One Platinum Prestige." By comparison, when Carrie Isaac, a young mother from Colorado Springs, visited the website, she was shown a card described as being for people with "average" credit.

The reason was buried in the computer code. Contained in the 3,748 lines of code that passed between Thomas's computer and Capital One's website were the credit card company's guesses about his income level ("upper-mid"), education ("college graduate"), and his town ("avon"). Capital One had assessed Carrie as having only "midscale" income with "some college" education. A Capital One spokeswoman told us, "Like every marketer, online and off-line, we're making an educated guess about what we think consumers will like and they are free to choose another product of their liking."

By 2012, when my team again tested for market manipulation, the techniques had become more widespread and increasingly sophisticated. We found that credit card companies were still offering different cards to different users. Discover was showing a prominent offer for the "it" card to computers connecting from cities including Denver, Kansas City, and Dallas, but not to people connecting from Scranton, Pennsylvania; Kingsport, Tennessee; and Los Angeles.

But we also found that websites were varying prices based on their guesses about where users were located. In our tests, Lowe's was selling a refrigerator for $449 to users in Chicago, Los Angeles, and Ashburn, Virginia. But it cost $499 in seven other test cities. Similarly, a 250-foot spool of electrical wiring was displayed at six different prices on Home Depot's website depending on the user's location: $70.80 in Ashtabula, Ohio; $72.45 in Erie, Pennsylvania; $75.98 in Olean, New York; and $77.87 in Monticello, New York. Both Lowe's and Home Depot said the variations were an attempt to match online prices to the closest store.

We found the most comprehensive price differences on the website of the office supply giant Staples, which appears to use data about visitors to guess where they live. It then displays different prices to different users based on its estimate of their geographic location. The end result: when Trude Frizzell logged on to Staples.com from her work computer in Bergheim, Texas, she saw a Swingline stapler listed for sale for $14.29. Just a few miles away, in Bourne, Kim Wamble saw the same stapler listed on the same website for $15.79. The difference was not due to shipping costs, which are calculated after purchasing the item. Rather, the prices seem to reflect how far Staples believes the user lives from a competitor's store. Staples confirmed that it varies prices by a number of factors but declined to be specific.

It's not illegal to charge different prices to different users, as long it is not based on race or other sensitive information that could constitute redlining. But offering price variations to different users can result in unfair results that are unintended. Our tests of the Staples website showed that areas with higher average income were more likely to receive discounted prices than lower-income areas. "I think it's very discriminatory," said Kim.

The worst types of financial manipulation exploit the poor, the old, or the uneducated. Consider the so-called sucker lists that data brokers compile of people who are old, in financial distress, or vulnerable in some other way to certain types of marketing pitches. Sucker lists are often sold to unscrupulous marketers who pitch fraudulent products.

In October 2012, the Federal Trade Commission fined one of the nation's largest data brokers, Equifax, and its customers a total of $1.6 million for abusing personal data by selling lists of people who were late in paying their most recent mortgage bills to fraudulent marketers. The lists were marketed with names like "Save Me From Foreclosure" and "Debt Regret." One of the buyers was a particularly seedy Southern California boiler room operation that allegedly bilked more than $2.3 million from at least fifteen hundred home owners who paid fees ranging from $1,000 to $5,000 for loan modifications that almost never materialized. Many of those home owners eventually lost their homes.

When I asked an official at the Direct Marketing Association whether there are any lists its members won't sell, such as "seniors with Alzheimer's who like sweepstakes," she sent me the organization's ethical guidelines, which prohibit the sale of lists that are "disparaging." Otherwise, it's fair game, apparently.

YOU CAN BE PLACED IN A POLICE LINEUP.

On April 5, 2011, John Gass picked up his mail in Needham, Massachusetts, and was surprised to find a letter stating that his driver's license had been revoked. "I was just blindsided," John said.

John is a municipal worker—he repairs boilers for the town of Needham. Without a driver's license, he could not do his job. He called the Massachusetts Registry of Motor Vehicles and was instructed to appear at a hearing and bring documentation of his identity. They wouldn't tell him why his license was revoked.

When John showed up for his hearing, he learned that the RMV had begun using facial recognition software to search for identity fraud. The software compared license photos to identify people who might have applied for multiple licenses under different aliases. The software had flagged him and another man, Edward Perry of Rehoboth, Massachusetts, as having similar photos and had required them to prove their identities.

John was a victim of what I call the "police lineup"—dragnets that allow the police to treat everyone as a suspect. This overturns our traditional view that our legal system treats us as "innocent until proven guilty."

The most obvious example of this is airport body scanners. The scanners conduct the most intrusive of searches—allowing the viewer to peer beneath a person's clothes—without any suspicion that the person being scanned is a criminal. In fact, the burden is on the individual being scanned to "prove" his or her innocence, by passing through the scanner without displaying any suspicious items. These dragnets can be Kafkaesque. Consider the no-fly list. People placed on the list are not told how they got on the list, nor can they argue against the decision.

John Gass luckily was given a chance to plead his case. But it was an absurd case. He was presented with a photo of himself from thirteen years ago.

"It doesn't look like you," the officer said.

"Of course it doesn't," John said. "It's thirteen years later. I was a hundred pounds lighter."

John presented his passport and his birth certificate, and his license was reinstated. But the officers wouldn't give him any paperwork to prove that it was reinstated. He wanted a piece of paper to show his boss that he was okay to drive again. "It was kind of like a bad dream," John said.

Angry at his treatment and his lost income, John filed a lawsuit against the RMV, claiming that he had been denied his constitutionally protected right to due process. The RMV argued that he had been given a window of opportunity to dispute the revocation because the letter had been mailed on March 24 and the license wasn't revoked until April 1. John didn't pick up his mail until April 5.

The Suffolk County Superior Court granted the RMV's motion to dismiss. Gass appealed, but the appellate court also ruled against him. "Although Gass's pique at having to defend his identity is understandable, it does not follow that his case raises larger legal questions that appellate courts must resolve at this time," the court stated.

John felt betrayed by the whole process. He now is very careful around state police because he worries that he won't be treated fairly. "There are no checks and balances," he said. "It is only natural humans are going to make mistakes. But there is absolutely no oversight.

"I do think we are trading our liberties for security," he said.

✦

These stories illustrate a simple truth: information is power. Anyone who holds a vast amount of information about us has power over us.

At first, the information age promised to empower individuals with access to previously hidden information. We could comparison shop across the world for the best price, for the best bit of knowledge, for people who shared our views.

But now the balance of power is shifting and large institutions—both governments and corporations—are gaining the upper hand in the information wars, by tracking vast quantities of information about mundane aspects of our lives.

Now we are learning that people who hold our data can subject us to embarrassment, or drain our pocketbooks, or accuse us of criminal behavior. This knowledge could, in turn, create a culture of fear.

Consider Sharon and Bilal. Once they learned they were being monitored on PatientsLikeMe, Sharon and Bilal retreated from the Internet.

Bilal deleted his posts from the forum. He took down the drug dosage history that he had uploaded onto the site and stored it in an Excel file on his computer. Sharon stopped using the Internet altogether and doesn't allow her son to use it without supervision.

They started talking on the phone, but they missed the online connections they had forged on PatientsLikeMe. "I haven't found a replacement," Sharon said. Bilal agreed: "The people on PLM really know how it feels."

But neither of them could tolerate the fear of surveillance. Sharon said she just couldn't live with the uncertainty of "not knowing if every keystroke I'm making is going to some other company," she said. Bilal added, "I just feel that the trust was broken."

Sharon and Bilal's experience is a reminder that for all its technological pyrotechnics, the glory of the digital age has always been profoundly human. Technology allows us to find people who share our inner thoughts, to realize we're not alone. But technology also allows others to spy on us, causing us to pull back from digital intimacy.

When people ask me why I care about privacy, I always return to the simple thought that I want there to be safe, private spaces in the world for Sharon and Bilal, for myself, for my children, for everybody. I want there to be room in the digital world for letters sealed with hot wax. Must we always be writing postcards that can—and will—be read by anyone along the way?

Do we want to live in a world where we are always at risk of being hacked? A world where we can always be found, we can't keep secrets, we can be watched even in our own homes, we can be impersonated, we can be trapped in a hall of mirrors, we can be financially manipulated and put in a police lineup? This book is my attempt to answer that question in two parts.

In the opening chapters, I explore why indiscriminate surveillance matters. To do that, I examine the legal and technical origins of our Dragnet Nation, the uses and abuses of surveillance, and its impact on individuals and society.

In the chapters that follow, I examine whether there is any hope of building an alternative world, where we can enjoy the fruits of technology without fear of being hacked. I test various strategies for evading dragnets, ranging from using a burner phone to establishing fake identities.

I hope that my exploration will help the conversation about privacy evolve beyond the simple anxiety of "Who's watching me?" into a more nuanced discussion of "Why does it matter?" and, ultimately, to a productive conversation about what we can do about it.

2

A SHORT HISTORY OF TRACKING

Seven weeks after the terrorist attacks that killed thousands of people and demolished the World Trade Center in New York, one of the nation's top code breakers walked out of the premier spy agency in the United States for the last time.

It was October 31, 2001. Lower Manhattan was still smoldering. Letters containing anthrax had been sent to members of Congress and media outlets across the nation. Bomb scares were reported seemingly every day. A jittery nation was at war with an unseen enemy.

But Bill Binney, a code breaker who had risen to the level equivalent to a general within the National Security Agency, wasn't joining the fight. He was retiring after more than thirty years at the agency. As he reached the bottom of the steps at the agency headquarters in Fort Meade, Maryland, he said, "Free at last. Free at last."

Binney had spent years trying to modernize the spy agency's surveillance methods so that it could monitor Internet communications that bounce all over the world, while still respecting the privacy of U.S. citizens' communications. But his efforts had been thwarted at every turn.

Now, his colleagues were telling him that the agency was collecting the communications of U.S. citizens without any privacy protections. He wanted no part of it.

As he left the Fort Meade compound, Binney was fleeing what he viewed as the scene of a crime. "I could not stay after the NSA began purposefully violating the Constitution," he later declared in court testimony against his former employer.

We have since learned, of course, that Binney was right. After the 9/11 terrorist attacks, the U.S. government established sweeping, possibly illegal dragnets that captured the phone call and e-mail traffic of nearly every American.

✦

In my quest to understand the history and origins of mass surveillance, I kept returning to the year 2001. Not only was it the year of the devastating terrorist attacks on the United States, but it was also the year that the technology industry was left reeling from the bursting of the dot-com bubble. These two seemingly unrelated events each set in motion a chain of events that created the legal and technical underpinnings of today's dragnets. For the U.S. government, the terrorist attacks showed that its traditional methods of intelligence gathering weren't working. And for Silicon Valley, the crash showed that it needed to find a new way to make money.

Both arrived at the same answer to their disparate problems: collecting and analyzing vast quantities of personal data.

Of course, each had a different purpose. The government was seeking to find and extract terrorists who might be hiding within the population. The tech industry was seeking to lure advertisers with robust dossiers about individuals. But, inevitably, the two became intertwined as the U.S. government used its power to dip into the tech industry's profiles.

Together, the government and the tech industry hatched our Dragnet Nation. This is the story of how it all began.

✦

In the eighteenth century, the British were having a hard time controlling their American colonies. The Americans were rebelling against British attempts to block trade between the colonies and other European countries and against British demands that they pay taxes without receiving representation in Parliament.

To combat the smuggling epidemic, the British instituted a new type of surveillance technique: general search warrants, known as writs of assistance, which allowed British officers to conduct what basically amounted to suspicionless house-to-house searches.

Americans were outraged that British officers could storm into any house at any time, even during a wedding or funeral. "It appears to me the worst instrument of arbitrary power," the lawyer James Otis Jr. argued in a famous speech in Boston in 1761.

Outrage over the general warrants helped prompt the American Revolution. And outrage over the general warrants are the underpinning of the Fourth Amendment to the U.S. Constitution, which states: "The right of the people to be secure in their persons, houses, papers, and effects, against unreasonable searches and seizures, shall not be violated, and no Warrants shall issue, but upon probable cause, supported by Oath or affirmation, and particularly describing the place to be searched, and the persons or things to be seized."

The Fourth Amendment is a bedrock principle for law enforcement officers in the United States. However, technology has enabled the exploitation of loopholes in the interpretation of the Fourth Amendment. Some of the most important loopholes are:

• **Public space.** The Fourth Amendment protects only "persons, houses, papers and effects." The Supreme Court has interpreted this language to mean that individuals have no reasonable expectation of privacy in public. However, technology has reduced the protective confines of private space by enabling surveillance of computer use in one's own home and drones that fly over backyards.

• **Third-Party Doctrine.** The Supreme Court has established the "Third-Party Doctrine," which states that individuals do not have a reasonable expectation of privacy in information they give to third parties— such as their bank or their phone company. As a result, even sensitive information that is stored with third parties, such as e-mail, can often be obtained without a search warrant.

• **Metadata.** Metadata is data about data—for example, the envelope containing a letter can be considered metadata; the data is the letter itself. The court has traditionally set lower legal standards for searches of metadata than for searches of data. For instance, the post office can take a photograph of the envelope of your letter without a warrant, but it cannot open the letter without a warrant. In the digital era, metadata can reveal a lot, such as all the phone numbers you call, the people you e-mail, and your location.

• **Border searches.** Courts have largely supported a "border search exception" to the Fourth Amendment, which allows government to conduct searches at the border without obtaining a search warrant. In today's electronic age, that means that agents can—and often do—download the entire contents of an individual's phone or computer at the border. U.S. Customs and Border Patrol says that it conducts about fifteen electronic media searches per day. In March 2013 the U.S. Court of Appeals for the Ninth Circuit in California set a new limit on device searches at the border, ruling in *United States v. Cotterman* that reasonable suspicion of criminal activity was required for a forensic search of a device—such as using software to analyze encrypted or deleted data, as opposed to performing a more cursory look at documents, photos, or other files.

In the digital age, these loopholes have become large enough to allow for the type of suspicionless searches that outraged the Founding Fathers.

✦

U.S. presidents have long been cautious about overstepping the bounds of the Fourth Amendment.

In 1981, when President Ronald Reagan authorized limited domestic spying in order to seek Soviet infiltrators, he ordered the intelligence agencies to use "the least intrusive collection techniques feasible within the United States or directed against United States persons abroad." Over the years, Reagan's directive has been interpreted to mean that domestic spying should be done cautiously, and only in cases where there is reason to suspect a crime.

But after 9/11, the requirement to establish some kind of suspicion before engaging in domestic spying was, for all intents and purposes, tossed aside. Documents revealed by the former NSA contractor Edward Snowden paint a devastating portrait of how a single decision made in the days after the attack opened the floodgates for vast domestic dragnets. According to a leaked draft of a 2009 inspector general's report, the NSA's domestic spying began on September 14, 2001, three days after the attacks, when the agency's director, Michael Hayden, approved warrantless interception of any U.S. phone call to or from specific terrorist-identified phone numbers in Afghanistan. On September 26, Hayden expanded the order to cover all phone numbers in Afghanistan.

But soon Hayden wanted more data. He believed there was an "international gap" between what the NSA was collecting overseas and what the FBI was looking at domestically. No one was monitoring communications to the United States that originated abroad. So Hayden worked with Vice President Dick Cheney, who asked his legal counsel to help draft a legal memo that would aid the NSA in filling the international gap. On October 4, President George W. Bush issued a memorandum titled, "Authorization for specified electronic surveillance activities during a limited period to detect and prevent acts of terrorism within the United States." The memo allowed Hayden to continue to target communications between Afghanistan and the United States without seeking approval from the Foreign Intelligence Surveillance Court, which normally oversees electronic surveillance that involves U.S. residents. The program was authorized for thirty days.

At the time, it seemed like an understandable emergency measure. In an era when terrorists could mask their Internet traffic by bouncing it all over the world, it was sometimes difficult to sort out U.S. from foreign communications. The order gave the NSA a temporary reprieve from sorting out U.S. communications during a time of crisis.

However, Hayden's narrowly crafted, short-term program eventually metastasized into a full-blown domestic spying effort. The thirty-day order was perpetually renewed and expanded. Within a year, it expanded beyond just U.S.-Afghanistan communications. The NSA used the presidential order to justify obtaining e-mail and phone communications from thousands of targets at a time. It also began obtaining bulk long-distance and international calling records, to conduct "chaining," that is, finding a person who called a person who called a suspected terrorist. And the NSA began collecting Internet traffic (who you e-mailed and Web pages you visit) from sources where a "preponderance of communications was from foreign sources" and there was a "high probability" of collecting terrorist traffic.

To collect all this data, the NSA sought cooperation from Internet and phone companies. The report states that seven companies (who are not named) were approached. Three declined to participate.

In 2005, the *New York Times* broke the story of the warrantless wiretapping program, describing it as a major shift in intelligence-gathering practices. The broad sweep of the program became clear a few months later when a retired AT&T technician, Mark Klein, went public with the news that the NSA had installed equipment in a secret room in AT&T's San Francisco office that could tap all the communications that flowed through that portion of the Internet. "This is the infrastructure for an Orwellian police state. It must be shut down!" Klein said in a public statement.

Then in May 2006, USA Today published an article stating that AT&T, Verizon, and BellSouth began providing the NSA with the phone call records of their customers soon after 9/11. "It's the largest database ever assembled in the world," said an unnamed official quoted in the article.

Under pressure, President Bush briefly shut down parts of the program. But in 2008, he signed into law amendments to the Foreign Intelligence Surveillance Act, which reinstated and legalized the wiretapping program and immunized the telecommunications providers against lawsuits for their previous participation in a possibly illegal program.

The FISA amendments established a new class of search warrants that allowed the government to intercept communications without obtaining the name of a target—essentially continuing the broad sweeps that it had conducted under warrantless wiretapping. But this time, a judge had to approve the algorithm being used to target suspects. The PRISM program, disclosed by Snowden, described the Internet companies that were complying with the algorithmic warrants. Yahoo! apparently fought to declare one of the warrants unconstitutional in a secret court hearing, but it lost and was forced to comply with the warrant under a threat of civil contempt.

Amazingly, it turns out that the warrantless wiretapping was one of the more restrained NSA programs, since it captured only U.S.-to-foreign communications. Far more sweeping were the vast amounts of phone and Internet traffic that the NSA began collecting within the United States. Because it was just "metadata," the NSA argued that sweeping up domestic phone calling records and Internet traffic was not violating Americans' privacy.

Snowden revealed a secret court order requiring Verizon to turn over daily calling records to the NSA. Soon after, Senator Dianne Feinstein of California confirmed that the NSA had been collecting domestic and international calling records from all the major telecommunications companies for seven years.

Snowden also revealed a 2007 memo written by Kenneth Wainstein, a Justice Department attorney, in which he pushed for the NSA to be granted legal authority to collect more Internet traffic within the United States. "Through the use of computer algorithms, NSA creates a chain of contacts linking communicants," Wainstein wrote. "NSA's present practice is to 'stop' when a chain hits a telephone number or address believed to be used by a United States person." He then asked the attorney general for permission to conduct "contact chaining" of U.S. residents.

Apparently, his wish was briefly granted. The Obama administration said that the Internet traffic-monitoring program ended in 2011 and was not restarted. But it remains likely that the NSA is still monitoring domestic Internet traffic under another guise.

Regardless, Snowden's revelations confirmed what many had long suspected: the creation of a tiny thirty-day dragnet covering U.S.-Afghanistan communications had mushroomed into a massive domestic dragnet.

✦

After 9/11, a massive rush of counterterrorism spending fueled dragnet surveillance at the state and local levels as well. Federal intelligence agency budgets ballooned to $75 billion in 2013, up from about $27 billion prior to the attacks. And some of that trickled down to the states in the form of grants.

Consider just the activities of the Department of Homeland Security. Since 9/11, the department has doled out more than $7 billion for grants to help "high-threat, high-density urban areas" to prevent and respond to terrorism. More than $50 million of DHS's grants were doled out to state law enforcement agencies to purchase automated license plate readers that allow them to keep tabs on citizens' movements in ways never before possible. The department also helped fund the creation of "fusion centers" in nearly every state that were tasked with crunching data from different agencies—and often from commercial data brokers—to look for clues that could prevent future acts of terrorism. And local police increasingly began tracking people using signals emitted by their cell phones.

At the same time, suspicionless investigations became more common. In 2008, the attorney general issued new guidelines that allowed the FBI to launch investigations without "any particular factual predication." Under the new rules, the FBI was charged with "obtaining information on individuals, groups, or organizations of possible investigative interest, either because they may be involved in criminal or national security-threatening activities or because they may be targeted for attack or victimization by such activities."

And in 2012, the Justice Department authorized the National Counterterrorism Center to copy entire government databases of information about U.S. citizens—flight records, lists of casino employees, the names of Americans hosting foreign-exchange students—and examine the files for suspicious behavior.

Previously, the agency had been barred from storing information about U.S. residents unless the person was a terrorism suspect or was related to an investigation.

Suspicionless dragnets had become the new normal.

✦

The terrorist attacks of 2001 also ushered in an era of dragnets in Silicon Valley.

Until the late 1990s, the consumer software industry was a retail business. Software was sold in shrink-wrapped boxes on store shelves. Of course, companies also bought industrial-grade software wholesale. But the popular market—consisting mostly of games and office productivity tools—was a retail business.

The Internet blew up the software business entirely.

The first real piece of Internet software was the Web browser Netscape Navigator, introduced in 1994. The prospect of the first truly mass-market software propelled Netscape to a stratospheric initial public offering. Its stock price shot up in its first day of trading, closing the day at four times its initial offering price. Netscape's cofounder Marc Andreessen, only twenty-four years old, suddenly found himself worth $171 million. The following year, Andreessen was pictured on the cover of *Time* magazine, barefoot and wearing a crown, next to the caption "The Golden Geeks."

But the profits never came. Microsoft began including a free Web browser, Internet Explorer, along with its Windows 95 operating system. As a result, Netscape was never able to charge for its software.

In 1998, the Department of Justice and attorneys general from twenty states and the District of Columbia sued Microsoft, alleging that it was acting as a monopoly in bundling Internet Explorer with Windows 95. But by the time Microsoft signed a consent decree in 2002, the damage was done. In 1998, Internet Explorer surpassed Netscape in market share, and by 2008 Netscape's software was officially abandoned.

The first truly mass-market software had been built. But it hadn't made any money. The lesson was clear: the retail software market was dead. But technology requires software. How was it going to be financed?

At first it seemed that advertising might be the answer. In the late 1990s, Silicon Valley was awash in dot-com businesses, many of them based on the premise that advertising would support their efforts. But the bubble burst in 2000. Yahoo!, whose revenue came mostly from online advertising, saw its market capitalization plummet from $113.9 billion in early 2000 to just $7.9 billion a year later.

The conventional wisdom was that online advertising had failed. "Two years ago, nearly all advertisers were saying, 'I have to be on the Internet,'" Pat McGrath, CEO of the Arnold McGrath ad agency, said in November 2001. "Today, they are stepping back and saying, 'Does the Internet make sense as one of the ways to promote this brand?'" McGrath's assessment was echoed across the industry. Wendy Taylor, the editor of Ziff Davis Smart Business, was the most succinct. "Online advertising is dead," she declared.

An industry with the best tools to measure the size of its audience in the history of advertising was accused of having no metrics to prove the effectiveness of its product. Internet companies began to search for even better measuring sticks. A great tracking technology called cookies could track Web users from site to site. But it wasn't clear if it was legal.

In 2000, a federal class action suit was brought against the online advertising company DoubleClick, alleging that its installation of cookies on the computers of website visitors was violating laws that limit wiretapping, hacking, and electronic surveillance. A year later, Judge Naomi Reice Buchwald, in the Southern District of New York, ruled that DoubleClick's actions were not illegal because websites authorized DoubleClick to install cookies on their visitors' computers. "We find that the DoubleClick-affiliated Web sites are 'parties to the communication[s]' from plaintiffs and have given sufficient consent to DoubleClick to intercept them," she wrote. Her ruling amounted to a free pass for corporate Internet surveillance: when a person visits a website, the website is free to invite others to secretly wiretap the visitor.

Finally, Silicon Valley had a business model: tracking.

✦

Of course, private companies have long collected data about their customers and employees. But buying and selling personal data didn't become an industry until the rise of modern computing.

In 1971, Vinod Gupta's boss asked him to get a list of every mobile-home dealer in the country. Gupta, a recent immigrant from India who had completed an MBA at the University of Nebraska, sat down with a bunch of yellow page directories and began creating his own list. He soon realized there must be a better way to create a marketing list. In 1972, he founded a company, American Business Information, which used the yellow page listings to build custom lists for marketers to use. The company, now known as Infogroup, soon branched out to include data from the white pages and began buying data from professional associations and scooping up any kind of public data available—from driver's license records to voter registration cards to court records.

"Just about every list is available," Gupta later said. "If you want left-handed golfers or left-handed fishermen or fly fishermen or dog owners, all those lists are available."

Across the country, in Conway, Arkansas, another company was tackling the same problem. In 1969, Charles Ward, a local businessman who was active in the Democratic Party, set up a small company called Demographics Inc. to help local candidates run direct mail campaigns. His company helped Dale Bumpers in his run for governor of Arkansas, and Lloyd Bentsen in his unsuccessful presidential bid, before eventually expanding beyond politics. In 1989, the company changed its name to Acxiom.

Acxiom soared in the 1990s, as businesses needed companies with computer expertise to manage their customer data. Between 1993 and 1998, Acxiom's revenue quadrupled to $402 million from $91 million. "The data has always been there," Donald Hinman, an executive at Acxiom, told the *Washington Post* in 1998. "It's just that now, with the technology, you can access it."

The new data troves fueled new businesses. The credit card companies Capital One and Discover found ways to slice and dice the population into profitable segments that they could target by direct mail. Selling data became a lucrative business for governments at all levels. The state of Florida alone makes about $62 million a year selling driver's license data. The U.S. Postal Service generates $9.5 million in revenue a year allowing companies like Acxiom to access its National Change of Address database.

In the 2000s, as the Internet became pervasive, marketers became interested in "fresher" data about where people were browsing online. The DoubleClick legal decision had spawned an entire industry devoted to following Web users' every click online. In 2007, all the Internet giants jumped into the online tracking business. AOL bought the behavioral targeting firm TACODA for $275 million, Google paid $3.1 billion for DoubleClick, and Microsoft paid $6 billion for the online ad company aQuantive. All those companies were in the business of building profiles of Web users.

The big data brokers reacted quickly. Acxiom, along with others, began working to merge its files with Web-browsing records, allowing advertisers to target online ads as precisely as they targeted their mail. At the same time, Acxiom started selling its data to companies such as Facebook that wanted to enhance their own tracking.

Online tracking also fueled a new industry: data trading. On exchanges similar to the stock market, advertisers bought and sold customer profiles in millisecond trades. It works like this: When you look at a digital camera on eBay, the Web page is embedded with code from a data exchange such as BlueKai. Once BlueKai is alerted that you are on the page, it instantly auctions off your "cookie" to advertisers who want to reach camera buyers. The highest bidder wins the right to show you a digital camera advertisement on subsequent pages that you visit. That's often why online ads appear to follow you around.

Due in large part to tracking, online advertising is growing fast. Industry revenues rose to $36.6 billion in 2012, up from just $7.3 billion in 2003. Tracking is so crucial to the industry that in 2013 Randall Rothenberg, the president of the Interactive Advertising Bureau, said that if the industry lost its ability to track people, "billions of dollars in Internet advertising and hundreds of thousands of jobs dependent on it would disappear."

Meglena Kuneva, a member of the European Commission, summed it up best in 2009 when she said: "Personal data is the new oil of the Internet and the new currency of the digital world."

✦

If you were to build a taxonomy of trackers it would look something like this:

GOVERNMENT

- **Incidental collectors.** Agencies that collect data in their normal course of business, such as state motor vehicle registries and the IRS, but are not directly in the data business.
- **Investigators.** Agencies that collect data about suspects as part of law enforcement investigations, such as the FBI and local police.
- **Data analysts.** A new class of agencies that scoop up and analyze data from government agencies and commercial data brokers, such as state fusion centers and the National Counterterrorism Center.
- **Espionage.** Agencies such as the NSA that are supposed to focus on foreign spying, but have turned their attention to domestic spying as well.

COMMERCIAL

- **Incidental collectors.** This is basically all businesses that collect personal information in the course of regular business, ranging from the local dry cleaner to banks and telecommunications providers.
- **The "Freestylers."** These are mostly software companies, such as Google and Facebook, which provide free services and make money from their customers' data—usually by selling access to the data to marketers.
- **Marketers.** The rise of Internet tracking as a basis for digital advertising business has put marketers primarily in the data business.
- **Data brokers.** These are companies that buy from incidental government and commercial collectors, analyze the data, and resell it. Some, like Acxiom, sell primarily to businesses. Others, such as Intelius, sell primarily to individuals.

• **Data exchanges.** Marketers and data brokers increasingly trade information on real-time trading desks that mimic stock exchanges.

INDIVIDUALS

• **Democratized dragnets.** Technology has become cheap enough that everyone can do their own tracking, with items such as dashboard cameras, build-it-yourself drones, and Google Glass eyeglasses that contain tiny cameras that can take photos and videos.

The trackers are deeply intertwined. Government data are the lifeblood for commercial data brokers. And government dragnets rely on obtaining information from the private sector.

Consider just one example: voting. To register to vote, citizens must fill out a government form that usually requires their name, address, and, in all but one state, birth date. But few voters realize that those lists are often sold to commercial data brokers. A 2011 study found that a statewide voter list sold for as little as $30 in California and as high as $6,050 in Georgia.

Commercial data brokers combine the voting information with other data to create rich profiles of individuals. For instance, the data broker Aristotle Inc. markets its ability to identify 190 million voters by more than "500 consumer data points" such as their credit rating and size of their mortgage.

And guess who buys Aristotle's enriched data? Politicians, who are sometimes using government money. Aristotle crows that "every U.S. President—Democrat and Republican—from Reagan through Obama, has used Aristotle products and/or services." In fact, an intrepid 2012 thesis by a Harvard undergraduate, Melissa Oppenheim, found that fifty-one members of the U.S. House of Representatives bought data from Aristotle using some of their congressional allowances, allowing them to identify their constituents by the age of their children, whether they subscribe to religious magazines, or if they have a hunting license. And thus, the data come full circle in what Oppenheim calls the "Dark Data Cycle." The government requires citizens to create data and then sells it to commercial entities, which launder the data and sell it back to the government.

The dark data cycle occurs with nearly every type of data. State auto vehicle records are swept into LexisNexis reports, which are enhanced with other data and sold to the Department of Homeland Security. Foreclosure records are compiled in state courts and then collected by data brokers such as CoreLogic, which sells packages of real estate data to clients including the government.

An even darker data cycle occurs in the secret Foreign Intelligence Surveillance Court, where the government can demand that private industry hand over data about their customers. In those circumstances, giant companies such as Google, Yahoo!, AT&T, Verizon, and Microsoft have been forced to hand over customer data to the NSA.

The reality is that corporate and government dragnets are inextricably linked; neither can exist without the other.

✦

Bill Binney suffered for speaking out against the NSA's dragnets.

While at the NSA, Binney had developed what he believed was a dragnet that respected and protected individual privacy. Called ThinThread, it was a clever program that intercepted tons of Internet and phone data, encrypted it, and analyzed it for patterns. It would be decrypted only if a specific threat was found and a court had approved a search warrant to decrypt the data.

But he couldn't get the program deployed. After several years of internal battles, during which Binney and his colleagues took their case directly to congressional leaders, the NSA's top leaders declined to support ThinThread. One reason: in the pre-9/11 era, the NSA's lawyers worried that ThinThread would violate Americans' privacy because it might collect domestic communications, even though they were encrypted. Another reason: NSA director Michael Hayden had thrown his support behind a much more expensive program called Trailblazer, built by private contractors, which also aimed to analyze the NSA's oceans of data but didn't use encryption. Trailblazer eventually was abandoned after massive cost overruns and technical failures.

In 2002, Binney's colleague Kirk Wiebe, who had worked on Thin-Thread, contacted the Department of Defense's inspector general to report what he believed was "waste, fraud and abuse" at the NSA. The inspector general's report, issued in 2005, was heavily redacted, but the few unredacted parts seemed to vindicate ThinThread.

In 2006, the *Baltimore Sun* published an article about the battles over

ThinThread. "NSA Rejected System That Sifted Phone Data Legally," the headline stated.

On July 26, 2007, the FBI raided Binney's home in suburban Maryland.

Binney was in the shower. "The guy came in and pointed a gun at me," he recalled. "I just said, 'Do you suppose I could put some clothes on?'"

Wiebe, who had retired from the NSA the same day as Binney in 2001, was also raided on this day. Neither Binney nor Wiebe was ever charged with a crime.

On November 28, 2007, the FBI raided the home of another Thin-Thread supporter, Thomas Drake, an NSA executive who had collaborated anonymously on the inspector general's investigation. Agents seized Drake's papers, computers, and hard drives and alleged that they found classified documents in the basement. Two and a half years later, Drake was indicted and charged with violating the Espionage Act because of his "willful retention" of classified documents.

Drake was financially devastated by the prosecution. He was five and a half years from retirement at the NSA. He lost his pension, which would have been $60,000 a year. He took out a second mortgage on his house and withdrew most of his 401(k) retirement plan to pay for his expenses. He was unemployable in the intelligence community, so he started working at an Apple retail store. After spending $82,000 on legal fees, he was declared indigent by the court and was represented by a public defender.

In 2011, after a wave of publicity about Drake's plight, the government dropped all ten felony counts against Drake, as a condition for Drake pleading guilty to a misdemeanor of "exceeding the authorized use of a government computer." During the sentencing, the U.S. District Court judge Richard D. Bennett called the government's two-and-a-half-year delay between the search and indictment "unconscionable." "It was one of the most fundamental things in the Bill of Rights that this country was not to be exposed to people knocking on the door with government authority and coming into their homes," he wrote. "And when it happens, it should be resolved pretty quickly."

Judge Bennett didn't overtly accuse the government of using its power to harass a whistle-blower. But he gave Drake the lightest sentence possible—one year probation, during which he was required to do twenty hours of community service a month and no fine. He closed the sentencing hearing by addressing Drake: "I wish you the best of luck in the rest of your life."

Prior to Drake's prosecution, Binney, Drake, and Wiebe had tried to reform the agency from within. But as Drake's trial approached, they went public. And after Drake's exoneration, they became full-time critics of the NSA, giving scathing interviews to media outlets and warning of the power of an unchecked agency that has information on everyone.

When I first met Binney, the first thing he said to me was that the amount of data being assembled by the NSA was "orders of magnitude" more than the world's most repressive secret police regimes, the Gestapo, the Stasi, and the KGB.

"It's a real danger when a government assembles that much information about a citizen," he told me. "Gathering that much information gives them power over everybody."

3

STATE OF SURVEILLANCE

Surveillance is not, in and of itself, a terrible activity.

Parents surveil their children in order to make sure they don't hurt themselves. Police officers surveil the population to catch criminals. Companies surveil their employees to catch thieves and cheaters. Journalists surveil powerful institutions to expose abuses.

But the modern era of dragnets marks a new type of surveillance: suspicionless, computerized, impersonal, and vast in scope. Some people believe this surveillance will keep society safer. Others believe it will usher in a police state.

To understand the worst-case scenario, I visited the world's best-kept archives of pre-electronic surveillance—the Stasi archive in Berlin. I wanted to see how the files kept by the Stasi, the East German secret police during the Communist era, compared with the information collected by today's commercial and governmental surveillance operations.

The Stasi was the largest secret police operation—on a per capita basis—in the history of the world. Famously repressive, it kept files on 4 million East Germans—or about one-quarter of a total population of nearly 16.7 million. The Stasi didn't have the advantage of today's technology— it had to steam open mail and listen to phone calls manually—but it had an extensive network of informants. In 1989, roughly one in fifty East

Germans between the ages of eighteen and eighty worked for the Stasi in some capacity.

As the East German regime was collapsing in November 1989, the Stasi began shredding the files they had kept on citizens. Outraged that the evidence of the regime's oppression was being destroyed, residents stormed the Stasi headquarters to halt the destruction of files. As a result, today's citizens can request to see files kept about them, and researchers have access to some files, with the names of the people who were monitored removed.

On a trip to Berlin in 2011, I stopped by the Stasi archive—formally known as the Federal Commissioner Preserving the Records of the State Security Service of the former German Democratic Republic—which is incongruously located in a cheerful, glass-paned office building in the heart of the city.

The Stasi records administrator assigned to my request, Günter Bormann, was immediately enthusiastic about my idea of comparing Stasi and modern surveillance. As I filled out the paperwork to obtain a set of Stasi records, he asked me what a typical Western data gatherer knows about me. So I asked if I could use his computer to show him a bit of what is known about me online.

I logged on to my Gmail account and navigated to the settings, where Google allowed me to view my previous Web searches, including books I had researched and photos I had viewed. It also listed the ninety-three people that I'd e-mailed or instant-messaged using Gmail.

Standing over me, Bormann was impressed. Social network mapping, he told me, "was very difficult for the Stasi." He sat down at his conference table and started drawing a few circles with connecting lines. "They tried to do social network mapping," he said, but even with all their informants they had a hard time building robust maps.

Inspired, I clicked on to my LinkedIn page—where I had installed a special plug-in that allows me to see a visualization of my social network. It was a beautiful map with nearly two hundred points strung together with colored lines. My New York work colleagues were all clustered in one corner in yellow, other media colleagues were clumped in a blue corner, and my connections from my time in California are on the other side of the map in a sea of orange and gray dots.

Bormann was even more impressed. "The Stasi would have loved this."

✦

Three months later, a packet of documents arrived at my desk in New York. Inside were more than a hundred pages containing two files in German. After a bit of searching, I found some Stasi experts to help me translate and interpret the files.

The surprising thing was how crude the surveillance was. "Their main surveillance technology was mail, telephone, and informants," said Gary Bruce, an associate professor of history at the University of Waterloo and the author of *The Firm: The Inside Story of the Stasi*.

The first file revealed a low-level surveillance operation called an *imforgang* aimed at recruiting an unnamed target to become an informant. (The names of the targets were redacted; the names of the Stasi agents and informants were not.) In this case, the Stasi watched a rather boring high school student who lived with his mother and sister in a run-of-the-mill apartment. The Stasi obtained a report on him from the principal of his school and from a club where he was a member.

The Stasi didn't have much on him—I've seen Facebook profiles with far more information—but they still tried to recruit him as an informant. He turned them down, citing some nonspecific health reasons. He was lucky that he was young and boring. Most people who were asked to be informants felt that they couldn't say no to the Stasi when presented with evidence of a minor infraction—such as watching West German television.

The second file documented a surveillance operation known as an OPK, for *Operative Personenkontrolle*, of a man who was writing oppositional poetry. It was a medium-size operation: the Stasi deployed three informants against him but did not steam open his mail or listen to his phone calls.

Stasi officers received bonuses when they launched OPKs, and an even more generous bonus if OPK was fruitful—in producing either an arrest or a new informant. Ultimately, however, the OPK of the poet was fruitless because the regime collapsed before the Stasi could do anything about him.

Six months later another, smaller packet arrived. This one contained about fifteen pages documenting specific Stasi surveillance tactics that I had requested.

In one file, Stasi agents recorded the movements of a forty-year-old man for two days—September 28 and 29, 1979. They watched him as he dropped off his laundry, loaded up his car with rolls of wallpaper, and drove a child in a car "obeying the speed limit," stopping for gas and delivering the wallpaper to an apartment building. The Stasi continued to follow the car as a woman drove the child back to Berlin.

"The targets were extremely circumspect . . . ," the Stasi officer, Lieutenant Colonel Fritsch, wrote. "Presumably . . . [they had been] tipped off . . . that observations were being conducted in the vicinity."

The agent appears to have started following the target at 4:15 p.m. on a Friday evening. At 9:38 p.m., the target went into his apartment and turned out the lights. The agent stayed all night and handed over surveillance to another agent at 7:00 a.m. Saturday. That agent appears to have followed the target until 10:00 p.m. From today's perspective, this seems like a lot of work for very little information.

The second file was simply a hand-drawn social network. On a single page of paper, agents had drawn forty-six connections, linking a target to various people (an "aunt," "Operational Case Jentzsch," presumably Bernd Jentzsch, an East German poet who defected to the West in 1976), places ("church"), and meetings ("by post, by phone, meeting in Hungary").

This was an impressive document. It had only one-quarter of the data compared to my two-hundred-plus contacts on my LinkedIn profile, but they were likely more relevant to the investigation than my far-flung network.

The Stasi would likely have conducted surveillance of everybody on the map, who were known as "secondary individuals," according to Gary Bruce. "You didn't have to do anything particularly oppositional to end up with a Stasi file," he said.

The problem was that a Stasi file—no matter how large—could affect whether a person got demoted or promoted, how long they would have to wait to get a car or an apartment, or whether their application to visit relatives in the West would be approved. As a result, even though the Stasi had files on only a quarter of the population, fear of becoming a target was pervasive.

In a 1990 survey, right after the fall of the Communist regime, 72.6

percent of former East German citizens described the Communist experience as "complete surveillance." In 1992, when asked to consider the statement, "One felt spied upon. You couldn't trust anyone," 43 percent described it as "True, that's exactly how it was."

In a study of psychological effects of Stasi surveillance, Babett Bauer interviewed about thirty individuals who had had direct encounters with the secret police. She found that their fear of another Stasi encounter had prompted them either to become model citizens or to withdraw from society. Bauer concluded that people who encountered the Stasi internalized repression into "the body's wrinkles and the brain's mechanisms."

✦

The power of observation to be repressive was the foundational idea of the "Panopticon"—a prison design proposed by Jeremy Bentham in 1787. His idea was that a perfect prison would allow prisoners to believe they were being watched at all times but allow the watchers to remain unseen. He designed a circular prison with a guard tower in the middle, but it was never built during his lifetime.

In 1975, the French philosopher Michel Foucault popularized Bentham's idea, describing the Panopticon as a "marvelous" instrument of power. "The more numerous those anonymous and temporary observers are, the greater the risk for the inmate of being surprised and the greater his anxious awareness of being observed," he wrote in his book *Discipline and Punish*.

Now that we live in a world of extensive surveillance, it would make sense that Foucault's "anxious awareness" would be our collective mental state. But it seems Foucault was only partially correct. As Babett Bauer discovered in her interviews with East Germans, people cope with surveillance as much by changing their behavior as through increased anxiety.

In 2011, Finnish researchers installed extensive monitoring equipment—video cameras; microphones; and computer, smartphone, and TV monitoring devices—in ten households for a year, to determine the long-term effect of ubiquitous surveillance. They found that the subjects of the study—who had obviously volunteered—"gradually became accustomed to surveillance" over the course of the study. However, the responses varied. One participant dropped out after six months, stating that the surveillance had curtailed his or her computer usage and affected his or her relationships. (The researchers did not reveal genders or identifying details of the subjects.)

Although the subjects knew that the data from the surveillance was not being disclosed to anyone except the researchers, and that they could turn off the system at any time, they still found the monitoring to be a source of "annoyance, concern, anxiety and even rage," the researchers wrote. The most hated monitors were the computer monitoring and the video cameras (which two participants admitted to turning off regularly).

Most participants changed their routines, particularly to be more cautious about where they undressed (cameras were not placed in the bedrooms or bathrooms) and where they held sensitive conversations.

"Two subjects started to spend more time in the bedroom, which was not covered by the microphones. Two others said that they would go to a café to discuss personal matters," the authors wrote. "One subject mentioned avoiding inviting many people home."

The lead author of the paper, a computer science researcher named Antti Oulasvirta, said that although people's overt concerns about privacy plateaued after three months, they all adjusted their behavior to adapt to the situation. But their adaptations were easily disturbed. "The required changes made the home fragile," he said. "Any unpredicted social event would bring the new practices to the fore and question them, and at times prevent them from taking place."

+

Another way to cope with ubiquitous surveillance is painted by the science fiction author David Brin, in his prescient 1998 book *The Transparent Society: Will Technology Force Us to Choose Between Privacy and Freedom?*

The book opens with a "tale of two cities." Both cities have surveillance cameras installed on "every lamppost, every rooftop and street sign." In the first city, all the images are piped into the central police station. In the second city, every citizen can access any camera through a wristwatch television.

Both cities are crime-free. But the first city is a police state, while the second city enjoys some freedom: "A late-evening stroller checks to make sure no one lurks beyond the corner. . . . An anxious parent scans the area to find which way her child wandered off. . . . A shoplifter is taken into custody gingerly . . . because the arresting officer knows that the entire process is being scrutinized."

Brin argues, convincingly, that the proliferation of cameras—and other surveillance technology—is the inevitable result of the progress of technology. To him, the important question is: Who controls the cameras? As he sees it, mutual surveillance—the citizens and the state watching each other—can transform ubiquitous surveillance from oppression to mutual accountability. And there is some evidence to support this view.

During the Cold War, mutual surveillance played an important part in preventing the United States and the Soviet Union from dropping nuclear bombs on each other.

After the Soviet Union launched Sputnik in 1957, America was consumed by a fear of the Soviet Union's capabilities and their implications. In 1958, Senator John F. Kennedy claimed that the United States was falling behind the Soviets and predicted that "by 1960 the United States will have lost . . . its superiority in nuclear striking power."

It wasn't until the United States successfully launched photoreconnaissance spy satellites that it was able to measure the missile gap. The images captured by the satellite showed that the true missile gap ran the other way: in 1961, the Soviets had just four intercontinental ballistic missiles, compared to America's stockpile of 170.

However, the United States still failed to notice the Soviet missile buildup in Cuba during the summer of 1962, an intelligence failure that brought the United States and the Soviet Union to the brink of a nuclear war. As a result, building better spy satellites became an important part of the Cold War race.

In 1972, the United States and the Soviet Union codified their spying in the Anti-Ballistic Missile Treaty, when each side agreed to use "national technical means" to verify the other's compliance with the treaty. Six years later, President Jimmy Carter acknowledged the importance of the spy satellites in a speech at the Kennedy Space Center. "Photoreconnaissance satellites have become an important stabilizing factor in world affairs in the monitoring of arms control agreements," he said.

Indeed, overt surveillance can be effective at changing human behavior. Studies have repeatedly shown that the simple suggestion of being watched can encourage people to behave more cooperatively—even if there is no actual surveillance being conducted.

The belief that another person is present triggers a state of "psychological arousal," even if that "person" is not real, according to Ryan Calo of the University of Washington. In one study, people who stared at a photo of a bug-eyed robot donated 30 percent more money into a communal pool in a computer game than those who felt they weren't being watched.

In 2011, researchers at Newcastle University in Britain hung posters of staring human eyes at eye level in random locations in the campus cafeteria for thirty-two days. They found that people were twice as likely to clean up after themselves when they finished eating, compared to the locations where posters of flowers or other benign images were displayed. The following year, a similar group of researchers at the university posted signs near the bicycle racks around campus that said, "Cycle Thieves: We Are Watching You," with text printed over a photograph of human eyes. Bicycle thefts decreased by 62 percent in the locations with the new posters, but they increased in those locations without posters (by 65 percent), suggesting that the thieves had moved their activities to "safer" locations. "The effectiveness of this extremely cheap and simple intervention suggests that there can be considerable crime-reduction benefits to engaging the psychology of surveillance, even in the absence of surveillance itself," the researchers wrote.

Surveillance theater—the pretense of surveillance, conducted by humanlike eyes or robots—does appear to cause people to treat each other better. But the jury is still out about whether surveillance conducted by cameras deters crime.

A 2008 analysis by the California Research Bureau of forty-four studies of closed-circuit television surveillance found that 43 percent of the studies showed no effect on crime, while 41 percent showed statistically significant crime reduction.

In 2011, the Urban Institute analyzed camera surveillance systems in Baltimore, Chicago, and Washington, D.C., and found similarly conflicted results. In Baltimore, the authors found that a network of five hundred cameras that was monitored around the clock by a team of trained retired police officers contributed to a 35 percent drop in incidents of overall crime per month in one neighborhood. But cameras in other neighborhoods proved less successful. Similarly, in Chicago, which has installed a multimillion-dollar surveillance program with more than eight thousand cameras, the Urban Institute found that the cameras contributed to a 12 percent drop in crime in Humboldt Park but provided no statistically significant decline in crime in West Garfield Park. And in Washington, D.C., the Urban Institute found that surveillance cameras had no statistically significant impact on crime.

One reason for the conflicting results: many factors can contribute to a drop in crime, and it's difficult to isolate camera surveillance from other factors, such as increased police patrols or improved lighting.

In 2004, Leon Hempel and Eric Töpfer, writing from the Center for Technology and Society in Berlin, analyzed studies of closed-circuit television (CCTV) use in Europe and found that many of the studies lacked control groups to compare crime trends in the areas where cameras were installed to crime trends in the wider areas without cameras, and lacked analysis of the displacement of crime from the target areas to other areas.

The few studies that have used control groups show little support for the theory that cameras can prevent crime. Another Urban Institute study from 2011 analyzing the impact of surveillance cameras on crime in parking lots—and using a randomized controlled trial method—showed that the cameras made no real difference. The study compared a year's worth of car-related crime in twenty-five parking lots near Metro stations in Washington, D.C., that had installed motion-activated cameras with identical crimes in twenty-five similar "control" parking lots with no cameras installed. Although these were digital still cameras, researchers posted signs that gave the impression of constant camera surveillance of the parking lot. The study found that "the cameras had no discernable impact on crime."

And some evidence even suggests that simple streetlights may be as good at deterring crime as surveillance cameras. In 2004, the criminologists Brandon Welsh and David Farrington analyzed thirty-two studies conducted in the United States, Canada, and Britain to determine whether CCTV deterred crime more effectively than simple streetlights. Their conclusion: streetlights and CCTV were equally effective in deterring property crime—and neither one was very good at deterring violent crime. They theorized that cameras and streetlights both "act as a catalyst to stimulate crime reduction through a change in perceptions, attitudes and behavior of residents and potential offenders."

The authors of the Urban Institute study speculated that cameras are effective only when they are actively monitored by law enforcement agents, who act quickly upon the information obtained by the cameras. "The technology is only as good as the manner in which it is employed," they wrote.

In other words, surveillance cameras work to influence human behavior only when people are convinced that a human being is on the other side of the camera watching them.

✦

It is also not clear that surveillance conducted by computer data analysis helps catch terrorists before they strike.

After all, several terrorist plots have slipped through the surveillance dragnets. Since 9/11 there has been a series of attempted terrorist attacks. The most notable include:

- **The Shoe Bomber.** In 2001, Richard Colvin Reid tried and failed to detonate a bomb in his shoe while on a flight from Paris to Miami.
- **The LAX Shooter.** In 2002, Hesham Mohamed Hadayet, an Egyptian, opened fire at the El Al ticket counter in Los Angeles International Airport, killing two and wounding several others.
- **The Fort Hood Shooter.** In 2009, U.S. Army major Nidal Malik Hasan entered a deployment center at Fort Hood in Texas, jumped on a desk, shouted "Allahu Akbar," and opened fire with two pistols. He killed thirteen people and injured forty-three others.
- **The Underwear Bomber.** On Christmas Day 2009, Umar Farouk Abdulmutallab attempted to detonate explosives sewn into his undergarments aboard a flight to Detroit from Amsterdam. His device did not explode, but simply ignited—injuring Abdulmutallab and two other passengers.
- **The Times Square Bomber.** In 2010, Faisal Shahzad, who had trained with terrorists in Pakistan, tried but failed to detonate a car bomb in New York's Times Square.
- **The Boston Marathon Bombers.** In 2013, Tamerlan and Dzhokhar Tsarnaev allegedly deposited homemade bombs near the finish line of

the Boston Marathon. The explosions injured hundreds of people and killed three, including an eight-year-old boy.

Surveillance advocates point out that these statistics don't take into account the attacks that were prevented—many of which remain secret. However, for the first time, we do have some evidence of deterred attacks.

In the wake of the Snowden leaks, General Keith Alexander, the director of the NSA, disclosed that the agency's controversial phone and Internet dragnets had "contributed to our understanding, and, in many cases, helped enable the disruption of terrorist plots" in fifty-four cases.

He didn't specify the exact cases—although he did say most of them were foreign—but he did highlight the case of Najibullah Zazi. In 2009, Zazi was arrested just days before he and friends were allegedly planning to carry out a suicide bombing in the New York City subway.

According to Alexander, Zazi was swept up in a dragnet called "Operation High-Rise." The NSA found e-mails from Zazi among e-mails between the United States and Pakistan that it was monitoring under the PRISM dragnet that sweeps up the U.S. end of international e-mails.

Within those communications, the NSA also found a telephone number. It then used the Patriot Act dragnet of all telephone calls placed in the United States to locate other numbers that were connected to the first number. "We found Zazi was talking to a guy in New York who had connections to other terrorist elements," Alexander said.

Once the FBI was alerted, its agents used traditional law enforcement techniques. They followed Zazi as he drove to New York City from his home in Colorado. When he arrived, the FBI asked the Port Authority to stop Zazi at a checkpoint on the George Washington Bridge, but nothing was found in his car. Zazi was allowed to drive away, but he was spooked by the surveillance. A few days later, he flew back to Denver without carrying out his plot.

Zazi was arrested in Colorado and later pleaded guilty to charges including conspiracy to use weapons of mass destruction and providing material support to al-Qaeda. He has not yet been sentenced.

But it is not clear that the government needed dragnets to catch Zazi. If Zazi was e-mailing with terrorists under surveillance, a search warrant would have sufficed to capture his communications. Similarly, once his phone number was identified, a judge would most likely have approved pulling the calling records for that phone.

When closely questioned by the Senate about whether the dragnets were "critical" to catching Zazi, General Alexander hedged. He said phone records were *not* critical and didn't answer whether the e-mail dragnets were critical to catching Zazi. And even President Obama was lukewarm when describing the use of NSA dragnets in catching Zazi. "We might have caught him some other way," he said in a television interview with Charlie Rose. "But at the margins, we are increasing our chances of preventing a catastrophe like that through these programs."

Is mass surveillance worth it when its fiercest advocates can only say that it "contributed to our understanding" of cases "at the margins"?

✦

Dragnets are also a double-edged sword. If intelligence agencies pick up a lead but don't pursue it, they are often blamed in the event of an attack. That's what happened in the cases of the underwear bomber, the Fort Hood shooter, and the Boston Marathon bombers. The perpetrators had all been flagged as terrorist threats at some time prior to their attacks.

In their book *Enemies Within: Inside the NYPD's Secret Spying Unit and Bin Laden's Final Plot Against America*, the journalists Matt Apuzzo and Adam Goldman chronicle how the New York Police Department's indiscriminate surveillance of Muslims in New York City failed to catch Najibullah Zazi and his friends, as they dreamed up their terrorism plot in Queens. The NYPD's "rakers" had surveilled Zazi's neighborhood restaurants, his mosque, and even the travel agency where he bought his airline tickets to Pakistan. "After years of raking, the NYPD knew where New York's Muslims were," Apuzzo and Goldman wrote. "But they still didn't know where the terrorists were."

The father of Umar Farouk Abdulmutallab, the underwear bomber, had warned the American embassy in Nigeria of his son's radical views and that his son had disappeared and might have traveled to Yemen. A White House investigation found that "several agencies" had obtained information about Abdulmutallab prior to the attempted attack but had not placed him on a watch list.

An FBI field office had been monitoring Fort Hood shooter Nidal Malik Hasan's communications with radical Islamic cleric Anwar al-

Awlaki but hadn't taken further action before he opened fire at Fort Hood. And the future Boston Marathon bomber Tamerlan Tsarnaev had been in the National Counterterrorism Center's database for at least a year prior to his attack.

Some research suggests that collecting vast amounts of data simply can't predict rare events like terrorism. A 2006 paper by Jeff Jonas, an IBM research scientist, and Jim Harper, the director of information policy at the Cato Institute, concluded that terrorism events aren't common enough to lend themselves to large-scale computer data mining.

After all, Zazi was buying nail-polish remover to build an acetone explosive, Abdulmutallab was sewing explosives into his underwear, and Hasan was sending fan mail to al-Awlaki. Each event had its own distinct patterns. By comparison, data mining for patterns works well in pursuing credit card and insurance fraud, where fraud is more common. Credit card companies develop "red flags"—such as transactions in foreign countries, that can alert them to a possible fraud. "Unlike consumers' shopping habits and financial fraud, terrorism does not occur with enough frequency to enable the creation of valid predictive models," Jonas and Harper conclude.

In 2008, the National Academy of Sciences convened dozens of experts to study counterterrorism data mining. The group reached a similar conclusion: "Highly-automated tools and techniques cannot be easily applied to the much more difficult problem of detecting and preempting a terrorist attack, and success in doing so may not be possible at all."

Some intelligence officials have hinted that they share the same pessimism about their ability to sort through vast amounts of data to predict the next attack. In a 2012 speech, Matthew Olsen, the director of the National Counterterrorism Center, said, "If there is another attack, the likelihood is that you could look back retrospectively and find some hint or some clue in the vast amount of data that we have access to."

And after the Boston Marathon bombings, the city's police commissioner, Ed Davis, went even further, telling Congress that more technological surveillance wouldn't have helped. "There's no computer that's going to spit out a terrorist's name," he said. Instead, the best leads come from people who alert "law enforcement when something awry is identified. That really needs to happen and should be our first step."

✦

So what can we conclude about life in a state of surveillance?

The evidence suggests that human surveillance, or perceived surveillance through pictures of human eyes or cameras actively monitored by humans, can modify behavior to promote positive social habits, such as clearing up dishes in a communal cafeteria, and sometimes can deter property crimes. However, there is some evidence that suggests that street lighting may be just as effective. Mutually assured surveillance also appears to have helped prevent mutually assured destruction during the Cold War.

However, surveillance does not appear to be good for predicting terrorism, as many terrorist events have slipped through the dragnets. Even the Stasi failed to predict the collapse of the East German regime in 1989. And the flood of surveillance data can be overwhelming and confounding to those who are charged with sorting through it to find terrorists.

But ubiquitous, covert surveillance does appear to be very good at repression. People who were indiscriminately and secretly monitored— whether in East Germany or in the Finnish study—were found to censor their behavior and speech.

The question then becomes: Are the benefits of ubiquitous, indiscriminate, dragnet surveillance worth living in a culture of fear?

4
FREEDOM OF ASSOCIATION

Yasir Afifi no longer believes in coincidences. If he sees the same car twice while driving, he tenses up and ponders changing his route. "Things that happen by coincidence I examine like a scientist," he says. Paranoia doesn't come naturally to Yasir. His temperament is sunny, his gait is springy, and his handshake is firm. Just twenty-three years old, he exudes the eternal optimism of a born salesman. But ever since Yasir found that he was being surveilled by the FBI, he has become extremely cautious.

Yasir moved out of his bachelor pad—which he shared with three friends—and married a woman with two daughters from a previous marriage. He spends evenings at home helping the girls with their homework. He has stopped using Facebook except for playing a few games. "I'm one of those guys now who believes that everything you type online or say on the phone goes into a database," Yasir says.

He avoids conversations about politics or religion. He started using a different name at work, Aladdin, because he didn't want his boss to Google his name and see news about his FBI surveillance. He is humorless about pranks that involve breaking the law. If a friend suggests an April Fools' joke, he says, "I would say, 'What you are saying is wrong, it's illegal.' Even if they say it's just a joke, I'll say, 'Delete my number.'" He estimates he has stopped hanging out with about 90 percent of his previous friends who, he says, "liked to go get drunk or high and do stupid stuff." He rarely speaks to his best friend from childhood who posts online about smoking marijuana and spends his free time playing video games.

Over a leisurely lunch at an Indian restaurant with Yasir and his wife, Angelina Asfour, I asked her how he had changed since the surveillance. She told me, "He's basically the same. He just doesn't have any of the same friends."

Yasir added: "It just made me really cautious about who I associate with."

✦

Categorizing people by their associations is a favorite tactic of repressive regimes. The Stasi were obsessed with identifying anyone with an association to West Germany. The Nazis were obsessed with identifying anyone with Jewish blood. The Iranians are obsessed with identifying anyone related to the United States. The Chinese are obsessed with identifying any potential opposition to the government.

That's why freedom of association is one of the rights enshrined in the United Nations Declaration of Human Rights, which was adopted after the atrocities of World War II.

Generally, freedom of association means that people should not be prevented from joining groups or, alternatively, coerced into joining groups. In the United States, the First Amendment protecting freedom of speech and freedom of assembly has also conferred the right to freedom of association.

In 1958, the Supreme Court ruled that the state of Alabama's attempt to obtain the membership lists of the National Association for the Advancement of Colored People was unconstitutional, because it could chill members' First Amendment right to freedom of association and that freedom of association was essential to the liberty promised by the Fourteenth Amendment. "Revelation of the identity of its rank-and-file members has exposed these members to economic reprisal, loss of employment, threat of physical coercion, and other manifestations of public hostility," wrote Justice John Marshall Harlan in his majority opinion. "Under these circumstances, we think it apparent that compelled disclosure of petitioner's Alabama membership is likely to affect adversely the ability of petitioner and its members to pursue their collective effort to foster beliefs which they admittedly have the right to advocate."

In today's world, however, the idea of protecting only members of a group is an outdated way of looking at freedom of association. Yasir didn't have to join a group like "Young Muslim Men of Santa Clara" for his associations to be noted by the authorities. His digital footprints left a trail of associations that could be scooped up by the FBI with very little effort.

In fact, it can be argued that the very purpose of much technology these days is to unveil hidden associations. Consider people who track their own movements using Fitbit pedometers and other technology tools—they are studying their own movements in order to better understand the hidden associations. Do they feel better on days that they walk more?

Or consider my husband, who has installed sensors in our walls to monitor our electricity, gas, and water usage. He is trying to unveil hidden associations. And it has worked: we now know that our toaster is incredibly inefficient and that our water usage is weirdly spiking. (I blame my daughter's long showers, but we haven't quite corralled the data to prove that yet.)

I'm all for learning from my own data. But the same technology that we use to monitor ourselves is also being used by others to monitor us and to build dossiers about our likes and dislikes, about our associations.

In today's world, every choice we make associates us with a person, a place, or an idea. Visit a political website; you are associated with its views. Sit in a restaurant near somebody who is being watched; your cell phone is now part of the "community of interest" that may be monitored by authorities. Those associations are scooped up and entered into databases where people use them to make predictions about your future behavior.

Even proponents of the so-called big data movement admit that these issues are perplexing. In their 2013 book *Big Data: A Revolution That Will Transform How We Live, Work, and Think*, Viktor Mayer-Schönberger and Kenneth Cukier state that as big data is increasingly used to make predictions about people's behavior, safeguards will have to be put in place, which may include the creation of a new profession of "algorithmists" who will conduct audits of big data usage. "Without such safeguards, the very idea of justice may be undermined," they write.

And no less a big data proponent than Eric Schmidt, the chairman of Google, warns in his book *The New Digital Age*, written with Jared Cohen, that the rise of "near-permanent data storage" will usher in an era where "people will be held responsible for their virtual associations, past and present." Although Schmidt and Cohen are mostly bullish about how technology will empower citizens, in a section of the book called "Police State 2.0," they warn, "Everything a regime would need to build an incredibly intimidating digital police state is commercially available now." In the hands of a police state, they write, "guilt by association will take on new meaning with this level of monitoring."

✦

The surveillance of Yasir Afifi appears to have started with an innocent question about why deodorant could not pass through an airport screening.

On June 24, 2010, a user of the social networking website Reddit.com named "JayClay" posted a question: "So if my deodorant could be a bomb, why are you just chucking it in the bin?"

His post generated hundreds of comments. Some Reddit users dubbed the deodorant ban "Security Theater." Others talked about items they had smuggled onto planes—nail clippers, bamboo needles, razors, knives. One user suggested that bombing a mall would be a "softer target."

On June 25, a user named "Khaledthegypsy" weighed in: "bombing a mall seems so easy to do," he wrote. "i mean all you really need is a bomb, a regular outfit so you arent the crazy guy in a trench coat trying to blow up a mall and a shopping bag. i mean if terrorism were actually a legitimate threat, think about how many fucking malls would have blown up already."

Khaledthegypsy signed off with a sort of joke: ". . . so . . . yea . . . now i'm surely bugged : /"

Khaledthegypsy was really Khaled Ibrahim, a nineteen-year-old community college student in Santa Clara, California, and Yasir Afifi's best friend. Khaled was more accurate than he knew. Four months later, he and Yasir went to get the oil changed in Yasir's blue Lincoln LS 2000 sedan. When the car was up on its hoist, Yasir noticed a wire hanging from the undercarriage. The wire was connected to what looked like a giant walkie-talkie stuck to the bottom of his car.

"That is not part of the car," Yasir told the mechanic.

When the mechanic tugged on the device, it came off easily; it had been attached to the undercarriage by a magnet. Yasir thought to himself: "This is either a very outdated type of tracking device or supposed to look like a pipe bomb."

Born and raised in Santa Clara, Yasir had moved to Egypt with his Egyptian-born father when he was twelve years old, after his parents' divorce. When he turned eighteen, he returned to the United States to go to a community college, get a job, and live on his own. Yasir and Khaled, whose family was also Egyptian, had been best friends in elementary school and reconnected when Yasir returned to the United States.

Soon after Yasir's return to the United States, he says, an FBI agent showed up at his door when he was out and left a card asking him to call. When Yasir called, the agent told him that the FBI wanted to talk to him because "we got an anonymous tip that you might be a threat to national security." Yasir said he would be happy to answer questions, but that he first wanted to consult a lawyer.

Yasir called a prepaid legal service, which advised him not to meet with the agent. So he declined the FBI's invitation and forgot about it. He threw himself into his business management classes and his job selling computer equipment to businesses in the Middle East.

But after he discovered the device under his car, his thoughts returned to the FBI. He threw the device in the backseat and drove home to show it off to his roommates.

One roommate was worried it looked like a bomb. Yasir wondered how much he could get if he sold the device. Khaled, more suspicious by nature, suggested first posting it on Reddit to find out what it was. And so at 10:15 p.m. Khaled uploaded a picture of the device to Reddit with a simple question: "Does this mean the FBI is after us?"

By midnight, Reddit commenters had identified the device as a Guardian ST820 GPS tracking unit manufactured by Cobham, a company that sells and markets its products exclusively to law enforcement agencies. In short: "Yes, FBI or Police is after you," wrote user "jeanmarcp."

At first, Yasir was excited. The post made the front page of Reddit. More than three thousand people commented on the article. Advice was raining in from all around. Yasir recalled thinking, "This is awesome."

The next day, his excitement began to fade. Yasir's roommates told him that a man and a woman were standing by his car in the apartment complex's parking lot. In a bit of bravado, Yasir went downstairs to confront them. They were still standing next to his car, which was parked inside the electronic gates that control access to his apartment complex. "Hi, is there something I can help you with?" Yasir asked. "You're standing right next to my car."

"Do you know your tags are expired?" the man said with a laugh.

"How is that your business?" Yasir asked. "Please step away from my car while I reverse."

For a moment, it seemed that Yasir would leave the strangers behind. He pulled out of the apartment complex and turned left onto the street. Then he heard the squeal of tires and saw two dark SUVs pull up behind him. They followed him for half a block, and then they flashed their lights. In his rearview mirror, he saw that a third car had joined—a black Chevy Caprice.

Yasir pulled over, having traveled only a few hundred feet. He was in front of the elementary school across the street from his apartment complex. Six people walked up to his car—the man and woman who had been beside his car and four agents wearing bulletproof vests holding guns.

Yasir's stomach felt fluttery and his hands went cold. But he tried to be tough. An agent identified himself as "police" and asked about his expired tag. "Is that why an army pulled me over?" Yasir responded. The police officer asked if he could search the car, and Yasir said yes. But instead of searching the vehicle, the police officer asked Yasir to step out of the car and speak to FBI agents standing behind the car.

Yasir got out of the car. The officer patted him down for weapons and then let him approach the FBI agents—the same man and woman who had been standing by his car earlier. The man identified himself as Vincent and the woman as Jennifer.

Vincent asked for the tracking device back. "I don't have it," Yasir said. "How do you know I didn't sell it?"

Vincent played tough, declaring the device to be federal property and threatening to bring federal charges against Yasir. "Give us the device or you can be arrested for obstruction of justice," Vincent threatened. Yasir asked for a lawyer but got no response.

Jennifer played nice. "We just want the device back, just give it back to us and we'll leave you alone," she said.

Yasir suggested that he could have his attorney contact them to make arrangements to return the device. But that only incensed Vincent, who yelled that Yasir must turn over the device immediately.

"Why are you doing this to me?" Yasir asked.

Vincent pulled out a piece of paper with Khaled's Reddit post about bombing a mall.

"This is why we were tracking you," Vincent said.

"Why don't you put this device under his car?" Yasir said.

"Oh, you guys are together every day," Vincent said.

"So what do you think about what he said?" Jennifer asked.

"That's so stupid," Yasir said. "Khaled is a very smart guy. But what he wrote was very stupid. . . . Why don't you go talk to him?"

Eventually, however, Yasir's toughness began to crumble in the face of men with guns. He agreed to return the device, which was sitting on the coffee table in the apartment.

Yasir, Jennifer, and Vincent walked across the street, back into the apartment complex, as his friends and neighbors watched. The four agents with guns followed them. Yasir buzzed them all into the electronic gates, and they walked up the outdoor stairs to his second-floor apartment.

As Yasir unlocked the door, Vincent tried to enter the apartment with him. "Step back from the door," Yasir said.

His roommates were watching TV in the living room. "Hey guys, there are FBI right outside the door," Yasir told them. Before they had a chance to respond, he grabbed the device and took it outside to give to Vincent.

"Are you going to arrest me?" Yasir asked.

"No," Vincent replied. "But we'd like to ask you a few more questions."

Now that the tracking device was out of his hands, Yasir was curious to hear more about how extensively he had been monitored by the FBI. So he agreed to a brief talk.

He walked with them back to their cars. The four agents with guns drove away, leaving Yasir alone with Vincent and Jennifer. She gave him a business card identifying herself as FBI agent Jennifer Kanaan.

They began peppering him with questions that seemed to be about jihad.

Had he traveled to Syria, Iran, or Afghanistan? No.

Had he ever had any type of overseas military training? No.

Was he religious? "I go to mosque on Friday," Yasir said.

Jennifer wrote down on her notebook, "Yasir Afifi is not a threat to national security," and showed the page to Yasir.

Now it was Yasir's turn to ask questions. "How do I know you guys aren't following me everywhere?" he asked.

Jennifer responded in Arabic. "I really like your taste in restaurants," she said.

Yasir was floored. "You speak Arabic. Are you kidding me?" he said.

She continued in Arabic: "We know where you go, we know what you do, we know you take your girlfriend to Santana Row," a shopping mall in San Jose.

"Wow, what else do you know?" Yasir asked.

"We know you have a new job—congratulations on your new job," she said. "We know you are going to Dubai in two weeks."

Yasir's heart sank. He had only talked about the job on the phone, and he had only discussed the Dubai trip in e-mails. The FBI must have been listening to his calls and reading his e-mails. He thought to himself: "Do you also know what color my boxers are?"

"I'm sure you're listening to my calls," he said.

"Oh, I can't tell you that," she replied.

"Am I going to see you guys again? Are you going to pull me over again with your army?" Yasir said.

"Don't worry about it, you're boring," she said. "You're probably not going to hear from us again. No need to contact a lawyer."

Yasir didn't heed the FBI's advice. After the agents left, a friend put him in touch with the Council on American-Islamic Relations, a Muslim legal advocacy group.

On March 2, 2011, CAIR attorneys filed a complaint in federal court alleging that the warrantless GPS tracking device violated Yasir's Fourth Amendment rights, that compiling files about his religious behavior violated his First Amendment rights, and that the surveillance created "an objective chill on his First Amendment activities," among other charges.

The complaint alleged that Yasir now felt fear "when expressing his political views and maintaining certain lawful associations" and that the surveillance "deterred others from associating with him, prospective employers most notably."

Yasir not only sought an injunction against future tracking, but also requested the data about his location be deleted from the government records.

The FBI won the right to file a secret response to Yasir's complaint. In its limited public filings, the bureau said that its investigation of Yasir was closed and that its warrantless tracking of Yasir was legal at that time. (Since then, the Supreme Court has said that it is not acceptable for agents to trespass when installing a GPS tracking device.) The government also argued that Yasir could not point to any concrete evidence of his First Amendment rights being curtailed in the future: "He has not demonstrated a concrete, imminent threat of such conduct occurring in the future."

✦

The First Amendment to the U.S. Constitution is a negative right. It states what *cannot* be done: "Congress shall make no law respecting an establishment of religion, or prohibiting the free exercise thereof; or abridging the freedom of speech, or of the press; or the right of the people peaceably to assemble, and to petition the Government for a redress of grievances."

As a result, it's not always easy to tell what the First Amendment is *for*. To help me sort through the legal thickets, I sat down with the renowned First Amendment scholar Lee Bollinger, who is also the president of Columbia University. "First Amendment theory can be described as paranoia," Bollinger said. The founders believed that a functioning democracy required freedom to criticize the government. As a result, an important test for any First Amendment legal case is: Does the activity in question limit participation in democratic debate?

The Supreme Court has been extremely cautious about curbing any activities if those restrictions might chill public participation in democracy. For instance, in 1964, the Supreme Court ruled that the New York Times Company was not liable for publishing an advertisement that included untruths about a public official because a "rule compelling the critic of official conduct to guarantee the truth of all his factual assertions . . . leads to a comparable 'self-censorship.'" And in 2000, the Supreme

Court ruled that the Boy Scouts of America did not have to accept a gay member because forcing groups to accept members would violate the freedom of expressive association. "The First Amendment protects expression, be it of the popular variety or not," Chief Justice William H. Rehnquist wrote.

But the high court has not been receptive to the argument that surveillance is harmful to free society. In 1972, the Court ruled 5–4 that U.S. citizens who had been spied on by a U.S. Army surveillance program could not demonstrate any specific harm and thus lacked a "personal stake in the outcome of the controversy" required for judicial redress. And again in 2013, the Supreme Court ruled 5–4 that U.S. citizens who had been spied upon by the NSA's warrantless wiretapping program could not prove "concrete, particularized and actual or imminent" injury that would require judicial action.

However, I was struck by the eloquence of the dissent from Justices William O. Douglas and Thurgood Marshall in the 1972 case. They called the army surveillance program a "cancer in our body politic" that is "at war with the principles of the First Amendment." They wrote: "When an intelligence officer looks over every nonconformist's shoulder in the library, or walks invisibly by his side in a picket line, or infiltrates his club, the America once extolled as the voice of liberty heard around the world no longer is cast in the image which Jefferson and Madison designed, but more in the Russian image."

✦

After their brush with the FBI, Yasir and Khaled were both paranoid about every car that drove by. But slowly, the fear wore off and a new feeling set in: acceptance of being watched.

"What can you do?" Khaled told me when we met at a Starbucks in Santa Clara, a year after the event. "We're about to lose all our privacy anyway. Technology took it away from us."

Khaled walked me through what happened after the FBI showed up at Yasir's door. A few days later, the FBI agent Jennifer called Khaled's cell phone and left a message. He didn't call her back. Since then, he said, he often got calls from a blocked number—when he picked up all he heard was a whooshing sound. "They'll call me twice a day for two days and then not for three weeks," he told me.

Initially, he looked under his car every time he got in, but after a while he stopped. He figured that if the FBI wanted to follow him, it would find a way.

His Reddit posts slowed to a trickle. Where he used to post long treatises about injustice, he switched to mostly short, noncontroversial comments.

Khaled also stopped hanging out with Yasir. When Redditers began pestering Khaled for news about the GPS tracking case, Khaled wrote, "He just kind of became a douche and flaky on us so we kind of fell apart."

When Khaled and I met, he had just returned from a visit to Egypt and he told me he was thinking of moving back there. He said that people in the United States are too complacent as they watch their rights slip away.

"Here it's the illusion of freedom," he said. "There it is actual freedom. You can do whatever you want."

✦

It was hard for me to argue with Khaled that he should be more optimistic about his freedom. Unfortunately, Muslims in America have often been treated as suspects in a police lineup ever since al-Qaeda's attack on America on September 11, 2001.

After 9/11, the FBI set up a "domain management" system to analyze where Muslims lived, using commercial data, and to target those communities with informants. Not surprisingly, this corresponded with an increase in terrorism prosecutions of Muslims. The investigative journalist Trevor Aaronson examined the 508 terrorism prosecutions brought by the FBI since 9/11 and found that nearly half of the cases involved the use of informants and one-third involved stings. Aaronson reported that informants often target vulnerable, desperate people and lure them into a phony terrorist plot. "There hasn't been yet a sting operation on people who had weapons themselves," Aaronson said. "It's almost universally the case that the entire means is provided by the FBI."

One of the most aggressive efforts to spy on Muslims has taken place in New York City, through a secret collaboration between the New York Police Department and the Central Intelligence Agency to infiltrate Muslim political groups, neighborhoods, events, and student groups in New

York and New Jersey. In 2008, an undercover agent accompanied a Muslim student group from the City College of New York on a whitewater rafting trip. In 2009, undercover NYPD officers set up a safe house near Rutgers University in New Jersey, but their cover was blown when the building superintendent suspected them of being a terrorist cell and called the police.

Consider the story of Asad Dandia, a twenty-year-old New York City student who was surveilled by an NYPD informant. In 2011, Dandia cofounded a charity called Fesabeelillah Services of NYC, which raised money to feed the homeless and indigent. In March 2012, he was contacted on Facebook by a man named Shamiur Rahman, who said he wanted to get involved with the charity. "We had several friends in common, and I was happy to help him in his quest for religious self-improvement, so I introduced him to my friends in FSNYC," Dandia wrote in a blog post describing his surveillance.

Rahman and Dandia, who were about the same age, became close friends. Rahman visited Dandia's parents' house several times, and once spent the night. Rahman was also nosy. "Rahman would ask everyone he met for their phone number, often within minutes of meeting them," Dandia wrote. "He also often tried to take photos with or of people he met through me."

On October 2, 2012, Rahman posted a message on Facebook revealing that he was an NYPD informant. He later told the press that he became an informant after a string of minor marijuana arrests and that he was paid as much as $1,000 a month. But Rahman eventually tired of spying on his friends and quit. "I hated that I was using people to make money," Rahman told the Associated Press. "I made a mistake."

Rahman's revelation shocked his friends. "When I learned the news, I froze," Dandia wrote in the blog post. "It was a terrifying feeling. I couldn't believe that an NYPD informant had been in my home." The incident also cast suspicion on Dandia's charity, which had been renamed Muslims Giving Back. The local mosque asked Dandia to stop holding charity meetings at the mosque and to stop soliciting donations from congregants. The charity suffered financially and emotionally, Dandia says. Dandia and other members have started blurring out their faces in photos they post to the charity's Facebook page. Dandia has joined in a lawsuit against the New York Police Department.

"I used to try to be as inclusive and public as possible about my charitable work—now, I communicate mainly with people I know personally," Dandia wrote.

✦

Yasir Afifi has also withdrawn behind a protective shield. He no longer hangs out with his childhood friend Khaled. He is busy working as a software salesman and taking night classes to complete his college degree. He saved up to buy a house, and his wife is pregnant.

"If you've grown up and your best friend hasn't, it's hard to hang out," he told me. "At this point in my life, me hanging out with him is a complete waste of my time."

Yasir can't afford to take chances. He believes he is still on some sort of watch list. When he and his wife returned from a trip to Puerto Vallarta, Mexico, in 2012, he was questioned for nearly an hour upon arrival, while federal agents searched his bags and asked questions. He said the agents took his wife's phone but that he refused to give them his phone. "They were asking questions they had no right to ask. They asked my wife why she broke up with her last husband," he told me. "I was so angry."

But he tries to keep his anger in check. "Would I like some policy where they stopped harassing Muslim Americans? Yes," he told me as we stood in the spot where he had been pulled over by the FBI. "Would I like if they wrote me an apology for putting [the GPS tracking device] on my car? Yes. But these are things I'm not depending on. I'm going forward with my life. I want to be wealthy. I want to have a nice family. I want the American Dream. I want others to have it, too."

A year after that conversation, Yasir achieved his dream. He and his wife bought a house in South San Jose. One hot day, I came to visit, driving my rental car to their cul-de-sac. I parked next to the small swimming pool shared by all the houses on the block.

Inside, Yasir showed me a brand-new leather couch set in the living room, the colorful bedspreads and curtains in the girls' bedroom. A grill was set up in the tiny side yard.

As I toured the house, I kept thinking about my relatives who immigrated to the United States from Russia at the turn of the twentieth century. They were escaping a world where Jews were persecuted for their beliefs.

They suffered a lot to come here—my great-grandmother worked in a sweatshop, my great-grandfather was a street peddler—but it was worth it for the freedom.

Yasir's family came here from Egypt to seek economic opportunity. Yasir has worked hard and achieved financial success here. But he has not tasted as much freedom as was promised. Instead, he has censored himself and repressed his associations.

Yasir has the freedom to buy grills and town houses and leather couches on credit, but apparently not the freedom to associate with people who make jokes about the government's ban on deodorant at airports.

5

THREAT MODELS

In a world where nearly everything is being monitored, it is easy to feel hopeless about privacy. Often, when I tell people I have just met that I write about privacy, their immediate response is, "I've given up. Privacy is dead."

In truth, I had kind of given up, too. For three years, I had been writing about the privacy invasions that technology had made possible. But I hadn't done much to try to protect myself. I told myself that it was because I was too busy, but in fact I was overwhelmed by the impossibility of it.

After many such conversations, I started to feel guilty. Was my reporting about privacy invasions actually contributing to the hopelessness?

I am a natural optimist: I wanted to believe there was hope. I am also a born contrarian: I wanted to disprove the doubters. And finally, I am stubborn: I determined that I would find some hope.

So I decided, against all odds, to try to evade the dragnets. I would attempt to avoid being monitored during everyday activities such as reading and shopping. I would obscure my location—at home and while out and about. I would seal my e-mails and texts with the digital equivalent of hot wax. I would find ways to freely associate with people and ideas. I would try to find a way to protect my kids from building a digital trail that would haunt them later in their lives.

It was a daunting task. "I can't do it," I told a close friend. "How would I live without a credit card? Without a cell phone? It would be irresponsible to my children."

But I realized that my questions were exactly what I needed to examine: Was it possible to live in the modern world and evade the dragnets? Had I somehow consented to ubiquitous surveillance—trading my data for free services or security—as the people in the surveillance business contend? What would happen if I tried to withdraw my consent?

✦

My first step was to identify the threats to my privacy.

In the computer security industry, identifying your adversaries is called building your "threat model." The idea is that you can protect yourself only against known threats. The computer security industry expert Bruce Schneier calls this the first lesson of security: security is a trade-off. "There's no such thing as absolute security," he wrote in the introduction to his book *Schneier on Security*. "Life entails risk, and all security involves trade-offs. We get security by giving something up: money, time, convenience, capabilities, liberties, etc." What you give up depends on what you are trying to protect and whom you are trying to protect it from.

Focusing on the wrong adversary can be disastrous. Consider the case of General David Petraeus, the former director of the Central Intelligence Agency.

In 2012, the FBI uncovered General Petraeus using a rather low-tech technique to conduct an extramarital affair with his biographer Paula Broadwell. Critics decried him for using a shared Gmail account, in which he and Broadwell left draft e-mails for each other—*Foreign Policy* magazine dubbed it "old spycraft." But the real problem was that the general had misjudged his adversary.

He and his mistress were trying to hide their affair from their spouses. In that case, a shared Gmail account, accessed from computers not in their homes, was sufficient protection. But they had not envisioned that the FBI would begin investigating Broadwell for sending threatening e-mails to a volunteer event planner in Tampa, Florida, named Jill Kelley. The FBI obtained the computer IP addresses from which the e-mails had been sent, most likely through a subpoena to Broadwell's e-mail provider.

FBI agents traced those IP addresses to a variety of public unsecured Wi-Fi connections, including several hotels, and then sought hotel guest lists for the dates the e-mails had been sent. The FBI soon found that Paula Broadwell was the common guest at those hotels on those dates. And from there it was a short step to search Broadwell's e-mail, via either a search warrant or subpoenas—and to discover her affair with Petraeus.

If the general and his mistress had attempted to outsmart the FBI, they would have at the very least needed to take steps to mask the IP addresses from which they logged in to their accounts, to use encryption, and to make sure their accounts were under fake names. Even then, there's no guarantee they wouldn't have been caught.

After all, perfect privacy is not possible, even if you identify your adversary correctly.

Consider another case: Theodore J. Kaczynski, the Unabomber. For a decade, Kaczynski lived as a hermit in a one-room cabin—with no electricity, plumbing, or telephone—in a remote area of Montana while conducting a series of bombings through the mail that killed three people and injured twenty-two others. But even the hermit could not evade the FBI forever. The FBI eventually tracked him down in his cabin due in large part to the fact that his brother stepped forward to provide an essay Kaczynski had written as a young man that could be compared to a linguistic analysis of his current writing.

And that is a good thing: society was better off when the FBI caught Kaczynski and ended his bombing spree. But the rest of us would be better off building our threat models.

✦

What is my threat model?

I'm a working journalist with a son in preschool and a daughter in elementary school. My husband is a professor who travels overseas often for his research.

If I were to describe my family in one simple word it would be "busy." We are always running in a million different directions. Privacy and security are exactly the kinds of things that fall through the cracks when you're always in a rush.

And yet I want to protect myself and my children from indiscriminate tracking. I want us to have the freedom to associate with people and places and ideas, without worrying about how those associations might constrain our future prospects.

I also want to protect myself against targeted threats against journalists. After all, the Obama administration has been extremely aggressive at prosecuting people who pass sensitive material to journalists. Since 2009, the administration has charged eight government whistle-blowers with allegations of violating the Espionage Act, a law that had been used just three times over the previous ninety-two years against government officials accused of providing classified information to journalists.

My concern is less about myself because it seems that the journalists don't end up in jail too often. Sadly, it is the people who leak information to journalists who end up in jail. I want to be able to give my sources a pledge of confidentiality that I can honor.

So, really, I have two threats: indiscriminate tracking and targeted attacks against journalists and their sources.

✦

When building a threat model, it's also important to assess your own strengths and vulnerabilities.

My strength is that I have been writing about privacy and technology for several years, so I have an army of experts I can call on for help and guidance. I am also lucky that I do not have any privacy issues that I have to "clean up." A few years ago, when my book about the social network MySpace was published, I worked to make my online reputation bulletproof. I conferred with search-engine optimization consultants who helped me build a website and sanitize my social network profiles so that my Google search results would be dominated by items I had written about myself, rather than items written by others about me.

Also, my kids are young and their data are not yet publicly available. The kids don't have cell phones or computer access. They have limited access to the iPad and they don't have any social media accounts (except for the ones that my daughter's school has set up for her within their walled garden). So I don't have a lot to "clean up" on their front, either.

But I have plenty of vulnerabilities. Probably my biggest issue is that I have no patience. I often take shortcuts instead of hunkering down to figure out why my technology tools aren't working. As a result, I am liable to leave myself vulnerable to exposure.

Another huge issue: my home address is known to the world. When my husband and I bought and renovated our home, I succumbed to the pleas of a colleague at the *Wall Street Journal* and blogged about the renovation for the newspaper's online real estate section. Although I never published the exact address of our house, at least one blog identified it from the photos. So one basic building block of privacy is already gone.

My husband also doesn't care about privacy. He is a professor, and he always jokes that if somebody broke into his files, the number of readers of his papers would double. Not only does he not care about privacy, but also his field of work is essentially privacy-invading. He is a mechanical engineer, and one of his projects is to install remote sensors to monitor energy usage. In fact, he installed energy sensors in our home without asking me. I only found out the day we were moving in and one of his graduate students was in the house finishing up the wiring for the system.

That said, the real-time energy monitors that he installed are actually kind of cool—we can see how much energy we're using at any given time, and we can learn from our patterns of usage. Of course, it's a little weird that his grad students are also monitoring our energy usage.

"What do you do on Fridays?" one of his students asked him one day. "Energy usage spikes on Fridays." It turns out that our cleaning lady comes on Fridays and runs the vacuum cleaner.

My kids also don't care about privacy. To them, "privacy" is just a word that means "no." Privacy is why they can't post videos on YouTube. Privacy is why I won't let them sign up for kids' social networks. Privacy is why I complain to their teachers about posting pictures of them on a non-password-protected blog.

In fact, my daughter thinks that privacy is something to be defeated. She delights in trying to guess my passwords. Once, she figured out my iPhone password, accessed my phone, changed the password, and then forgot what she changed it to, leaving me locked out and forcing me to do a factory reset to gain access to the device.

So I will be fighting this fight alone, at least on the home front. My fellow soldiers will be a ramshackle network of technologists, hackers, and concerned citizens around the world.

✦

Now I needed a battle plan for how to defend myself. And I needed to determine how far I was going to go: Was I going to live in a bunker? Was I going to change my name?

I read a few books about protecting privacy and they were startlingly extreme. In *How to Be Invisible: Protect Your Home, Your Children, Your Assets, and Your Life*, J. J. Luna writes that "your journey to invisibility must begin with the first step: *separating your name from your home address.*" If your address is already publicly known, he advises moving.

Luna suggests setting up a limited liability company in New Mexico that owns your assets—house, car, and so on. He goes on to suggest that you cannot send your children to public school because that will reveal your address. "There are only two remedies for this danger," he writes. "Either homeschool your kids or put them in a private school willing to guarantee their privacy."

I can't afford to put my kids in private school or to quit my job and homeschool my children. Nor do I want to pursue either of those options.

Luna's privacy threat model? Private investigators. And even if you follow all of his advice, he says, a private investigator with unlimited funds will still be able to find you eventually.

In *One Nation, Under Surveillance*, Boston T. Party, the pen name of Kenneth W. Royce, writes that "the law no longer works because America has spun off her legal axis." He advises readers to hoard their guns, grow their own food, homeschool their children, and boot up their computers from a CD containing an operating system called Puppy Linux.

His threat model is a hostile government that he perceives to be ready to strike at civilians.

I'm not that paranoid yet. I don't believe that the government is a lost cause. I still believe in the legal system and that our system of checks and balances is mostly working. I'm not ready to start hoarding guns and growing my own food (aside from a few tomatoes and basil in the back-yard each summer). And I'm not planning to start homeschooling, or to move to an all-cash economy.

I am trying to defend against a different threat: the rise of indiscriminate tracking—the dragnets that aim to capture every element of our lives in a permanent record. I worry that this indiscriminate tracking will prevent me from associating with certain ideas and people, that it will cause me economic distress, and that it will create a culture of fear. At its worst, I am concerned that indiscriminate tracking could enable the creation of a totalitarian surveillance state.

✦

To build my threat model, I consulted with experts of all kinds—from high-level government officials with security clearances to hackers who build anti-surveillance tools. Each had a different suggestion. For example, some advised me to use different computers for different purposes—one for banking, one for personal, one for professional; others recommended running software that would separate my single computer into three separate compartments, emulating a three-computer setup; others said there was no point in trying to compartmentalize, as my data would end up getting mixed up anyway. After many such conversations, I came to realize that there was no silver bullet.

I would have to come up with my own battle plan. I built a spreadsheet, outlining the threats and my proposed tactics to counter each threat. Some threats would likely be relatively easy to counter; to avoid online ad tracking, I would install different types of anti-tracking software and evaluate which one worked best. But other threats were trickier; I didn't know a good tactic to counter automated license plate readers that would photograph my car's plate when I drove past. One expert suggested that I could cover my license plate with a spray or a glass that could foil the infrared cameras. But in New York, where I live, it's illegal to cover a license plate in a way that "distorts a recorded or photographic image of such number plates."

I realized that before I chose my tactics, I needed to develop some guidelines to govern my behavior. So I developed my own rules of engagement.

DON'T BREAK THE LAW. I am not trying to evade taxes or break the law. So I will engage only in actions that are legal. That means not obscuring my license plate.

Sometimes it's not clear what is legal. Consider fake driver's licenses.

I asked Mark Eckenwiler, a former surveillance lawyer at the U.S. Department of Justice, for advice about whether fake IDs are legal.

Mark pointed me to the statute that makes it illegal to use someone else's identification to commit a crime. But he also pointed me to a 2009 Supreme Court ruling that interprets the statute to mean that the offender must know that he is misusing the credentials of an actual person. That could imply that it's acceptable to use a fake driver's license for a fictitious person. But then he pointed me to the mail fraud and wire fraud statutes that state that it is illegal to engage in "any scheme" to obtain money or property by "false or fraudulent promises."

Not surprisingly, Mark declined to give me official advice about whether to get a fake ID. However, the cases seemed to indicate that I probably would be safe with a fake ID in a fictitious name if I didn't use it for any type of fraud.

But even so, I decided not to get a fake ID. I'd rather be on the safe side of the law.

CONTINUE TO LIVE IN THE MODERN WORLD. I am not interested in disconnecting from technology. I believe technology has empowered people to make great changes in the world. I simply want to limit the harmful downsides of a technology-saturated life.

As a result, I won't be able to achieve perfect privacy. With a talented and determined adversary, almost any measure can be circumvented. John J. Strauchs, a former CIA agent who is now a security consultant, told me a story about how he was hired to break into the headquarters of a well-protected financial entity that had three rings of guards stationed outside. So he smuggled in an infiltrator in the trunk of an unsuspecting employee's car.

Similarly, most of the actions I will take can be circumvented. For instance, if I use codes to scramble the contents of an e-mail, an adversary could still install software on my computer that captures my keystrokes before they are encrypted.

My goal is not to win at all costs. My goal is simply to force my adversary to work harder. I may not be able to prevent myself from being surveilled on public streets, but perhaps I can force my adversary to watch hours of videotape rather than simply track my location through a series of easily analyzed GPS coordinates.

USE CONVENTIONAL TOOLS. In his delightful book about industrial food, *The Omnivore's Dilemma*, Michael Pollan prepares a meal by hunting and gathering. He kills a pig, hunts mushrooms in the forest, and picks cherries from a neighbor's tree. He calls it the "perfect meal."

Some of my hacker advisers take a similar approach to technology. They don't trust tools they can't build, modify, or design themselves. They circumvent the software installed on their phones in order to run software of their choosing. They boot their computers from CDs rather than running a traditional operating system.

This may be the "perfect" way to protect one's data, but it is sadly out of reach for me. I am tech-savvy enough to manage my own website, but I don't trust myself to start modifying my phone software. Nor do I think that it is the right approach. The beauty of the modern era is that these powerful technologies are finally simple enough for regular people to enjoy their benefits.

And so, as a corollary to my guiding principle of living in the modern world, I am also going to eschew some of the most extreme measures taken by the kill-your-own-food hacker crowd. Instead, I will use conventional tools that are within reach of most people with some amount of tech savvy. (I will not pretend that your grandmother can do everything that I'm going to do. But certainly your teenager will be able to.)

AIM FOR ZERO DATA RETENTION. The best way to protect my data is not to give it away. And the best way to do that is to use services that don't store data.

Of course, such services are rare, but they do exist. Consider my doctor's office, which is located in a midtown Manhattan skyscraper. Like most New York buildings post 9/11, the doormen demand identification from visitors. But my doctor's office wants to protect patient privacy. So the doctor's office assigns each patient a code to give to the doorman instead of identification. That way, the doormen are appeased and yet they have zero data stored about the patients.

During my journey, I will seek to do business with companies that store the least amount of data that is sufficient to complete their task. In some lucky cases, that will be zero data. In other cases, it will be minimal data.

USE THE MUD-PUDDLE TEST. One way to determine whether I have minimized my data trail is to use what some security engineers call the "mud-puddle test." It goes like this: imagine you drop your device in a mud puddle, slip in the mud, and crack your head so that you forget your password to access your data. Now, can you get your data back from the service you were using? If the answer is yes, then you have left a data trail. If the answer is no, you have successfully avoided leaving a data trail. Of course, you also don't have your data.

The problem with the mud-puddle test is that you lose either way. But it's a good reminder that if you are using a service that lets you recover your lost password, then the service has access to your data. I will use the mud-puddle test to evaluate the services that I use.

ENGAGE IN DATA POLLUTION. When I can't minimize my data trail, I can try to pollute it by using fake names and providing misinformation.

It's embarrassing to admit that lying is hard for me. It makes me physically uncomfortable to lie—even if I am just putting a fake name into a Web form. I start to feel hot and my pulse starts racing.

But the fact is that I have nothing to be ashamed of. Until recently, anonymous transactions were the norm for many daily activities. We paid cash. We called from phones that didn't have caller ID. We sent letters that sometimes didn't have return addresses.

So I vow to remind myself that the people asking me to fill out forms online in order to accomplish simple tasks don't always deserve truthful answers. It's a difficult path for a girl who was such a Goody Two-shoes in elementary school that I used to stay in at recess and clean chalkboards for the teachers.

But I will try to make data pollution a key part of my privacy arsenal.

PROTECT MY TRAFFIC. I plan to work hard to protect myself against analysis of my "traffic," that is, the people with whom I e-mail, call, and instant message.

People worry about the contents of their e-mails, texts, and instant messages being intercepted. But traffic analysis can often reveal as much or more than the contents of a message. If I am exchanging six messages a day with a drug dealer, do you really need to know what we are saying?

The volume of messages alone will land me on a list of suspected affiliates of drug dealers.

Computers are also much better at analyzing lists of to/from to find patterns than they are at sorting through huge amounts of text for patterns. As a result, indiscriminate trackers will almost always focus on traffic patterns first. So I will put a top priority on defending my traffic patterns.

USE REAL-TIME COMMUNICATIONS. The Wiretap Act requires police officers to get a "super-warrant"—which is harder to get than a regular search warrant—before intercepting real-time communications such as phone calls, video chats, and instant messages in the United States.

Once those communications are stored, however, the data can often be obtained without a search warrant. So a good way to avoid being tracked is to use real-time communications and not store the communications. (Unless, of course, you are actually a criminal suspect and the police have obtained a super-warrant to intercept your real-time communications—in which case, good luck to you.)

It's not easy to turn off storage of texts and instant messages, particularly because you often can't control whether the recipient is storing the information. But, luckily, most voice and video discussions are not stored by default.

As a result, plain old-fashioned domestic telephone calls are still one of the most private ways to communicate.

SPREAD DATA AROUND. The only thing worse than losing a credit card is losing your entire wallet. Similarly, losing some data is not as bad as losing all of your data. So I will endeavor to spread my data around—in order to minimize the damage from inevitable leaks, data breaches, government spying, and so forth.

For example, I will have to choose which among Google's many services I will retain—e-mail, search, maps, and Android phone. Considering that in the last half of 2012 alone, the government made 21,389 requests for information to Google, it makes sense not to store all of my valuable data on Google's computers.

Of course, there is no way to completely avoid having some data stored in a vulnerable database—unless I decide to store all my data at home. But I hope that by spreading my data around, I can mitigate the risk of exposure.

PAY FOR PERFORMANCE. Many of the hackers who build privacy-protecting technology are adherents of the free software movement. They believe that users should be able to build and modify the software that they use, so that they are not trapped in systems they do not control.

Theoretically, free (as in freedom to modify) software does not need to be free (as in price). But in reality, most profit-seeking companies prefer not to open up their code to outside tinkering. And so most free-to-modify software ends up being free-in-price.

The unfortunate result is that without a revenue stream, much of this software withers from neglect when the programmers who built it for free in their spare time move on to other hobbies. So in my quest to protect my privacy, I will aim to support (through donations or purchasing software) projects that pay their programmers a living wage, in the hope that the project will continue.

TRANSPARENCY RULES. Trackers who let me see the data they have about me are less offensive than trackers who will not let me view my data.

Transparency is the key. I feel better about my credit report because I have a chance to review it and dispute any errors I find. But most companies that track my movements won't show me the data they hold about me. That feels unfair. So I plan to take a more generous approach toward trackers that provide transparency. And I will be even kinder to trackers who let me delete my data, correct it, or download it and take it with me.

PRIVACY AS PROTEST. I always ask for a pat-down instead of going through the body scanners at the airport. The pat-down is very invasive: one time the screener stuck her hand a little too deep into my pants when patting down my waistband; another time, the scanner pulled my waistband away from my back with such force that I almost fell over. In many ways, it's more invasive than the automated scanners.

But my purpose in opting out of the scanner is simply to register my protest against the procedure. The body scanners are the rare form of indiscriminate tracking that is not covert, and so I take the opportunity to contribute my voice to the opposition. I view it as similar to recycling at home. The cans and bottles that I dutifully separate are not likely to change the fate of the planet. The miles that I drive in my car are much worse, ecologically speaking. But recycling is a kind of gateway drug; it makes larger changes seem within reach.

It is my hope that my small privacy protests will make larger changes seem within reach.

DON'T SUCCUMB TO FEAR. It's likely that taking steps to protect my privacy could land me on a "red flag" list of possible suspects.

Federal prosecutors have argued in an Arizona case that the defendant had no reasonable expectation of privacy because he used a fake name to sign up for a prepaid wireless card.

And NSA documents revealed by Edward Snowden show that the NSA is storing encrypted communications of U.S. citizens, even though its own guidelines say that "domestic communications will be promptly destroyed." But messages that contain "secret meanings" can be retained, meaning that my encrypted e-mails are likely placing me on some kind of red flag list at the NSA.

But I don't want to succumb to fear that my privacy-protecting actions will land me on a watch list. Instead, I plan to count those red flags as part of my political protest against the dragnets.

✦

In some ways, this new world that I am entering is familiar to dissidents in repressive regimes: a world where quiet conversations in a café are safer than phone calls, e-mails, and other electronic communications.

To understand the life I was embarking on, I reached out to a man who has deeply examined the challenges faced by dissidents—Mike Perry, a developer at the Tor Project, which makes software designed to help people evade censorship and surveillance. After 9/11, Perry was outraged at the privacy invasions of the Bush administration, so he started volunteering as a computer programmer for Tor. He began taking his privacy seriously.

When he was looking at technical material on Amazon with his boss and the director of engineering, he was bothered that he was seeing personalized recommendations for books on political and personal topics.

He decided that even Amazon recommendations were too "personal" for him, so he began erasing his data trail.

Perry and I met in a park in San Francisco. (Public places are apparently good places to have private conversations as long as you don't use trigger words such as "bomb" that cause people to listen carefully, according to John Strauchs.) Perry looked like your basic issue hacker—skinny, slightly pale, and clad in all black. He told me some of the basics of his operational security (although not all, since that would compromise his security).

Perry describes himself as a "surveillance vegan"—by which he means that he is as strict about avoiding surveillance as vegans are about avoiding animal products. (His two exceptions: he still books plane tickets and sometimes stays in hotels under his own name.)

Even his closest friends don't know where he lives, although some of them have tracked him to the city block on which he lives. (His family visited once but they don't have the exact address.) One friend even dropped a prepaid cell phone enabled with GPS into his bag in a fruitless effort to locate him.

He receives mail in several places, including a Laundromat, a UPS box, and a "business box" that allows him to get packages under other names. He also uses multiple disposable phones. He pays cash for prepaid phones that are designated for different relationships. One is for official business, one is for personal business, and another is for communicating with Tor. "I try to keep different topics to different phones," he told me. He tries to remove the batteries from the phones when he is not using them.

Perry believes in using multiple disposable identities that are specific for each relationship. That means that he sets up multiple e-mail and instant messaging addresses. After our talk, he set up a dedicated instant messaging address for me to reach him. He said he would delete it after our conversations were complete.

Perry's life sounded challenging. I asked how it had affected him.

"To be honest," he said, "it's affected my ability to have close relationships." He said his surveillance-avoidance techniques contributed to breakups with two girlfriends and made it difficult to keep in touch with several friends who didn't want to keep a dedicated encrypted chat program open in order to talk to him.

This was starting to sound like a young man's game. After all, Perry is a single man who works from home. I'm a mom with two kids who goes into an office every day. It was going to be hard for me to run my life out of a Laundromat, with multiple phones for each person with whom I communicate.

But in his gentle way, Perry assured me that he was probably doing it all wrong anyway and that I didn't have to be a surveillance vegan. "Some people are only 'surveillance flexitarian,' and that's cool too," he said.

Then he took the muni train with me to my destination. He walked me out of the station to my parking garage. Then he went back inside the subway, heading home—wherever that might be.

6
THE AUDIT

"**Y**ou should know your data," Michael Sussmann told me, over a late breakfast at a café near Capitol Hill.

Sussmann, a former federal prosecutor in the Department of Justice's computer crimes and intellectual property section, had been out late the night before. A devoted Bruce Springsteen fan, he had driven two and a half hours with his wife to see the Boss play in Charlottesville, Virginia. Sussmann was bleary-eyed but had kindly agreed to help me build my threat model.

"It's boring," he admitted, but audits are usually the first thing he does for his clients. Sussmann is now a partner at the law firm Perkins Coie, where he advises companies such as Google on Internet privacy issues. "We start with an org chart and then begin to find out every bit of data this company collects, from every source," he told me.

He raised a good point: if I didn't know where my data was, how could I protect it? For me, however, the challenge was not to locate my data internally; it was to locate it externally. So I decided to begin my privacy quest by trying to find my data.

✦

I started with the most obvious sources of data—Google, Facebook, and Twitter, the companies I've called the Freestylers. What did they know about me?

To find my Google data, I visited the website of the Data Liberation Front, a quirky Google project that lets users download the data that they have stored with Google. Using the Data Liberation Front's "take-out" menu, I downloaded the contacts for 2,192 people whom I have e-mailed since I started using Gmail in 2006. I also got a few photos I had stored on Picasa (Google's photo service, which I had forgotten I used). And I pulled down twelve documents that I had shared with people using Google Drive (but not all 204 that had been shared with me by others).

But that was about it. When I tried to download the history of websites I have visited, the Data Liberation Front declared: "There is no current way to escape from Google Web History."

I found a bit more information on my Google Dashboard—a page that contains information about my activity on various Google services that was buried in my Gmail account settings. The Dashboard noted that of the 2,192 people I've contacted on Gmail, the person I contact the most is—not surprisingly—my husband. It also noted that I have had 23,397 e-mail and chat conversations on Gmail.

Strangely, my Web search history wasn't on my dashboard. It was hidden away in a section of my account called "Other Tools." There, I found that Google had apparently been logging my Web searches from the time I opened my account in 2006. Apparently, I conduct hundreds, and sometimes thousands, of Google searches per month!

Google had helpfully sorted my searches by date and by category (maps, travel, books, etc.), and they were a horrifying insight into what Buddhists call the "monkey mind," leaping from place to place restlessly.

Consider November 30, 2010: I started the day reading some technology news. Then, suddenly, I was searching for "Pink glitter tiny toms" for my daughter. Then I was off to the thesaurus to look up a word for an article I was writing, then to OpenTable to book a restaurant reservation, and then a visit to Congress to download the text of privacy legislation. Phew.

My searches not only illuminated my inner thoughts, but they also revealed my whereabouts. A bunch of searches for "Berlin city map" were conducted during my trip to Berlin; "Hyatt Regency Pune" was in the midst of my annual trip to see my in-laws in India; my search for "DFW airport, Irving, TX → 3150 Binkley Ave., Dallas, TX 75205" was during a business trip to Dallas.

This was more intimate than a diary. It was a window into my thoughts each day. I felt nostalgic perusing my searches for nursing pillows after my son was born and my searches for good Mexican restaurants during a family vacation in Arizona.

I really wanted to download the data. But there was no way to easily get it. A Google spokesman, Rob Shilkin, told me, "There are lots of products that are not a part of Takeout—we started with five products in 2011 and have been steadily adding." He added that I could delete my Web history. But once I had seen it, I didn't want to delete it. I wanted to own it.

Facebook was considerably less forthcoming with my data. I clicked on "Download a copy of my data," and Facebook sent me an archive that was notable for what it did not include. It did not include my list of friends, my posts, likes, or comments on other people's posts. Instead, my Facebook archive contained a few photos I thought I had deleted, friends I had deleted, and a comprehensive list of when and from where I had logged in to my Facebook account (mostly my home, my office, and a few business trips). It turns out that the posts and likes are in another section of Facebook called the "Activity Log." But it, too, was weirdly incomplete. My activity log contained only a few posts, no likes, and no comments. And it couldn't be downloaded.

My Facebook data were a pale shadow of what Max Schrems got when he obtained his data from Facebook in 2011. Schrems, a law student in Vienna, requested his data from Facebook under European privacy laws and received 1,222 pages of personal data. Not only did it list all his friends, his posts, and so forth. It also had a lot of data that Schrems thought he had deleted—friend requests that he had rejected, pokes he had removed, and wall posts and status updates that he had deleted.

In August 2011, Schrems filed a complaint with the Irish Data Protection Commission (Facebook's European offices are in Ireland) alleging that much of the data stored by Facebook violates European Union data protection laws. The European Union requires holders of personal data to be transparent about their data collection practices and to keep data only as long as necessary for the purpose for which it was collected.

As a result, the Irish commission reviewed Facebook's practices and recommended some "best practices," including better explanations of its policies around deleted content. A year later, Facebook changed its data use policy and stated explicitly that "information associated with your account will be kept until your account is deleted." In 2012, the Irish commission reviewed Facebook's compliance and found that the company had implemented "most" of its suggestions. But the agency found that Facebook was still not providing fully verified account deletion "beyond all doubt."

In short, it seemed that Facebook planned to keep my data—whether or not I deleted it. But I wasn't likely to obtain a comprehensive set of my Facebook data anytime soon.

Getting my data from Twitter was easy. I simply pressed a button labeled "Request your archive." Twitter promptly sent me an e-mail with a handy Excel spreadsheet containing my 2,993 tweets since I opened my account in 2008.

It wasn't always this easy. Twitter didn't give users an opportunity to download their entire archive of tweets until 2012—even though since 2010 it had been offering similar data to companies who paid to subscribe to the entire Twitter stream in order to monitor trends.

My tweets were less intimate than my Google searches. Many were an extension of my work—tweeting articles by colleagues or myself and live-tweeting at events. But there were some tweets I had forgotten. On March 9, 2009: "My first night of real sleep in an entire year—baby finally slept thru the night. Hallelujah."

In total, the Freestylers had compiled a pretty revealing portrait of my life over the past few years. It was far more comprehensive than any of the files I had reviewed from the Stasi archive.

And yet, as creepy as it was, much of it made me nostalgic. This was a digital record of my life.

It reminded me of the time that I ran into a friend and her husband at the playground in our neighborhood in Manhattan. As we watched our daughters—who are the same age—play on the jungle gym, the husband asked me about the articles I had been writing regarding privacy.

"I used to care more about privacy," he said. I braced myself for the usual "I have nothing to hide" argument. But he surprised me with an entirely different approach. He said he realized that he "liked the idea of leaving artifacts" about his life more than he worried about his privacy. In short, he said, all this data were providing "immortality."

Looking at my old tweets and Google searches, I couldn't help but think of my talk with my friend's husband. Of all the arguments for ubiquitous data collection, immortality did seem like a good one.

✦

I got another glimpse at immortality when I peeked at the information that data brokers have about me. This happened when I was sitting on Mike Griffin's deck overlooking Chesapeake Bay in the Baltimore suburbs.

Mike is a "repo" man who stumbled into the automobile surveillance business. He is tall and thin and filled with nervous energy. He seems to subsist entirely on coffee and cigarettes.

I was doing research for an article about the rise of automated license plate readers and decided to pay Mike a visit. He runs one of the largest private license plate snapping operations in the United States. His fleet of ten camera-equipped cars log three hundred to four hundred miles a day, scanning plates in the Baltimore and Washington, D.C., metropolitan areas. Each month, his two shifts of drivers collect data about the location of one million plates.

Mike primarily uses the data to spot cars that are wanted for repossession. The technology has boosted his captures to fifteen cars a night, up from about six per night without the cameras. But Mike says his ultimate goal is to sell access to his data to bail bondsmen, process servers, private investigators, and insurers. "In the next five years, I hope my primary business will be data gathering," he told me.

He mused about one possible buyer for the data: a company called TLO. I had been hearing about TLO for years. The founder, Hank Asher, was legendary. A former drug smuggler turned law enforcement buff, Asher was the most flamboyant guy in the data brokerage business.

Asher made millions through owning a business that painted high-rise buildings in Florida and retired at thirty. He moved to Great Harbor Cay in the Bahamas, drove a fast boat, flew a twin-engine Aerostar, and developed a cocaine habit. Eventually, after agreeing to fly a few loads of cocaine to Florida, he realized he'd gone too far. He quit cold turkey and decided he wanted to clean up drug smuggling on the island.

He started working with the U.S. Drug Enforcement Administration and noticed that the agency needed better databases. In 1992, he launched a product called AutoTrack that would change the data-collection industry.

AutoTrack was a better way to search public records: Asher bought data from the Florida Department of Motor Vehicles and made it easily searchable. Suddenly police could look up a person's driving and vehicle records just by searching an address or part of a social security number or fragment of a name. Previously, police had to enter a person's entire name, gender, and birth date to obtain a plate. AutoTrack changed the way police investigations were done. Journalistic investigations, too. I've used AutoTrack many times to find the names and addresses of people I was investigating.

Eventually, however, Asher's flamboyance and drug history caught up with him, and his company bought him out for $147 million. Undeterred, Asher soon started another company with a very similar product called Accurint. After 9/11, he put together a program called MATRIX that would create a "High Terrorist Factor" list, but it ran aground on privacy concerns. Again, Asher resigned from his company under pressure.

In 2009, Asher made another run at the business, founding a database company called TLO, standing for The Last One, as in the last one he planned to launch. He turned out to be right about that; he died at age sixty-one in 2013.

Mike said TLO's data were good and cheaper than data provided by LexisNexis, which years earlier had bought Asher's two previous firms. TLO charged only 25 cents to conduct a simple search and $5 for an advanced search. By comparison, LexisNexis's PeopleWise service charged $1.95 for a basic report and $24.95 for a premium report.

"Can I see my report?" I asked.

"Sure," he said.

In less than a minute I was holding a four-page report, containing all my previous addresses—dating back to the number on my dorm room in college: #536B. There was not a single piece of inaccurate information in the report.

It took my breath away. I had forgotten the number on my dorm room, the address of the group house in Washington, D.C., that I had shared with five other recent college graduates, and my brief tenure in a New

York City studio before moving in with my husband. Each address brought back a wave of memories.

This was, in some ways, even deeper than the data the Freestylers had about me. After all, this was my real life, dating back decades. Talk about immortality.

✦

As I sought out my information from other data brokers, my love affair with immortality lost steam. I compiled a list of more than two hundred commercial data brokers, and I was pretty sure I hadn't identified all of them. This wasn't immortality, this was prostitution.

Some of them were well-known names, like the credit-reporting agency Experian. But most were tiny outfits in the voyeuristic "lookup" business—websites that let people look up information about other people for a small fee, or sometimes for free in return for selling advertising.

There are very few barriers to entry in the lookup business. Consider the story of BeenVerified.com. In 2007, Josh Levy and Ross Cohen decided to offer cheap online background checks. The two set up shop with a $200,000 investment. By 2011, the company said it had revenues of $11 million, and just sixteen employees. Not bad work if you can get it.

The U.S. data business is largely unregulated, which is not the case in most western European countries. Those countries require all data collectors to provide individuals with access to their data, the ability to correct errors in the data, and, in some cases, the right to delete the data.

After reading the fine print on 212 websites, I learned that only 33 of them offered me a chance to see the data they held about me. But upon closer examination, not all of them were real offers. Some required me to set up accounts in order to see my data.

I contacted twenty-three data brokers and received my data from thirteen of them. Some asked me to send my requests by postal mail, along with a copy of my driver's license. Others allowed e-mail requests. Most of the responses I got were from the biggest players in the industry.

Epsilon, one of the largest direct marketers, with more than $3 billion in annual sales, sent me a sparse two-page report identifying my name, address, age, and political affiliation. It listed recent purchase categories in extremely broad categories—apparel, media, business, health, home office, and sports. The most specific information was a description of my household interests: cycling, running, and sports. For someone who hasn't gotten on her bike in five years, that is more aspiration than reality.

I was shocked that Acxiom, the data-gathering giant with annual sales of around $1.1 billion, asked me to send a $5 check as a processing fee to obtain my data. But I sent it in, gritting my teeth. One month later, Acxiom sent me a nine-page report with my social security number, birth date, voter registration, and addresses dating back to childhood. None of the information that Acxiom sells about my interests was provided. Acxiom's reluctance to share was particularly galling, since it brags in its annual report that it has more than "3,000 propensities for nearly every U.S. consumer." One of its main products is the PersonicX database, which lumps people into seventy "clusters" within twenty-one "life stage groups."

Thanks to the journalist Dan Tynan, who does great work covering privacy issues, I found a page on Acxiom's website that lets you enter your age, marital status, income, and age of children to determine your PersonicX cluster. When I entered my real information (which was a bit scary), Acxiom reported back that I was in a cluster called "Fortunes and Families"—"one of the most educated and wealthy of all the groups." People in this cluster are more likely to have attended graduate school (yep) and be Asian (yep, that's my husband). Also true: "Their busy lives make Internet shopping a necessity rather than a preference." However, the stock photo on the "Fortunes and Families" cluster was a little absurd—a picture of a man and a woman standing in front of a private jet. We're not private-jet wealthy. We're not even business-class wealthy. We are strictly coach class.

Other Acxiom clusters have names like "Truckin' and Stylin'," "Married Sophisticate," "Urban Scrambler," "Rural Rover," and "Lavish Lifestyle." However, it's not clear which cluster Acxiom has actually assigned me to, since its demonstration website doesn't ask for names. Acxiom later introduced an online service that would let people see their data if they entered their name, address, birth date, e-mail address, and last four digits of their social security number. I was reluctant to hand over so much sensitive information but, once again, I gritted my teeth and submitted my information. The resulting demographic data were remarkably poor: Acxiom said I was a single Asian parent, with a seventeen-year-old child, who drives a 2009 Toyota Corolla—all of which is incorrect. However, the shopping data were impressive: it correctly flagged that I prefer online shopping over off-line shopping and identified categories in which I had spent money, such as linens, housewares, and "women's apparel—underwear and hosiery."

Datalogix, which claims to have data on "almost every U.S. household and more than $1 trillion in consumer transactions," took three months to respond to my request. But one day a FedEx envelope arrived containing two sheets of paper from Datalogix listing my "interest segments." It was a mishmash. Yes, I am a "mom" and a "foodie" and an "online buyer" of "women's fashion & apparel," but calling me a "fashionista" and "young and hip" is likely a bridge too far.

Similarly, my family does buy energy-efficient lightbulbs and organic milk, but I was surprised that this qualified us as "green consumers" and "health food" purchasers. And some data were outright wrong: we have no pet and no television, thus we have never purchased any "pet supplies" nor have we watched "Spanish language television."

Other Datalogix categories were deliberately obscure. "Political views" and "political geography" were among my interest categories, but the report did not disclose what views they believe I hold. Similarly, my household income and home value were listed as categories but not disclosed.

Infogroup merely sent me an e-mail containing my name and address—the same information that I had provided in order to access my dossier. Gee, thanks.

I got better results from LexisNexis, another giant in the field. Four days after I submitted my request, LexisNexis mailed me a free ten-page "Accurint Person Report," containing every address I've lived at since 1989.

Like the TLO report, it was disturbingly accurate. It had captured the one month I spent at my parents' house while looking for an apartment in San Francisco in 1996. It grabbed the two months that I spent living in my boss's attic while interning at the *Washington Post* in 1992. Under "Possible Associates," it listed my husband and his mother, and dates that she had visited him in his New York apartment.

Thomson Reuters's Westlaw was the most generous, kindly sending me two free reports: a thirty-four-page "summary" that was mostly correct except for listing my brother as the head of my household and an eight-page "comprehensive" report that listed my license plate, mortgage information, and employer. The Westlaw comprehensive report was the only report I saw that listed the sources from which it obtained my historical addresses—all were from credit-reporting agencies.

Some companies' offers of access seemed to be little more than window dressing. Intelius, one of the largest of the online people-search sites, which had $150 million in sales in 2010 (the last year that this information was publicly available), offered a website called TrueRep.com that allows users to see their data. However, the service was not advertised on any of the Intelius sites that I found. And when I visited TrueRep to find my data, it didn't work. After I contacted the company, it fixed the "bug" and I was able to access my data—first I had to answer a set of personal questions, such as when my house was built and what model car I drive. Strangely, once I passed those questions, the report didn't provide any details about my house and car. Obviously, Intelius must have more information that it is not disclosing, though it did report the correct names of my parents, husband, and brother. But it had two incorrect addresses for me—one in the Bronx and one at the United Nations.

Still, on average, the data brokers were largely correct about me. They correctly located most of my addresses and relations. And in large part they correctly identified me as a harried working mom, prone to choose convenience over thrift.

✦

I hoped I would find even more accurate information in the one realm of commercial data brokerage that is regulated—the credit scoring industry.

The Fair Credit Reporting Act, enacted in 1970, requires anyone who uses a credit report, and some other types of reports, to provide people with notice if they suffer an "adverse action" such as being turned down for a job, insurance, or a loan because of data in the report. That notice must provide information about the data gatherer who provided the information. However, until recently, people couldn't easily access their reports before being turned down for something.

In 2003, Congress passed a law requiring the big three credit-reporting agencies—TransUnion, Experian, and Equifax—to provide free annual access to credit reports from AnnualCreditReport.com. However, those free reports do not include the actual credit "score" on which consumers are judged.

When I requested a free copy of my credit report from TransUnion, my first clue that the data were wrong was when I couldn't correctly answer the security question designed to verify my identity: "Which two of the following five employers have you worked for?" I had worked for only one of the companies on the list, but I couldn't get past that question until I clicked on two companies. So I chose one at random and got into my report anyway. Hmm, so much for security. (Turns out I wasn't the only one to notice that the security questions were easy to circumvent. In March 2013, it was revealed that hackers had answered security questions and obtained credit reports for public figures ranging from First Lady Michelle Obama and FBI director Robert Mueller to celebrities Beyoncé and Paris Hilton, which were then posted online.)

When I got into my credit report, I saw that it listed me as working for a company called Borjomi 1 Inc. as of 1/30/2011. A quick Web search suggested that Borjomi 1 Inc. was a Brooklyn-based distributor of bottled mineral water from the republic of Georgia. It also listed a garbled previous address for me: "304 06920304 T75 Apt 79."

My experience was not unusual. The latest review of credit report accuracy by the Federal Trade Commission determined that 26 percent of people found at least one significant error on at least one of their three reports.

✦

I soon found even worse data about myself in an unregulated corner of the data broker industry—the data-scoring business.

I stumbled on this arena when I received my data from a company called eBureau. It was a one-page report that indicated that I had no children, had not completed high school, and had an income of $35,000—all of which are far from the truth.

With a bit of research, I discovered that eBureau was a hot new start-up in the field of data scoring—where companies use widely available personal data to create new categorizations of people. There are companies that analyze the popularity of your tweets and Facebook posts to determine if you are "influential." And there are a bunch of companies aiming to use new sources of data—such as personality or mobile phone behavior—to develop alternative credit scores.

Based in Chicago and founded in 2004, eBureau is trying to build a better credit score and has raised $38 million from venture capitalists for its predictive "scoring" system. The company says it analyzes information about people and predicts their "contactability" and "lifetime customer value" so that marketers can decide whom to target. eBureau promotes its scores as helping people with limited banking and credit histories obtain financial services and allowing debt collectors to predict the likelihood of collecting on an account. In a marketing sheet for its "income estimator," eBureau says its scores can be used to evaluate "newly admitted hospital patients for charity care program eligibility."

When I contacted eBureau about the inaccuracy of my data, I received an e-mail from "eBureau Compliance" noting that some of its data was labeled as estimates. In addition, the company noted that it "secures its information from third-party sources and neither eBureau nor its information providers, vendors, licensors, agents or affiliates warrant that the information is accurate or error free." It said that if my information was inaccurate, I could opt out; I availed myself of the offer.

Even creepier was a company called PYCO, which claimed it might be able to determine my personality type based on just my name and address. In its marketing materials, PYCO says it has created an "algorithm to reverse-engineer the data on a person's behavior—relationships, transactions, activities, interests, hobbies, purchase behavior, and so on." PYCO obtains data from the big data brokers and analyzes certain life decisions and translates what they might mean about your personality. For example, getting married can mean willingness to make a commitment. It then uses that data to determine things such as if you are extroverted or introverted or if you are a leader or a follower.

PYCO says it has built profiles for 181 million U.S. adults. But it said it didn't have one for me.

✦

Finally, I sought to extract my data from the U.S. government. Obviously, the National Security Agency was not going to give me my files (others have tried and failed to get those), but some other agencies might.

The Privacy Act, passed in 1974, gives individuals the right to see their government files and to correct the information in those files if it is incorrect. But the Privacy Act has a giant loophole: agencies can exempt themselves from provisions of the law.

As a result, it's not easy for individuals to obtain their files. Consider the story of an Ohio resident named Julia Shearson who was flagged as "armed and dangerous" and a "suspected terrorist" when she drove up to a U.S. Customs and Border Protection checkpoint after a weekend in Canada in 2006. Federal agents detained her and her four-year-old daughter for several hours before releasing them.

Shearson, who is a convert to Islam, wanted to know why she had been placed on a terrorist watch list. So she requested her files from Customs and from the Department of Homeland Security under the Freedom of Information Act and the Privacy Act. But the data she received did not include the reason she was targeted. So she sued the agencies for violating the Freedom of Information Act and the Privacy Act. They responded that they were exempt from providing information about the watch list.

Shearson obtained some documents in 2008 but was never able to find out why she was flagged. In 2011, the U.S. Court of Appeals for the Sixth Circuit ruled that if the government had unlawfully maintained records of First Amendment protected activity, it could be held liable for damages. The case was remanded to a lower court. Shearson settled for damages in 2013, after more than seven years of legal battles.

Still, I figured I would see what I could get about myself. I requested my FBI files and was informed that it had no records for me (phew!) but that this response "neither confirms nor denies the existence of your subject's name on any watch lists."

My request to the U.S. Customs and Border Protection agency proved more fruitful. About three months after I filed my request, I received a fat envelope full of data—a fairly speedy response by government standards.

For help interpreting the files, I called Edward Hasbrouck, a San Francisco–based independent travel writer who worked in the travel industry for fifteen years. He had requested his own records after the U.S. Customs agency revealed in November 2006 that it had begun using a system of records called the Automated Targeting System (ATS), which compiled travel records for U.S. citizens for the purpose of "risk assessment." He initially submitted a request for ATS records in 2007 and renewed his request in 2009. A year later, he sued the agency, alleging that its refusal to turn over his complete Customs files was a violation of the Privacy Act. He lost when a federal court said that it was legitimate for Customs to retroactively exempt his files from the Privacy Act, even after he requested them. Hasbrouck agreed to look at my files and help me decode them.

The first eight pages were from the TECS database—an updated and modified version of the former Treasury Enforcement Communications System—which is a kind of super-database that includes data from various parts of the Treasury Department and the Department of Homeland Security. My TECS file contained information about my international arrivals and departures dating back to 1990. For each crossing, it noted the airport, date and time, and a blacked-out category called "result" that Hasbrouck said was likely to be an indication of whether I was sent for secondary screening.

It was a limited peek at my travel history. The airline flights included my arrival time in the customs hall, but not where I was flying to or arriving from. There was only one "VEH" vehicle crossing—when I crossed into Canada at Niagara Falls in 2003.

A much more robust view of my travel was contained in a second set of documents—thirty-one pages of detailed international travel reservation information from a database called PNR, which stands for Passenger Name Records.

PNRs didn't used to be in government hands. They are commercial records held by the airlines. But after the 9/11 terrorist attacks, Congress hastily passed the Aviation and Transportation Security Act, which required the airlines to provide their commercial reservation data to the Customs agency "upon request." In typical fashion, "upon request" soon became codified as requiring the airlines to give the agency electronic access to the entire airline reservation databases.

Now, airlines routinely contribute their customers' international travel reservations to Customs and Border Protection's Automated Targeting System—which assesses the "risk" that individual travelers pose to the United States. The agency says that it uses the reservation data for five years but stores it for counterterrorism purposes for fifteen years.

After 9/11, European governments objected to this change, arguing that it violated European privacy laws. After a protracted legal and diplomatic battle, during which the European Court of Justice briefly invalidated the agreement, the Europeans eventually gave in and signed a deal. After all, they didn't want their citizens to lose the right to visa-free travel to the United States. And they did win some concessions—there are limits on how long the United States can store and use PNR data, and sensitive data may be accessed only on a "case-by-case" basis.

I understood that battle once I looked at my files. Each PNR was incredibly detailed, containing every single interaction, from the initial making of the reservation to the boarding of the plane.

My full credit card number was in there several times, as were my e-mail address, my birth date, my passport number, and all of my phone numbers—work, home, and cell. My fellow travelers' information was there as well—my husband's e-mail address, my children's birth dates, and all of our passport numbers. My children's names (they were identified as CHD 1 and CHD 2) and our meal requests were the only information that appeared to be redacted.

Hasbrouck deciphered the cryptic instructions that the airlines use to communicate in their mainframe systems. "OSI YY TCP-4PAX-RECLOC 5CLMWQ/5BUOEM" was an all-system message alerting airline staff that my family wanted to sit together to complete a party (TCP) of four passengers (4PAX) despite having two separate reservations in two different record locators (RECLOC).

It appeared that my corporate travel agency was also contributing information to the federal government. For a trip to London, the agency sent Customs my hotel reservation (Bloomsbury Hotel, queen bed), my corporate credit card number and expiration date, my employee ID number, my department budget code, and an internal code indicating that I was "NOT VIP."

Even more troubling, the agency had sent the government the "purpose of travel" field that reporters fill out when booking a trip. That description is forwarded to a reporter's boss for approval.

Luckily, I am super-paranoid, so I write only "conference" or "reporting trip" in those fields. But I'm sure some of my colleagues might have written more extensive descriptions of their plans. It's not at all far-fetched to imagine that some reporters have written in that field something like: "reporting trip to meet government whistle-blower John Smith in Maryland."

I called up our attorneys at the *Wall Street Journal*, and they were surprised that reporters' travel plans were being sent to the government. After looking into it, a spokeswoman told me that the problem was inadvertent and isolated to international travel on one particular air carrier. The *Journal* suspended travel on that carrier until the technical glitch could be fixed. "We are working closely with our travel agency to resolve this matter as quickly as possible," she told me.

In the meantime, detailed information about my reporting trips was sitting in government files and being analyzed for my terrorism risk. And there was nothing I could do to remove it.

✦

My audit was deeply unsettling. I had obtained only a tiny amount of the information available about myself. And even this tiny amount was disturbingly comprehensive. It included:

- Every address I had lived at dating back to college.
- Every phone number I had ever used.
- The names of nearly all my relatives (as well as in-laws).
- A list of nearly three thousand people with whom I exchanged e-mail in the past seven years.
- Records of about twenty-six thousand Web searches I had conducted every month dating back seven years, neatly sorted into categories such as "maps" and "shopping."
- A glimpse of my shopping habits.
- My internal communications with my employer, the *Wall Street Journal*, about reporting plans.

Most of my data were held by commercial data brokers. But all of it could be easily swept into government dragnets.

I couldn't help but compare my data to the Stasi files I had reviewed, with their rudimentary surveillance and limited windows into people's lives. Even in their wildest dreams, the Stasi could only fantasize about obtaining this amount of data about citizens with so little effort.

7
THE FIRST LINE OF DEFENSE

Before I had a chance to launch my privacy project, I was hacked.

It was Labor Day weekend of 2012. My brother and his fiancée had taken my kids camping, and my husband and I were excited to finally have a chance to hang around the house on our own.

We woke up lazily on Saturday morning. And because we weren't in our usual rush to feed the kids and get them to swim practice, I sat down at my computer to check e-mail and Twitter. Immediately, I spotted several comments from people who said they had received spam messages from my Twitter account. I checked my sent messages and saw that I had sent out dozens of messages to my friends asking them to click on links.

It was obvious what had happened: my account had been hacked.

"Apologies to those who received DM spam from me. I was hacked. Am cleaning up the mess now," I tweeted at 9:27 a.m. It took me an hour to delete more than one hundred messages that had been sent from my account. Luckily, that was the extent of the damage.

It could have been much worse. My password was a single six-digit dictionary word that I had used as a base for nearly every account since I first logged on to the Internet. A smart hacker could have tried several other accounts and likely broken into those, as well.

I knew better than that. As a reporter who covers technology, I knew that I should use long, complicated passwords and that I should have different ones for each account. The embarrassing truth was that for nearly a year, I had been debating about the best password strategy. I considered coming up with a key phrase and varying it slightly for each website, but worried that a single hack would force me to change every password. I examined various types of password-management software, but I couldn't decide whether I trusted free or paid software more in this situation, and I worried about managing the software across the different computers that I use at home and work. I had also considered a strategy that my hacker friend Michael J. J. Tiffany suggested—a "method of loci"—in which you teach yourself to memorize super-long passwords by using memory techniques that the ancient Greeks used to remember long poems. But whenever he talked to me about how easy it was, it sounded difficult.

In short, I had been paralyzed by the password issue for about a year, during which time I kept all my passwords at their absurdly hackable level, thinking that I wouldn't change them until I figured out my optimal strategy.

✦

The hack was a wake-up call: before I could tackle privacy, I needed to clean up my approach to security.

The two are sometimes considered to be at odds with each other. After all, we are constantly being asked to give up privacy in the name of security. Consider just a few instances: airport body scanners, programs to scan the Internet for terrorist keywords, cameras on every street corner.

"We have a saying in this business: 'Privacy and security are a zero-sum game,'" Ed Giorgio, a security consultant who used to work at the NSA, once told the *New Yorker*.

But in fact privacy is nothing without security.

"We have to cast aside the notion that our liberty and our security are two opposing values that are on the opposite sides of a seesaw, that when one is up the other necessarily must be down," said Secretary of Homeland Security Janet Napolitano in a 2012 speech. "The plain fact of the matter is that you cannot live free if you live in fear. Security is a prerequisite if we wish to exercise the rights we cherish."

She was right. Before I could start protecting my liberties, I needed to secure my digital domain. After all, what was the point of defending myself against indiscriminate tracking if I left myself open to hackers and other intrusions?

I wasn't prepared for how difficult this project turned out to be.

✦

The problem with computer security is that most of the advice we are given is absurd.

Consider the issue of child predators. When I was writing my book about MySpace in 2008, online child predators were the bogeymen of the moment. The advice being peddled by all the experts was to keep the family computer in the living room and police your children when they used it. It was absurd advice and impossible to follow. Most parents work— whether it is in an office or running a household. And most kids multitask when they are on a computer—they are simultaneously doing homework, instant messaging with their friends, and surfing the Web. The idea that parents can supervise all those activities while also earning a living wage and getting dinner on the table is ludicrous.

I've come to think of warnings like this as similar to the labels on mattresses that say it's illegal to remove the scratchy label, or the labels on the hair dryer cords that read: DO NOT REMOVE THIS TAG! These labels are designed for one audience only: lawyers. The rest of us either blithely ignore the labels or feel guilty about ignoring them.

Similarly, much of the advice that we receive about computer security is impossible to follow. Consider the computer security advice I found in a simple Web search: run antivirus software; install a firewall; back up your files; turn off your Wi-Fi network when you're not using it; don't connect to public Wi-Fi spots unless you are using encryption; lock your laptop with a security cable when you are in a hotel (!); avoid websites that contain JavaScript; uninstall old software; don't use Microsoft Outlook or Adobe Reader; record the IMEI (International Mobile Equipment Identifier) number of your phone in case your phone is lost or stolen. Some of that is good advice—backing up files and being wary of public Wi-Fi networks, in particular—but most people who aren't computer professionals have a hard time sorting out the necessary from the unnecessary.

One reason for all the confusion: the computer security industry has to get us really scared in order to convince us to pay for their products. It is in their interest to exaggerate the threats. Remember the Y2K worldwide computer meltdown that didn't occur?

An interesting data point: most of the computer security professionals I know do not rely on antivirus software. Instead, they keep their software up to date, and they are choosy about what software they install. Most important, they do not click on links or open documents if they are not entirely sure of their origin. Some of the most paranoid computer security professionals I know also have minimal information about themselves available on social networks.

Passwords are the best example of the absurdity of computer security advice. The conventional wisdom is that you should change your password every three months; it should be made strong with multiple symbols and letters; and it should not be written down anywhere.

Those rules are treated as gospel at my office. Every three months, I receive an e-mail reminding me to reset my password. Before this regime started, I had a reasonably long password—about eleven characters long, if I recall correctly. But the constant pressure to make a new password has steadily degraded my ingenuity. In 2012 I gave up and just made each password into the month that the e-mail reminder arrived. So when the March e-mail password reset reminder arrived, I changed my password to March2012! (with the requisite exclamation point to satisfy the symbol police). In June, I changed it to 2012June?, and on like that. I had dropped to nine easily guessable characters.

There is ample evidence that I am not the only one cutting password corners. In 2010, computer security researchers analyzed a database of thirty-two million passwords (which was hacked and briefly posted online) and found that the most popular password was "123456," followed by "12345," "123456789," and "password." The researchers, at the computer security firm Imperva, found that about 30 percent of the passwords were fewer than seven characters long and that nearly 50 percent used names or dictionary words. The result: "In just 110 attempts, a hacker will typically gain access to one new account on every second or a mere 17 minutes to break into 1000 accounts."

A more recent study, from 2013, suggests that not much has changed. The British telecom regulator Ofcom found that half of all adult Internet users in the United Kingdom use the same password on most, if not all, websites they visit. Additionally, 26 percent said they used a very easily guessable password such as their birthday or name.

Thankfully, computer scientists have also concluded that our terrible passwords are not our fault. In his well-regarded textbook *Security Engineering*, Ross Anderson of the University of Cambridge Computer Laboratory writes, "The password problem has been neatly summed up as: 'Choose a password you can't remember, and don't write it down.'"

In 2004, the Institute of Electrical and Electronics Engineers published a study on "Password Memorability and Security"—with Anderson as one of the coauthors—that concluded that the deficiencies of passwords are due in part to the instructions people are given, if they are given any at all, when creating passwords.

The authors conducted an experiment in password creation among approximately three hundred students. One group was asked to create their own passwords, at least seven characters in length and containing at least one nonletter. Members of a second group were given a sheet with numbers and letters on it and were told to choose eight at random with their eyes closed. And a third group was asked to create a password based on a mnemonic phrase, such as "It's 12 noon I am hungry" to create the password "I's12Iah." The researchers then tried to break the passwords using various hacking techniques. They cracked about one-third of the passwords in the first group (where users created a password without much advice) and fewer than 10 percent of the passwords in the two other groups. "We suggest changing the advice given to users for selecting passwords," the researchers concluded. In some cases, users should be given instruction on how to create mnemonic passwords, and in other cases it might be better for institutions to simply assign passwords to users. On their own, they said, "users rarely choose passwords that are both hard to guess and easy to remember."

In 2010, computer scientists at University College London also laid the blame for bad passwords at the doorstep of institutional password policies. The authors studied "password use in the wild" at two major organizations and found that excessively strict password rules—forcing users to create strong passwords and to change them frequently—caused stress for users and caused them to write their passwords down, thus thwarting security. "When the requirements of the policy exceed users' capabilities, they are forced to develop more complex—or, alternatively, less secure—coping techniques," the authors wrote.

And by the way, many computer security experts say it's perfectly fine to write down your passwords, as long as you keep them in a safe place.

In 2005, Jesper Johansson, who was then senior program manager for security policy at Microsoft, spoke at a security conference and berated the industry for giving bad advice about passwords. "How many have [a] password policy that says under penalty of death you shall not write down your password?" asked Johansson. The majority of the audience raised their hands. "I claim that is absolutely wrong. I claim that password policy should say you should write down your password. I have 68 different passwords. If I am not allowed to write any of them down, guess what I am going to do? I am going to use the same password on every one of them. Since not all systems allow good passwords, I am going to pick a really crappy one, use it everywhere and never change it. If I write them down and then protect the piece of paper—or whatever it is I wrote them down on—there is nothing wrong with that. That allows us to remember more passwords and better passwords."

The research made me feel better about my weak passwords. But it still didn't solve my problem of how I was going to come up with dozens of strong passwords.

After all, there are only so many mnemonics I can remember. And many websites are not worth the mental effort.

✦

The morning I was hacked, I changed the passwords on my key accounts— e-mail, banking, and social networks. Instead of using variations of a single six-character dictionary word, I made longer combinations of letters, numbers, and symbols, and I wrote them down on paper.

It was just a stopgap measure. I knew my passwords still weren't good enough. They were mostly variations on a single passphrase. But whenever I tried to think up new phrases, my mind went blank. I was reminded of a study that claimed that 38 percent of adults would rather do household chores, such as cleaning a toilet bowl or doing the dishes, than create a new username and password.

After a few weeks of mental blankness, I gave up. I decided to install password-management software. Drawing on my philosophy to "pay for performance," I chose 1Password because it was a paid service and well reviewed. I hoped that meant it was a real business that wouldn't go under and would provide good customer service.

1Password is essentially a password vault; you store all your passwords in its software. You unlock the vault with a single master password. To ensure that the passwords are totally secure, they are not stored at 1Password's offices in Canada, but on your machine in an encrypted file. If you forget your master password, you lose access to all your passwords. In other words, 1Password passed the mud-puddle test.

Putting all my passwords on my computer was scary. But confronted with my blank mind and my inability to generate passwords, I took the plunge. I downloaded the software and began the process of entering passwords as I encountered them online.

It truly was a slow process. I had forgotten how many frequent flier, hotel, and random commerce sites I had accounts with. On some sites, I used 1Password's password generator to create a password with the right length and mix of letters, numbers, and symbols. On less important sites, I simply entered my weak password and promised myself I would improve it later.

In the course of three months, I loaded up fifty-one passwords into 1Password. But I still felt leery about putting sensitive passwords such as banking and e-mail and important work files into 1Password. I kept those on paper. Immediately, I had a problem: I had no idea what any of my passwords were. The ones that I created through 1Password were an incomprehensible string of letters, numbers, and symbols, like qwER43@! The ones that I made up myself were words with symbols and numbers interposed, such as Tr0ub4dour&3. None of them was easy to recall.

I was surprised at how often I needed my passwords when I was away from my computer. My husband called to ask me for the password to my Amazon account so he could use my free shipping—and I had to tell him that I was at lunch and didn't have it. He e-mailed me to ask for the password to one of my frequent flier accounts; I didn't have that one, either. When I got a new cell phone, I kept trying to set up my Twitter account when I was away from my desk—and then realized I didn't know my Twitter password. (1Password has a phone version, but I felt it was too risky to store all my passwords on my phone.)

At first I was annoyed. But eventually I came to see these password emergencies for what they really were: nonemergencies. It turned out that the tweet could wait, and so could the Amazon order.

✦

Meanwhile, I started trying to secure my data in other ways.

To combat impersonation (a.k.a. identity theft), I bought a shredder and started shredding documents containing personal information. And I bought a wallet that blocks radio-frequency identification signals on my credit cards and passport, which can be skimmed by hackers.

To ensure that my data would be safe in case of a more serious hack, I bought an external hard drive and started backing up my files regularly. (Yes, I had not been backing up before. Terrible, I know.) To foil hackers who might make it into my machine, I encrypted my hard drive (which on a Mac was a one-click operation).

I put a sticker over my Web camera so that hackers couldn't use it to remotely spy on me. I bought a privacy filter that shields my laptop screen from people trying to read over my shoulder or from the seat next to me on a plane.

To combat hackers who try to steal passwords from Wi-Fi connections in coffee shops, I installed software called HTTPS Everywhere, which ensured that my connections to the Internet were encrypted whenever possible.

I also started being much more cautious about my use of Wi-Fi in general. Instead of relying on my home Wi-Fi router, I plugged my computer into a hard-wired Ethernet connection. When traveling, I started using a portable Wi-Fi hot spot that I carried with me. The connection was sometimes spotty, but it made me feel a lot better than connecting to all those intrusive hotel Wi-Fi systems that force your Internet traffic through their system.

I also set up double password systems—known as two-factor authentication—when it was available. On Gmail, that meant installing an app that gave me a code to enter in addition to my password. At my bank, that meant rooting around in the online settings until I found a way to require a "pin" number before authorizing any payments.

But I set up those systems only at places where I didn't have to give out my phone number. Twitter offered two-factor authentication, but only for people who are willing to receive text messages from them—so I declined.

I also tried using a system called "Little Snitch" to monitor all the connections my computer was attempting to make, but quickly abandoned it. It turns out that I didn't really want to know how many connections my computer was making at any given time. I found that I had to approve seventy-six connections just to open my Web browser, to connect to Gmail, and to start streaming music on Spotify. Each request looked like this: "Allow outgoing connections to port 80 (http) of d1hza3lyffsoht .cloudfront.net until Spotify quits." My two choices were to allow "forever" or just "until quits." After an hour I had made ninety-seven extremely ill considered choices, I realized that I had no idea what I was doing, and I uninstalled the software.

As I investigated security options, I decided that the biggest problem was that I didn't know whom to trust. I knew enough to be wary of cynical attempts to prey on my fear. But I didn't know enough to actually test the products to see how well they worked.

So far, I was mostly using tools from people I knew or tools that were well established. I knew and trusted the technologists at the Electronic Frontier Foundation who made the HTTPS Everywhere software. Little Snitch was a well-known program. Similarly, 1Password was well established. But I didn't know what to think about an encrypted cloud service called SpiderOak that I was considering. I wanted to store my data in the cloud in case something went wrong with my backup, and to be able to access my files from anywhere. But SpiderOak wasn't well known.

I couldn't get a good sense of the company from its website. I liked that it didn't look like most computer security websites—which tend to sport a black background and lots of references to "military-grade encryption." SpiderOak was a sunny orange and touted its "zero-knowledge privacy environment," which is similar in concept to the mud-puddle test. SpiderOak had also been recommended to me by Christopher Soghoian, a technologist at the American Civil Liberties Union. But a website and a recommendation were pretty thin gruel for someone seeking a full meal. So I e-mailed the CEO, Ethan Oberman, and set up a time to meet him the next time I was in San Francisco.

We met at a trendy coffee shop. With his blond hair and muscular arms, Ethan looked more like a jock than a computer geek. I was immediately skeptical.

Over coffee, he told me his story—and indeed, it was not the typical computer geek narrative. He grew up in a tony Chicago suburb, went to a prep boarding school, Hotchkiss, and then to Harvard. He was, as I had guessed, a hockey player and captain of the Harvard lacrosse team. After graduation in 2000, he went to work for his dad's business—which helped magazine publishers manage their circulation lists. The company wanted a digital strategy, so Ethan built an e-mail marketing operation within his father's company. But a few years later, he was tired of working for the family business. He took a break and traveled. He also bought his first Macintosh computer. When he had to call his mom to ask her to e-mail him a file from the tower PC that he stored in his parents' closet, he realized there was a market opportunity.

There were plenty of "backup services" such as Xdrive and Mozy, but they offered backup for only a single machine. He also wanted to synchronize his data across machines. "Backup is not sexy," he told me. "It's like brushing your teeth. What's really sexy is accessing your data everywhere."

Sexy wasn't quite what I was looking for; I wanted more specifics about the company's zero-knowledge promise. For that, Ethan cheerfully referred me to his business partner Alan Fairless. (To be fair to Ethan, he probably wasn't used to journalists who wanted anything more than a sexy quote for their article.) Still, Ethan seemed to have the finances in hand. He told me that the company was profitable and made money by selling subscriptions rather than advertising. This fit with my pay-for-performance guiding principle.

Two weeks later I spoke by phone with Alan Fairless, Ethan's partner and SpiderOak's chief technology officer. Alan explained that he was the one who had pushed for encrypting the data. "It was important to me that it was encrypted before it left my computer." He explained how SpiderOak takes users' passwords and turns them into unique methods of encryption. The encryption is only as strong as the password a user creates. "There is no requirement on how long the password has to be," he said. "We decided that it was not a good idea to make users change their computer password selection methods at the same time that we tell them that if they forget their password their data is gone."

Given what I had learned about passwords, I appreciated SpiderOak not forcing users into an unwinnable situation. Alan really won me over when he told me that "the threat model is that we are protecting the user against ourselves, which also turns out to be a good way to protect the user against the rest of the world." He said that the company had already received law enforcement requests for data but once the officers learned that SpiderOak had no way to decrypt the data the requests were dropped.

I breathed a sigh of relief. Straight talk about threat models and passwords made him credible to me. And SpiderOak passed the mud-puddle test. I signed up for a subscription. But the whole experience seemed an absurd way to shop for computer security. Was I really going to have to visit all my technology providers to determine their trustworthiness?

And after all that, my security on SpiderOak still relied on the strength of my password.

✦

It used to take some skill to crack a password. Now anybody can do it.

Increased computing power has helped password crackers work faster. And the increasing availability of huge lists of leaked passwords has allowed programmers to write programs that make password cracking more accurate. To show how easy it has become, the journalist Nate Anderson cracked eight thousand passwords in one day using a free online program called Hashcat. "Even though I knew password cracking was easy, I didn't know it was *ridiculously* easy—well, ridiculously easy once I overcame the urge to bash my laptop with a sledgehammer and finally figured out what I was doing," he wrote.

The way password cracking works is as follows (greatly simplified):

- A hacker obtains a list of passwords to crack.
- These lists are usually encrypted—or "hashed."
- The hacker then attempts to decode the hashes.
- Usually, the hacker first attempts to run a "dictionary" attack—meaning he or she compares the patterns of the hashes with traditional dictionary words.
- The hacker then compares the patterns of the hashes to well-known databases of leaked passwords.
- The hacker then tries a "brute force" attack—which attempts options in simple sequences such as "aaaaaa," then "aaaaab," then "aaaaac," etc.

Brute force attacks are what the computer security researcher Robert Graham calls "an exponential problem. The amount of time it takes quickly grows out of all reasonableness." For that reason, Anderson ran brute force attacks only on passwords that were six digits long. If he had tried for passwords of nine or ten characters, he estimated it would take weeks or months to crack. And he was able to crack only eight thousand of the seventeen thousand passwords he attempted. "The lesson was clear: I *could* crack every last hash in the file—but I'd probably need the better part of a year to do it, assuming my machine didn't simply collapse under the strain," he wrote.

One lesson from the world of password cracking is that people who store passwords should do a better job of hashing. The industry best practice is to "salt" hashes—meaning that if a user creates a six-character password, the hasher would add several unique characters to it, making it longer, before hashing it. That makes it harder to break.

Sadly, salting is not common enough: recent hacks at LinkedIn, Yahoo!, and eHarmony revealed troves of unsalted hashes that were quickly broken.

For those who have to make passwords, the lesson from the world of password crackers is simple: make longer passwords and avoid simple dictionary words or well-known passwords (such as "password1").

✦

The measure of password strength is something computer scientists call "entropy." Higher entropy means harder to break. Jeffrey Goldberg, a password expert at AgileBits, the makers of 1Password, told me that entropy is a measure of "how many ways you could get a different result using the same system." Short, simple passwords, such as dictionary words, have very low entropy because they can easily be guessed. Longer passwords that contain many types of symbols, letters, and numbers often have larger entropy because it takes more guesses to figure them out.

Julian Assange knew this when he created the following password to the WikiLeaks cables database: AcollectionOfDiplomaticHistory-Since_1966_ToThe_PresentDay#. It is fifty-eight characters long, with very few symbols, and easy to remember. Of course, the reason we know his password is that the *Guardian* newspaper published it in a book about WikiLeaks. So, obviously, it wasn't a secure password in other respects.

Entropy is frustratingly difficult to estimate. A long password can have low entropy if it is comprised of simple words and easy grammar. I started to become obsessed with measuring the entropy of the passwords I had created. One day I was sitting outside my daughter's dance recital when I stumbled on an online entropy estimator that had been built by Dan Wheeler, an engineer at Dropbox. His estimator measured the "entropy" of each password, as well as the "time to crack," and I was immediately entranced by the thrill of testing my newly created mnemonic passwords. I recklessly started entering all my passwords.

I started with my bank password (created by me using mnemonics, twelve characters long). Ooh, very exciting. It had fifty-six bits of entropy and would take "centuries" to crack!

Then I tried my Gmail password created by 1Password (eighteen characters). It had eighty bits of entropy and would take "centuries" to crack. However, I hate that password: I can never remember it.

But my *Wall Street Journal* e-mail password (nine characters) was disappointing. I created it using the mnemonic method, but it had only twenty-eight bits of entropy. It would take just seven hours to crack!

Oh dear. How is this? The password I use to protect my 1Password account (another homegrown mnemonic that was seventeen characters long!) had thirty-seven bits of entropy and could be cracked in five months. Ugh.

This was an addictive but depressing sport. A pattern was emerging— my 1Password-created passwords were super strong; my homegrown passwords varied from strong to super weak.

The worst of my homegrown passwords: the password to log in to my computer could be cracked in four minutes. My password to log into my blog could be cracked in an "instant."

As the thrill of cracking them all wore off, I realized that it had been spectacularly stupid to enter my passwords into an unknown cracking system while using Wi-Fi. Even though it was my own portable Wi-Fi spot, an encrypted Web connection, and a website that promised not to store the passwords, my passwords could still somehow end up in a database used by password-cracking teams.

Now I had two reasons to make new passwords: (1) the fact that my passwords didn't have enough entropy and (2) my own stupidity.

✦

In my search for high-entropy passwords, I considered a wide variety of options, including passwords created using obscure languages and long passphrases like the one used by Julian Assange.

But again I ran into the problem of my own mind. I could come up with one or two words in an obscure language, or one or two passphrases, but eventually I knew that I would run out of ideas and start using weak passwords.

Studies show that even when people are making longer passwords, they tend to take shortcuts. In 2012, researchers at the University of Cambridge studied the use of passphrases on Amazon.com and found that many were based on well-known movies or music or phrases, such as "dead poets society," "three dog night," and "with or without you." As a result, many passphrases are just as weak as regular passwords. "Our results suggest that users aren't able to choose phrases made of completely random words, but are influenced by the probability of a phrase occurring in natural language," wrote the authors, Joseph Bonneau and Ekaterina Shutova.

The study confirmed my suspicion: I needed a system where I didn't have to think.

I found what I needed in a password system called Diceware. It is deceptively simple: you roll a six-sided die five times and use the results to pick numbers from the Diceware word list, which contains 7,776 short English words. Each word is numbered. It looks like this:

16655 clause
16656 claw
16661 clay
16662 clean
16663 clear
16664 cleat
16665 cleft
16666 clerk

Diceware's creator, Arnold Reinhold, recommends using a string of at least five words. So the resulting passwords look something like this:

alger klm curry blond puck. You can make the password stronger by adding more words, or by adding a few letters, symbols, or capital letters. But even the simple Diceware string of five lowercase five-letter words would take more than eighteen hundred days to crack, according to Bruce Marshall, founder of PasswordResearch.com.

Using dice ensures that you pick the numbers randomly. There are also, of course, software and websites that will generate random numbers for you. But Reinhold and other security experts caution against using unknown random number generators, which could be built by adversaries seeking to crack your password system. In fact, documents released by Edward Snowden show that the NSA had authored one of the scientific standards for a random number generator and could break it.

Excited by the prospect of not having to think about passwords ever again, I printed out the thirty-seven-page Diceware word list, punched holes in the paper, and put it in a binder. But I was daunted by having to roll the dice hundreds of times for all the passwords I needed to create. The binder sat on my desk until I thought of a brilliant idea: enlist my eight-year-old daughter who was sitting around the house bored, in the time-honored tradition of kids out of school during the summer. I told her I would pay her to make passwords for me.

Within an hour, she presented me with a piece of paper with five hand-made passwords—and demanded cash. I paid her $3.50.

Excited by the easy money, she e-mailed her grandparents, her uncle, and a few family friends to let them know she was starting a password-making business. This is what she wrote:

> Subject: My Buisness [sic]
>
> I'm starting my own password business where I make passwords. 5 passwords cost's $3.50 cents. 5 passwords per page. Hope you try them.

My mom immediately wrote to me asking if my daughter's e-mail account had been hacked. I assured her that it was a real business, and she signed up for some new passwords. By the end of the summer, my daughter had made about fifty passwords for family and friends and raised her prices to $1 per password.

I was thrilled. I now had a bunch of passwords stored in 1Password that I didn't know, and a dozen strong memorable passwords for my key accounts. And, as an unexpected bonus, I had finally persuaded my daughter to care about privacy—or, at the very least, to care about profiting from privacy.

8

LEAVING GOOGLE

On June 8, 2004, an FBI agent showed up at the public library in Deming, Washington, demanding to know the names of people who had checked out the book *Bin Laden: The Man Who Declared War on America* by Yossef Bodansky.

Nothing like that had ever happened before in Deming, a tiny town near the Canadian border with a population of just 353 people. Deming is not known as a hotbed of terrorism; if Deming is known at all, it is as a place to fuel up for gas and beer in the foothills of the North Cascade Mountains.

Even so, the librarians were prepared. A year earlier, the Whatcom County library system's attorney at the time, Deborra Garrett, had trained the staff on how to handle law enforcement requests. Librarians became information defense warriors during the 1980s, when FBI agents started showing up at college libraries demanding to know which books had been checked out by foreigners. Subsequently, forty-eight states adopted laws in some way protecting the confidentiality of circulation records.

So when the FBI agent showed up in Deming, the librarian on duty refused to hand over the records. Instead, she promised to pass on the agent's request to her lawyers and showed him the door.

When Garrett got the request, she called the FBI agent and asked what he wanted. He said that a reader had called the agency to report that someone had scribbled a handwritten note in the margin of the book that said, "if the things I'm doing is considered a crime then let history be a witness that I am a criminal. Hostility toward America is a religious duty and we hope to be rewarded by God."

After the conversation, Garrett discovered that the quote was from a 1998 interview with Osama bin Laden. She sent the interview to the FBI agent, thinking "that would be the end of it," Garrett said. But a few weeks later a grand jury subpoena arrived for the library records, along with a request for the librarians not to discuss the order.

The Whatcom County library was in a difficult situation. Complying with the subpoena would mean abandoning principles the librarians believed in. Fighting the subpoena was going to be difficult, as the law requires compliance with a lawful grand jury subpoena. The library was going to have to fight to narrow the subpoena. Garrett suggested that it could rely on a 1998 precedent: a federal court in Washington, D.C., found that the bookstore Kramerbooks & Afterwords did not have to turn over records of Monica Lewinsky's book purchases because of First Amendment protections of reading material.

The library trustees were worried. If they fought and lost, they would face a terrible choice: turn over the information and betray their principles or possibly face jail time for refusing to comply with a subpoena. The trustees discussed the issue and decided to fight. "It was a frightening stand to take," recalled Amory Peck, chair of the board of trustees of the Whatcom County library system. "But we could do no less. We could do no less than protect a very basic right of our patrons: their ability to read widely, curiously, broadly, maybe even dangerously . . . in complete certainty their choices would be confidential."

After Garrett filed a motion to quash the subpoena on First Amendment grounds, the FBI withdrew the subpoena. "In my view, this case illustrates what happens when people know their actions are going to be reviewed by a court," said Garrett, who is now a judge. "It keeps people honest."

✦

I couldn't realistically expect my Internet providers to mount such a spirited defense of my reading materials.

Of course, they do try to defend their customers. Google has a phalanx of great lawyers. In 2006, Google challenged a Justice Department request for two months' worth of search records, winning the right to narrow the request to just fifty thousand URLs instead of the billions requested. In 2007, Amazon successfully fought a government subpoena that sought the identities of people who bought books from a used bookseller on its site. The government sought to interview the book buyers as part of its tax fraud investigation into an Amazon third-party bookseller, but Amazon refused to hand over the names. The court agreed that "it is an unsettling and un-American scenario to envision federal agents nosing through the reading lists of law-abiding citizens while hunting for evidence against somebody else."

But when it comes to surveillance, Internet companies often lose the fight because the law is stacked against them. There are no Internet equivalents of the state privacy laws that protect library circulation records. First Amendment claims are often dismissed for lack of actual harm. And most technologists haven't adopted a view of themselves as fighters for intellectual freedom, as librarians often do.

The relevant law governing most surveillance of Internet communications is the Electronic Communications Privacy Act of 1986, which was designed to expand the protections that were in place for phone calls and regular mail to the digital realm. However, at the time, the law didn't envision that people would store so much information on computers and services outside their home. As a result, stored communications, such as e-mails and cell phone location records, can often be obtained by the government without a search warrant. The law only requires the government to show that the data are "relevant and material" to an investigation.

Thus it is easier for law enforcement to legally read people's e-mail than to open their postal mail. Not only that, courts often seal the court orders related to electronic surveillance so that users are never notified that a search had been conducted. As a result, the gatekeepers of our data are hampered in their fight to protect their customers. In 2012, Microsoft produced customer data for 83 percent of law enforcement requests. That same year, Google handed over data about its users in about two-thirds of the cases where information was requested.

The leading Internet companies, including Google, Apple, and Facebook, have joined a coalition that is pushing to amend the electronic communications privacy law to require search warrants for e-mail and cell phone location records. But so far their efforts to reform the law have not been successful.

The few instances where we have learned that companies fought government surveillance have not ended well. Consider just two cases—a small Internet provider, Sonic.net, and Internet giant Yahoo!. In 2011, Sonic.net went public with the fact that it had fought—and lost—a secret court order demanding the e-mail addresses of people who had corresponded with a WikiLeaks volunteer, Jacob Appelbaum, in the course of two years. Challenging the order was "rather expensive, but we felt it was the right thing to do," said Sonic's chief executive, Dane Jasper. By speaking to me, Jasper was defying the court's gag order that prevented him from discussing the government's request. (Jasper later said that he was unaware that the gag order remained in force when he spoke to me.)

As for Yahoo!, in 2008 the Foreign Intelligence Surveillance Court rejected its challenge to a warrantless order for user data. Yahoo! argued that the government's broad requests were unconstitutional, but the court ruled that the company had not proved that anyone was harmed by the surveillance: "Notwithstanding the parade of horribles trotted out by the petitioner, it has presented no evidence of any actual harm, any egregious risk of error, or any broad potential for abuse in the circumstances of the instant case."

There have been many more cases. But the same thread runs through them all: the Internet companies' hands are often tied when it comes to surveillance.

◆

I don't dislike Google.

In fact, Google has tried hard to be transparent about surveillance. It was the first big Internet company to start publicly reporting the number of law enforcement requests it received. It has been active in the coalition pushing for reform of the electronic communications privacy law. And Google is appealing the government's gag order that prevents it from revealing how many requests it receives from the Foreign Intelligence Surveillance Court.

But Google has also repeatedly abused users' trust. In 2010, Google launched a social networking tool called Buzz that automatically listed people as "followers" of people with whom they frequently e-mailed or chatted on Gmail. Users who clicked on a button "Sweet! Check out Buzz," were not adequately informed that the identity of their closest Gmail contacts would be made public. Google later agreed to settle charges by the Federal Trade Commission that Buzz was deceptive, and paid $8.5 million to settle a class action lawsuit about Buzz. In 2012, my colleagues and I broke the news that Google was bypassing the privacy settings of the Safari browser used by millions of iPhone and other Apple users by using a special computer code to trick their browsers into allowing Google tracking. Later that year, Google agreed to pay $22.5 million to settle the FTC charges that its Apple circumvention had violated the terms of its Google Buzz settlement. The $22.5 million settlement was, at the time, the FTC's largest civil penalty of the kind. And in 2013, Google agreed to pay $7 million to settle with thirty-eight attorneys generals from thirty-eight states who claimed that Google violated people's privacy when its Street View cars inadvertently collected personal information from Wi-Fi networks.

I also have too much data stored with Google. My audit revealed that Google had stored all of my searches dating back to 2006 and had identified all 2,192 people that I had e-mailed in that time. Given the outdated privacy laws, I couldn't expect the company to keep all that data secret. I needed to go on a Google data diet.

I started by quitting Google search.

I'd been annoyed about the change in Google's privacy policy, announced in 2012, that allowed Google to combine information from its various services, for example, using information about my searches to show me customized ads on Gmail. Google also doesn't delete search history related to my account unless I delete it myself. If I search from a computer where I am not signed in to a Google account, it will remove some identifiers from the data after nine months. Theoretically, that means the government can ask Google for all my searches dating back to 2006. No such requests have been disclosed publicly, but the availability of search history seems like an open invitation for fishing expeditions.

My searches are among the most sensitive information about me. If I'm looking into buying a burner phone, all my searches are about burner phones. If I'm researching an article about facial recognition technology, all my searches are about facial recognition technology. Basically my searches are a fairly accurate prediction of my future actions.

To replace Google search, I found a tiny search engine called DuckDuckGo that has a zero-data retention policy. It doesn't store any of the information that is automatically transmitted by my computer—the IP address and other digital footprints. As a result, DuckDuckGo has no way to link my search queries to me. "When you access DuckDuckGo (or any Web site), your Web browser automatically sends information about your computer," the company's privacy policy states. "Because this information could be used to link you to your searches, we do not log (store) it at all. This is a very unusual practice, but we feel it is an important step to protect your privacy."

As soon as I switched, I realized how dependent on Google I had become. Without Google's suggested searches, and Google's perfect memory of what I usually search for, each search required more work from me. For instance, DuckDuckGo doesn't know that I live in New York City, so when I mistyped "Naturaly History Museum," it brought up the Natural History Museum of Los Angeles. For comparison, I checked Google: sure enough, it corrected my spelling and guessed I was in New York, listing the American Museum of Natural History in Manhattan at the top of my results.

DuckDuckGo's lack of knowledge about me forced me to be smarter in my searches. For instance, I noticed I had become so lazy that I had been typing URLs—such as CNN.com—into the Google search bar instead of the navigation bar, even though I knew exactly where I was going. So I began typing in the addresses into the correct spot on my Web browser.

The next thing I noticed: I had been Googling Web pages that I visit very regularly—such as my kids' schools and my yoga studio schedule—instead of just bookmarking them. And so I began bookmarking them.

In fact, I had gotten so accustomed to letting Google do my work that I found it a bit jarring to have to finish typing an entire word without Google finishing it for me. Without Google's suggestions, however, I found that I was less distracted to search for things I didn't need. No more typing in the letter *a* and having Google suggest "amazon," and then suddenly remembering I needed to order something from Amazon .com.

With DuckDuckGo, I usually found what I wanted, although sometimes it was strange to be confronted with just three results. I was so conditioned to seeing "millions" of results for everything on Google.

But DuckDuckGo had some black holes. I desperately missed Google Maps and couldn't find any other online maps that I liked as much. And I missed the Google News section.

Before going to a friend's dinner party, I searched to remind myself of the promotion he had just landed at Columbia University. There had been some recent news about it, but all my searches on his name alone, Sree Sreenivasan, and his name and Columbia, turned up nothing. Finally, I tried "Sree, Columbia and News" and an article popped up. The news was there. I just had to retrain myself to use DuckDuckGo's structure for news searches.

It dawned on me that I had tuned myself to Google. I had always thought of Google as a clean sheet of paper—possibly because of its nice white interface—but in fact I had molded my questions to adjust to how Google likes to answer questions.

Now I was tuning myself to a different service, DuckDuckGo, which had different ways of answering questions. It was like a new relationship; I was discovering my new partner's quirks and foibles. And it was empowering; I was tuning myself to a partner that didn't have a hidden agenda of tracking me.

I had broken free from Google, and the world was still on its axis. I had mastered another service and could still find the information I needed. The whole experience reminded me of a quote from Marc Andreessen, the man who created Netscape, the first Web-browsing software, back in 1994. "The spread of computers and the Internet will put jobs in two categories," Andreessen said in a 2012 interview. "People who tell computers what to do, and people who are told by computers what to do."

Mastering my switch to DuckDuckGo made me feel I had a better chance of being in the category of people who tell computers what to do.

✦

After using DuckDuckGo for a few months, I started to feel a bit uneasy. Who were these guys that I was trusting? And why was their logo a duck with a bow tie? It seemed kind of weird.

For all my dislike of Google's tracking practices, I had developed an emotional snapshot of Google as a place with all the cheerful arrogance of an Ivy League university. It had principles but few scruples: it took a high-profile brave stand against censorship in China but was making money off my personal data every day.

I was having a hard time getting the same kind of mental image of the principles and scruples behind a cheerful duck in a bow tie.

And so I boarded a train to Philadelphia to meet the people behind the duck. From Philadelphia, I rolled for another twenty minutes through leafy suburbs and past the Bryn Mawr College campus before arriving at my destination, Paoli. It was easy to spot DuckDuckGo's founder, Gabriel Weinberg, in the parking lot—he was the one whose car had duck stickers on it. Other than his shock of auburn hair, he looked like any other geek with his thick-framed glasses and a hoodie. I jumped in the car and we drove two minutes to his office.

To my surprise, we pulled into the parking lot behind a stone castle with colorful round turrets. "You work in a castle?" I said.

Yep, he did. DuckDuckGo's offices were on the second floor, the walls decorated with ducks. Weinberg had a polka-dot couch in his office and a play area near his desk for his kids. He told me that his focus for the company wasn't initially about privacy. He just wanted to build a better search engine. After selling a social networking website called the Names Database for $10 million in 2006, he and his wife moved to Valley Forge, Pennsylvania, so she could be close to her work at the pharmaceutical giant GlaxoSmithKline.

A freshly minted millionaire, Weinberg experimented with a bunch of projects. He made his own TV studio, worked on a social network for golfers, and started a service that sought to use crowdsourcing to find better search results. As he played around with search, he started to get increasingly annoyed by Google search results that were filled with the equivalent of spam.

So he decided to build a better search engine. "I wanted to go back to the Google old days when the focus was on quality links," he told me. Privacy came up only after he launched the first version of the website to the technology community, and some users asked about the site's privacy policies. "Honestly I hadn't given it one thought at all until then," Weinberg told me. "So I took a hard look at search privacy. I thought it was pretty creepy what a search engine could have on someone—it's arguably the most sensitive data you could have on someone on the Internet. I decided the coolest course of action would be to take it completely out of my hands—and not store the stuff. After doing that, I realized this is kind of a core thesis for the company."

By 2011, he had embraced privacy completely. He bought a billboard in San Francisco that said, "Google Tracks You. We Don't," and accepted an investment from a venture capital firm, Union Square Ventures, that was betting on the emerging market for privacy tools.

Over take-out sandwiches, a few of his engineers joined us to discuss the challenges of building a search engine from scratch. We talked about the challenges of building better maps and my frustrations with their news search results. Keeping DuckDuckGo privacy-friendly was difficult. The engineers had to build many of their technical tools from scratch. For instance, they had to build their own blogging software because the free blogging software contained tracking technology.

"It's like you guys are survivalists," I told Weinberg. "You have to grow your own food and stock your own guns."

As we talked, I was surprised at how earnestly they approached building a better search engine. Somehow, with the polka-dot couch, the ducks, the castle, and Weinberg's auburn hair, I had allowed myself to be lulled into thinking that it was more of a hobby than an actual company. But they appeared to be dead serious.

It reminded me of when I was a reporter at the *San Francisco Chronicle* in the late 1990s. I was dismissive of this newfangled search engine Google. I remember thinking: How could its reliance on machine-based page ranking be better than the hand-curated results on my favorite search engine, AltaVista?

Now I was sitting on a polka-dot couch in suburban Philadelphia wondering how a few guys working in a castle could pose a threat to a search engine that pulls in nearly $30 billion a year.

And yet, in the technology industry, some of the best ideas sound crazy at first.

✦

I really didn't want to quit using Gmail. Most of my hacker friends used it—even the ones who were paranoid about privacy. And Gmail makes it so easy to share documents and to chat with other Gmail users.

But it was hard to justify using an e-mail service that admitted to reading my mail. Of course, Google says (and we have no reason to disbelieve them) that humans aren't reading my mail. It's only computers that scan my e-mail for keywords, and then insert ads based on those keywords.

But that's what the National Security Agency says about domestic spying, too. Yes, its computers are scooping up all sorts of U.S. data "inadvertently" in the course of foreign espionage. But it "minimizes" data about U.S. citizens so that humans don't see it except under certain conditions, such as during an intelligence investigation or if it contains evidence of a crime.

Ultimately, the question is the same as for all dragnets: Will the data be abused eventually? The answer seems doomed to be yes. In 2010, Google fired an engineer for snooping on teenagers' Gmail chats—and said it was the second time an engineer had been fired for snooping on user data. In 2008, two former NSA intercept operators revealed that they and their colleagues had listened in on hundreds of Americans' phone calls—including phone sex.

Still, I kept delaying my departure from Gmail. It was just so easy and friendly and searchable.

Finally, it was a project at the Massachusetts Institute of Technology that convinced me to find a new e-mail service. A group of researchers there built a tool called Immersion that allowed people to visualize the metadata in their Gmail accounts.

It was a little hair-raising to authorize Immersion to access my Gmail account, but the developers promised they would delete their findings. So I took the plunge. After a few minutes of calculating, Immersion presented me with a beautiful graphic showing my connections to my top 504 e-mail "collaborators"—people with whom I have exchanged more than three e-mails. According to Immersion, my top "collaborator" was my best friend, followed by my husband. (Gmail had already reported to me that my husband was my most frequent e-mail partner. I'm not sure which report is correct.)

The graph of my collaborators looked like this:

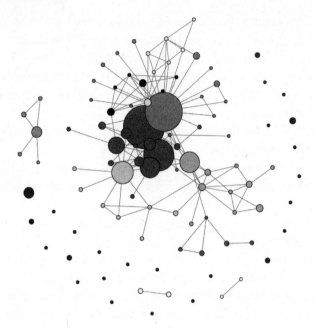

The graphic made it crystal clear that I e-mailed about a dozen people far more than anyone else. It reminded me how unique my social network was.

Disturbed, I set about trying to disentangle myself from Gmail.

I briefly considered running my own e-mail server at home after I ran across a blog post called "NSA Proof your e-mail in 2 hours." But I abandoned the idea eight paragraphs into the post when the author stated, "I'm going to assume you're running Debian Wheezy." It was clearly too technical a job for me.

So I looked around for privacy-protecting e-mail services. It turned out that there were dozens of them—with names such as Hushmail, Neo-Mail, and CounterMail. I really liked CounterMail—a paid e-mail service that passed the mud-puddle test—but I had to rule it out because it was based in Sweden. As a U.S. citizen, my e-mail is protected by law. The NSA has to at least "minimize" its spying of U.S citizens' e-mails. But if the NSA thinks I am a foreigner, there are far fewer restrictions.

That left only a few options based in the United States, including Lavabit, a Texas service that seems to have been used by Edward Snowden, and Riseup, a service run by a collective in Seattle. After studying their privacy policies, I decided Riseup was slightly more appealing. Both stored minimal user information and passed the mud-puddle test. But Riseup also stripped out location from e-mail addresses, while Lavabit said it retained the location in e-mail addresses so it could be used by law enforcement.

Joining Riseup wasn't easy. It was free but I needed to get "invited" by a member. Luckily, I was able to arrange an invitation through Christopher Soghoian, a technologist at the American Civil Liberties Union who also happens to be one of the most paranoid people I know (and I mean that as a compliment).

Invitation in hand, I started the signup process. But I was soon stumped by the social contract that I was asked to sign:

We ask that you do not use riseup.net services to advocate any of the following:

- Support for capitalism, domination, or hierarchy.
- The idea that class oppression supersedes race or gender oppression.
- A vanguard strategy for revolution.
- Population control.

If you disagree with this, then riseup.net is not for you.

Most of it was pretty unobjectionable. I was not planning to use Riseup to foment revolution, to push population control, or to argue either side of the class v. race/gender oppression debate. Nor was I likely to advocate for domination or hierarchy.

But disavowing "support for capitalism" was difficult. After all, I worked for the *Wall Street Journal*—a newspaper that once promoted itself with the tagline "Adventures in Capitalism." But, I argued to myself, my job as a reporter is to be a watchdog of capitalism, not to support capitalism unreservedly. Maybe I was parsing words, but I decided I could agree to Riseup's social contract.

I wasn't done yet. I had to find a way to manage my e-mail from my computer instead of from the Web. Riseup lets users store only a small amount of data on its servers, which keeps its costs down and, more important, means that there is less data for the government to grab from

Riseup. Of course, Riseup promises it will "actively fight" any attempt to obtain user data—but that is always an easier fight if there are no data to fight over.

With or without Riseup's quotas, I should have been storing my old e-mails on my computer instead of in Gmail's "cloud." The 1986 Electronic Communications Privacy Act allows the government to obtain e-mails stored with a third party after 180 days without a warrant, so storing old mail anywhere outside the home is, unfortunately, an invitation to government dragnets.

I searched around for e-mail software that was privacy-friendly. The best option was a free open-source project, Thunderbird, which supported encrypted e-mails. But Thunderbird's biggest backer, Mozilla, withdrew support for it in 2012.

Hewing to my guiding principle of "Pay for performance," I purchased a paid version of Thunderbird, called Postbox. (I also donated to the Riseup collective, in the hopes of keeping the e-mail service alive.) I downloaded all my Gmail into Postbox and set up Riseup to work with Postbox. Once I got it working, I felt an amazing sense of freedom. Suddenly, I could easily switch between e-mail providers; I could receive an e-mail in Gmail and reply from my Riseup account.

Strangely, I was tentative at first about using my Riseup account. I was worried that people wouldn't want to be linked to e-mails from an anticapitalist collective. So I e-mailed a few people who I thought would be most worried—people in top government jobs and high-ranking business executives—and asked if they minded me e-mailing them from an anarchist collective address.

The responses ranged from "Huh?" to "What?" Nobody seemed to care. It occurred to me that when I joined Gmail, I never asked anyone to "agree" to have his or her e-mails scanned by Google.

(It is worth noting that a few non-Gmail users have joined a class action complaint against Google over this very issue, on the theory that Google is violating the Wiretap Act when it scans e-mails they send to Gmail users. Google argues that there is implied consent, "just as a sender of a letter to a business colleague cannot be surprised that the recipient's assistant opens the letter." I'm not sure I buy that argument. After all, I always ask before opening my husband's mail.)

I realized I was doing my e-mail contacts a favor by switching to a service that wasn't going to scan their messages. I stopped asking and began using Riseup for all my professional contacts.

But I didn't pull the plug on Gmail entirely. I decided to keep it, just as I have kept my AOL account all those years. AOL has slowly devolved into my e-mail address for online shopping. I decided to keep Gmail and use it only to handle my "mom" e-mails—setting up playdates for my kids, signing my kids up for camp, and communicating with school through the inevitable Google shared documents.

As a final step, I downloaded all my shared Google documents onto my hard drive. Now I would rarely need to log in to Google's website again. And frosting on the cake: in case I decided to sneak in an occasional Google search, it wouldn't be tied to my identity if I wasn't logged in to Google. (Although the searches would still be tied to my computer IP address, unless I masked my address by using anonymizing software.)

I felt as if I had scaled a kind of technological Everest. I had taken control of my e-mail. It no longer controlled me.

❖

My euphoria was short-lived.

In August 2013, Edward Snowden's e-mail service, Lavabit, abruptly shut down. The founder, Ladar Levison, wrote that he shut down rather than "become complicit in crimes against the American people." Levison said he was planning to take his fight to the Fourth Circuit Court of Appeals, implying that he had already fought—and lost—in a lower court.

As in so many electronic surveillance cases, Levison received a gag order that prevented him from discussing the request. But after some documents were unsealed in the case, Levison disclosed that he had been asked to hand over the encryption keys that would have unlocked all of his users' communications. In other words, he'd been asked to breach the mud-puddle test. "It was the equivalent of asking Coca-Cola to hand over its secret formula," Levison said.

That kind of thing had happened to an encrypted e-mail service before. In 2007, Hushmail, a privacy-oriented e-mail service, strongly suggested that it may have been ordered by a court to install software that could intercept a user's password when that user logged in to the service, thus allowing the government to decrypt the user's data.

I could understand why Levison decided to shut down on principle rather than breach his users' privacy. But I couldn't help also feeling for the four hundred thousand people who lost their e-mail accounts without any notice. "Years of email accounts, saved email and important details all gone without any notice. Disgrace of a company," wrote one user on Lavabit's Facebook page. "This is horrible. . . . Thanks for screwing up my life," posted another user.

It could have been me. Lavabit had been my runner-up choice for an e-mail service.

After Lavabit shut down, another privacy-protecting company, Silent Circle, abruptly shut down its e-mail service. The company said that it had not yet received any government requests, but it wanted to act before any requests arrived. "We see the writing on the wall, and we have decided that it is best for us to shut down Silent Mail now," the company wrote.

Suddenly, Riseup was among the last privacy-protecting services standing. The Riseup collective posted a message reassuring users that it would fight any attempts at government surveillance and was working to build a "radical new infrastructure" that would better protect users' e-mails. However, this message was not entirely reassuring.

"We would rather pull the plug than submit to repressive surveillance by our government, or any government," the collective's leaders wrote. And they reminded users to download and back up their e-mails.

As I triple-checked that I was backing up my e-mails onto my hard drive and into my encrypted cloud service, I thought about how absurd my privacy journey was becoming.

I was hoarding all my data in case of an apocalypse. And even more strangely, the apocalypse seems to be right around the corner. I was turning into a data survivalist.

9
INTRODUCING IDA

da Tarbell was an investigative journalist who exposed the abuses of the Standard Oil Company at the turn of the twentieth century. She is also my alter ego.

Creating a fake identity was a key part of my strategy of data pollution. In cases where I couldn't avoid a dragnet, most likely when buying things or logging in to websites, I would try to contribute Ida's information to the dragnet rather than my own. After all, there is no reason that every single website that requires a log-on needs to know my real name.

Of course, a determined adversary would likely be able to connect the dots between Ida and me. But I wasn't looking for perfect; I just wanted to force the trackers to put some effort into tracking me specifically, rather than sweeping up data about me effortlessly.

I chose Ida because she is part of a generation of journalists that I admire. Known as "muckrakers," investigative journalists such as Ida Tarbell and Upton Sinclair exposed the underbelly of the industrial revolution, from monopolistic price gouging by the trusts to working conditions in slaughterhouses. Their work led to laws that reined in the worst excesses of the era.

I believe that today we are at a similar turning point. As our nation shifts toward an information economy, there are few laws policing the booming industry giants and few governmental or nonprofit institutions with the technical savvy to police the information economy. And so it falls to today's muckrakers—investigative journalists and conscientious objectors like Edward Snowden—to reveal the underbelly of the information revolution. I hope that once we see the abuses clearly, we will be able to find a way to restrain the excesses of the information age.

But I wasn't sure how to create an online identity for Ida. I had already decided that I wasn't going to create a fake driver's license. But everything else—fake e-mail addresses, phone numbers, mailing addresses—was fair game.

I soon found myself on a slippery slope of lies.

✦

I started small. I set up a Gmail account for Ida, which meant creating a birthday and a zip code for her. I decided that she lived in Berkeley, California, and was born in 1966.

Then I started making reservations in the name of Ida Tarbell at a few restaurants. The problem was that Ida didn't have a cell phone—and restaurants often asked me for a phone number when I made the reservation.

I was able to convince some restaurants to give me a reservation without a phone number, by promising that I would call them to confirm the reservation. They said okay, and often if I forgot to call they still kept the reservation.

But I found that lying was difficult for me: I got a little bit red and hot whenever I had to say the name Ida. I soon realized that Ida needed an OpenTable account—to book online reservations—so that I wouldn't have to lie on the phone.

But when I tried to sign up for OpenTable, it asked for a cell phone number. I knew that I should just enter a random phone number such as 212-555-1212, but somehow I couldn't do it. I abandoned the sign-up screen.

This was the same problem I had with passwords. The problem wasn't the technology. The problem was my mind.

✦

I'm a terrible liar.

I squirm and I don't make eye contact and my face gets hot and red. Or I giggle. I'm such a terrible liar that a colleague once took me aside and told me that I should never attempt to lie because I can't do it correctly.

I had always believed that it was easier to lie online. Some studies show that avoiding the physical cues that accompany lies can make lying online easier. But I wasn't finding the process any easier online. I didn't understand why until I stumbled on the research of Jeff Hancock, a psychologist at Cornell University who studies online deception.

In a 2012 study, Hancock asked 119 college students to create a traditional résumé or a public LinkedIn profile, and then analyzed the truthfulness of the results. The students who created traditional résumés were more likely to exaggerate information about their previous work experiences than those who created LinkedIn public profiles. But the LinkedIn folks were more likely to lie about their hobbies and interests. On the whole, Hancock said, "those LinkedIn resumes were more honest on the things that mattered to employers, like your responsibilities or your skills at a previous job."

In an earlier study, Hancock compared people's real height, weight, and age with what they stated in an online dating profile. Most people exaggerated, but only by a little bit. Most of the men lied about their height, Hancock said. "In fact, they lied about their height about nine tenths of an inch, what we say in the lab as 'strong rounding up.'"

Hancock believes that people can be more honest online than in person if they believe they will be held accountable for what they write. In other studies, he found that lies increase when the conversation is more ephemeral—whether an online chat or a face-to-face conversation. Truthfulness increases when the people knew each other in real life. In short, Hancock speculates that it is harder to lie when you are creating a permanent record for which you know you will be held accountable. After my data audit, I am keenly aware that everything I do is being recorded. So it makes sense that I have a hard time lying online.

Now that I understood the situation, I faced a difficult choice: Was it ethical for me to try to overcome my aversion to lying? To answer this question, I found myself in the company of philosophers. One of the strongest views on lying was held by the eighteenth-century German philosopher Immanuel Kant, who argued that lying was always wrong—even if a murderer shows up at your door seeking an innocent victim.

As a mother, I found it easy to discard Kant's extreme view. Any mother knows that sometimes you have to lie to your children. When my son's fingertip was sliced off in an accident and we were in the emergency room, I did not tell him the truth—which was that the surgeon was stuck in a blinding snowstorm and was not sure he would be able to get to the hospital in time to sew it up. I told him that everything was going to be okay. (And, yes, the plastic surgeon was able to stitch up my son's finger—but it took him nearly five hours to get to the hospital.)

So, in my mind, some lies are acceptable. But which ones? I found myself attracted to the "publicity test" described by the Harvard writer and philosopher Sissela Bok: "Which lies, if any, would survive the appeal for justification to reasonable persons?"

Some of the questions she asks:

- Are there truthful alternatives to your lie?
- What is the moral justification for telling the lie?
- What is the relationship that exists between you and the person you are lying to?
- What goods and bads will be brought about by your lie?
- What would happen if everyone in your situation lied?

Here, I felt myself to be on fairly solid ground. I was planning to use my fake identity for commercial transactions with companies that I believed were asking for more information from me than necessary to complete a transaction.

I can walk to a newsstand, hand over cash, and anonymously buy a copy of a newspaper. But every online newspaper wants me to fork over my identity—even if it is only for a "free" subscription. Similarly, I used to go to my local bookstore and buy books in cash. Now, all the bookstores are dying, and Amazon is my local bookstore. But why does Amazon need anything more than my money? Do restaurants where I book a reservation really need anything more from me than my money?

Some, if not all, of this information was clearly going to be used against me. Consider two examples.

In 2012, the International Air Transport Association adopted new rules that would allow the airlines to present different prices to different customers. The *New York Times* editorial board warned that the new pricing model will likely be used to present higher prices to people who try to shop anonymously and to people who appear to be able to pay more.

In 2013, Blue Cross Blue Shield of North Carolina said it began buying information from data brokers about the spending habits of more than three million people that it covers. The insurer said it could flag people who purchase items such as plus-size clothing and send them information about weight-loss plans.

To me, all this was the beginning of an era of financial manipulation. Big companies were seeking to use personal data to gain leverage over me. So I felt my lie was justified as a way of rebalancing the relationship.

However, Bok's last question gave me pause. What would it be like to live in a world where everybody had fake identities?

I tried to envision that world. It would be a world where you couldn't trust people you didn't know in real life, where you wouldn't open e-mails from people claiming to be a friend of a friend and where you couldn't trust reviews from an untrusted source. Maybe it was even the kind of world where a famous football star could be hoaxed into falling in love with a woman he met online; the woman was really a fictional identity created by a man who was in love with him. (For those who don't know, I just described the story of the Notre Dame linebacker Manti Te'o.) Maybe I don't have a good enough imagination, but it sounded a lot like the world we live in today.

And what about the appeals to reasonable persons? The people I consulted thought I was silly to even ask about the ethics of a harmless lie. My husband thought fake names were okay as long as I didn't get a fake ID card. My children's godmother thought it was a no-brainer; she already had several different fake e-mail addresses that she used for different aspects of her life. A colleague thought it was a great idea and started setting up fake name accounts right away.

It was admittedly a small sample, but I decided that my lying passed the publicity test.

✦

With my newfound commitment to lying, I regrouped and started again with Ida's online identity. This time I was serious: I was going to get a credit card for Ida Tarbell.

I got the idea for Ida's credit card from the cryptographer Jon Callas. He had come to my office to show me apps he had built that let you encrypt calls and texts from your iPhone. I mentioned to him my struggles to build a robust alternate identity. Without missing a beat, he pulled out his wallet and fanned out an array of credit cards with different names—including one with the name Dale B. Cooper, after the FBI special agent in the '90s TV show *Twin Peaks*.

It's easy, he told me. Just tell the credit card company that you want a new card with a new name added to your existing account. Parents do it for their kids all the time.

Aha. Now I got it. It was a threat model problem. Hiding my identity from the credit card company wasn't the threat. Hiding my identity from everywhere that I spend money was the threat. If I was suspected of a crime, a prosecutor could send a subpoena to American Express to learn the true identity of Ida Tarbell.

I decided to do it. I tried requesting a new card through the American Express website, but the website said that I needed to call. Finally, I called from the office late one night when no one was around. I still felt shy. I didn't want anyone in my family—or at the office—to overhear me.

Of course, the customer service representative was completely unruffled by my request for an additional card to be linked to my account. He asked Ida's birth date—luckily I had one from making the e-mail account. When he asked for Ida's social security number, I just said I didn't have one. He didn't even blink, just moved on. The card would be in the mail within a few days, he said.

A few days went by, and no card. A week, then two weeks. Finally, I called and requested another card. A week went by and that card didn't arrive, either.

Meanwhile, I started getting e-mails and calls from American Express asking for Ida's social security number. The automated calls said, "Press 1 if you are Ida, press 2 if not. Press 1 if Ida is available, 2 if not." I felt trapped by the questions: I wasn't Ida or not Ida. So I hung up.

I started to wonder if the missing social security number was delaying the card. But I forced myself to call one more time. The representative said she would overnight me a new card.

The next day it arrived—nice and shiny and green with Ida's name in raised letters. I had never loved a card so much. That evening, when my husband came home from work, I showed the card to him proudly.

"Oh!" he said. "Why didn't you tell me you were Ida Tarbell? I have been throwing out her mail for weeks."

Note to self: in the future, warn husband before setting up fake identity.

✦

Now Ida needed a new mailing address.

Having seen my files from data brokers, it was clear to me that if Ida started receiving mail regularly at my address, she would eventually show up as an associate or family member in my records.

I considered getting Ida a post office box, but the post office requires users to present identification when picking up packages. That wasn't going to work. I checked with the UPS Store, but it had the same policy requiring identification when picking up packages.

So I convinced a friend to accept mail and packages for Ida. My friend lived in a big apartment building where everyone's mail is sorted into mailboxes, similar in size to post office boxes. All I had to do was tape Ida Tarbell's name inside the mailbox and, presto, Ida had an address.

With a credit card and an address, Ida's possibilities were limitless. Still, I wanted to be cautious with her online accounts.

I consulted with Michael Sussmann, the former Justice Department prosecutor who now works as outside attorney for companies such as Google. He told me that most Web services keep the registration Internet address forever, so it is worth being mindful of the location from which I set up my accounts.

So I launched Ida's online life by taking my laptop to a café with free Wi-Fi. I sat down, ordered a cappuccino, opened up my laptop, and launched Tor, the anonymizing software that masks the Internet address of your computer by routing traffic around the world. This time, I appeared to be in Germany.

Browsing on Tor is slow. As a test, I typed New York University's Web address, www.nyu.edu, into the Tor browser and into the regular Firefox Web browser and clocked each of them. It took twenty seconds to launch in Tor and three seconds to launch in Firefox. At least I had plenty of time to sip my coffee as I browsed on Tor.

I started by signing up for a free e-mail account for Ida from Microsoft's Outlook.com. I steeled myself and entered 212-867-5309 as her backup phone number (after the famous '80s song by Tommy Tutone). I turned off Microsoft's targeted ads feature.

Feeling quite pleased with myself, I also set up an OpenTable account for Ida, using the Outlook address. I left the phone number entry blank. (I don't know why that hadn't occurred to me earlier.) And then I set up an Amazon.com account for Ida, using my friend's mailing address and Ida's credit card number. I declined Amazon's offer to provide Ida with the "Amazon betterizer," which would provide her with more personalized recommendations.

The first book I ordered was a used copy of *Surveillance in the Stacks: The FBI's Library Awareness Program*. Published in 1991, it is a librarian's recounting of the FBI's efforts in the 1980s to enlist librarians to spy on books checked out by foreigners, the program that prompted nearly every state to adopt laws protecting the confidentiality of library circulation records.

This was my privacy joke: using a fake name to order a book about why privacy of books should be protected.

✦

It took me a while to learn when to deploy Ida and when to be myself.

Ida ordered all my books from Amazon. She made all my restaurant reservations. And she paid for my meals in restaurants when I was meeting someone for an interview. Soon, I had half a dozen online accounts for Ida. I built a spreadsheet with all of her log-ins and passwords.

But I learned there were some things Ida couldn't do. I tried to use Ida's credit card in a Modell's sporting goods store and the clerk asked for identification to match my credit card. So I paid cash. The same thing happened at Old Navy, but not at the rag & bone designer store, where Ida purchased a sweater, no problem. It seemed that Ida needed to stick to designer stores.

Ida also made me aware of where I was known. When I sat down at my favorite bar near my office, the bartender greeted me by name with,

"Hi, Julia." I was surprised she knew my name—although we have often chatted at the bar, I didn't remember telling her my name. I realized she must know me from ringing up my credit card purchases. I also realized I would arouse suspicion if I suddenly switched identities. So when it came time to pay the bartender, I tucked my Ida Tarbell card back in my purse and pulled out my Julia Angwin card.

The more I used Ida, the more I worried about overusing her identity. Soon she was going to have a credit score of her own. Already, Ida was getting credit card offers in the mail from other companies. (American Express says it doesn't sell its customers' names, so it's not clear how Ida got on the marketing lists.) If I wasn't careful, Ida was going to end up on my data broker reports listed as an "alias."

I realized I wanted more fake identities to lessen the burden on Ida.

✦

I didn't have the mental energy to build another Ida, what with thinking up her birthday and her hometown and her passwords, and summoning the courage to lie about her.

I wanted an easier, faster way to create fake identities.

I found that there were plenty of services that let you create disposable e-mail addresses—mostly to prevent spam. For instance, if I created an account at a website called spamgourmet.com, I could create unique e-mail addresses for each website that I logged in to.

Once again, however, I was lazy: I didn't want to think up new e-mail identities. So I started using a free service called MaskMe, from a privacy start-up called Abine, which would create a new fake e-mail address for every account. For instance, when ForeignPolicy.com asked me to create an account to read an article, MaskMe created an e-mail address for me to use to log in: 18123a18@opayq.com. MaskMe forwarded to me all e-mails sent to that address. But if a website sent too many e-mails, I could instruct MaskMe to block them.

I enjoyed blocking e-mails. After receiving three e-mails from Klout, a social influence ranking company that I had logged in to during my audit, I blocked them. After seven e-mails from RecordedFuture.com, a big data analysis company, I blocked them.

I also signed up for a premium service from MaskMe for $5 a month, which issued me a new phone number that I could then forward to any phone. Now, I could enter my phone number onto forms without worrying about receiving annoying marketing calls.

I was starting to get the hang of this lying business. The best way to do it was to automate it.

◆

But it was hard to automate deception at the cash register.

Of course, I could always use cash. Unloved and untrendy, cash is mostly anonymous. U.S. notes contain serial numbers and some true privacy paranoids will exchange cash to avoid being tracked by the serial number. But for my threat model—avoiding dragnets—cash is fine.

However, carrying a lot of cash is unwieldy and often impractical. I tried to wean myself off credit cards, but I still preferred them—mostly because I like to keep track of my spending and I hated stuffing my wallet full of cash receipts and trying to remember to log them later.

I tried using a $200 prepaid debit card, which I bought at a drugstore for cash. I used it for small purchases—lunch near my office, coffee, a pair of $27 shorts at J.Crew. I liked how the receipts said "MyGiftCard" where the name would normally be located, and cashiers didn't blink when I handed it over. But as the balance on the card declined, I stopped using it. I felt silly asking a clerk to charge $5.32 to the card and have me pay the rest in cash. And yet I hated wasting the last dollars.

So I tried another route: a disposable credit card number. These are onetime numbers that can just be used at a single merchant. In effect, they are prepaid debit cards issued for each transaction. I got my disposable credit card numbers from MaskMe Premium, the same service that gave me disposable e-mail addresses and phone numbers.

My first attempt to use my disposable credit card number was a disaster. I wanted new yoga tops to replace the ones I had that were fraying. So I found the tops online and put them in my online shopping basket. I then entered my real name and address for shipping and billing. Once the website calculated the price—including shipping—MaskMe generated a credit card number that I could use for the exact amount of the transaction. But the card was rejected. I tried again but got the same message: PAYMENT AUTHORIZATION TRANSACTION DECLINED.

Now I was in a bind. MaskMe seemed to think I had paid. The credit card number stated that the money had been spent. But the website didn't think it had been paid. My money was lost somewhere in the ether.

After an hour on the phone with Abine, I figured out my mistake: I needed to enter Abine's address as my billing address. In the meantime, I called the website, canceled the transaction, and ordered the tops over the phone using my regular credit card number.

A week later, I tried again, buying a CD of kids' folk songs from the Smithsonian—using Abine's address as my billing address. This time it went through, no problem. Phew. Of course, this whole thing seemed a bit silly because I was still providing my real name and address for the goods to be shipped. I decided to try to find a more anonymous currency.

I hoped to buy bitcoins, a virtual digital currency that was all the rage in the hacker community. But I couldn't find a place that would let me buy bitcoins with a credit card. They all wanted my bank account number or a wire transfer—apparently because people often call their credit card company complaining that they didn't receive their virtual coins.

Bitcoins can be used on online "black markets" that can sell drugs and weapons. However, some brick-and-mortar businesses have started accepting bitcoins. In May 2013, Kashmir Hill, a reporter for *Forbes*, lived for a week only on bitcoins—subsisting mostly via a food delivery service in San Francisco that accepted the currency.

However, all Bitcoin transactions are logged and publicly viewable. People's names are not attached to their transactions, but a determined investigator could likely identify people behind certain Bitcoin transactions. This was not the anonymity I was seeking.

✦

The deeper I looked at anonymous digital transactions, the less I liked them. They seemed to be havens for criminals.

In 2007, a digital cash start-up, E-gold, was charged with money laundering. The indictment said the company knew that its services were used by identity thieves, child pornographers, and other criminals. The following year the company and its owners pleaded guilty to money laundering. And in 2013, federal prosecutors shut down the anonymous online currency exchange Liberty Reserve, charging that it was a $6 billion money-laundering operation for child pornographers and other criminals.

"If Al Capone were alive today, this is how he would be hiding his money," said Richard Weber, the head of the Internal Revenue Service's criminal investigation division.

Some have even predicted that truly anonymous financial transactions could cause society to break down. In 1996, self-proclaimed Internet anarchist Jim Bell posted on an Internet forum an essay titled "Assassination Politics," describing how anonymous cash could enable the establishment of cash prizes to people who correctly "predict" somebody's death. "It would be possible to make such awards in such a way so that nobody knows who is getting awarded the money, only that the award is being given." Bell described this death prediction market as a way to punish "violators of rights" by putting a price on their heads. "Consider how history might have changed if we'd been able to 'bump off' Lenin, Stalin, Hitler, Mussolini, Tojo, Kim Il Sung, Ho Chi Minh, Ayatollah Khomeini, Saddam Hussein, Moammar Khadafi, and various others, along with all of their replacements if necessary, all for a measly few million dollars," he wrote.

Bell's idea of placing "bounties" on the heads of government officials wasn't well received. In 1997, IRS agents raided Bell's home. He was charged with obstruction of justice and using fake social security numbers. He was sentenced to eleven months in prison.

Bell was clearly staking out an extreme position. But his essay made me reconsider Sissela Bok's ethical question: What would happen if everyone in your situation lied?

I started to think that what I really wanted was not anonymity but immunity. I wanted to be immunized from the consequences of my inconsequential transactions. I didn't want people having lunch with me to be suspected of passing information to a journalist. I didn't want my purchases to peg me as a "high spender" so that I would never be offered discounts online. I didn't want to be suspected of being an anarchist after exploring bitcoins. However, I did not expect or want immunity from criminal transactions.

My desire for immunity from the consequences of commerce reminded me of the anthropologist David Graeber's beautiful meditation on the meaning and moral implications of debt. In his book *Debt: The First 5,000 Years*, Graeber describes how there are debts that should never be paid, such as our debt to our parents or a debt for an unsolicited kindness.

Only some debts can be settled with money. Those debts have certain characteristics, he says. They are debts between "potential equals" but "who are not currently in a state of equality" who use money to set matters straight. "Debt . . . is just an exchange that has not been brought to completion," he writes.

I realized that the immunity I wanted was similar to what a debtor seeks: I wanted my debts to be fully discharged—returning me to a state of equality with my debtor—once my transaction had been completed.

But in the personal data economy, it seemed that I would never be free of my debts. All my transactions would haunt me forever, stalking me and informing the choices that were presented to me. And so, until I could find a better way, I was going to have to rely on Ida and my masked identities to settle my debts.

10
POCKET LITTER

was standing under the world clock tower on Alexanderplatz in Berlin, feeling nervous. I had just arrived in the city and had arranged to meet Jacob Appelbaum, the computer security researcher whose e-mail had been secretly investigated by the U.S. government after his involvement as a volunteer for WikiLeaks was publicly disclosed in 2010. But I didn't have any way to get in touch with him—no cell phone number, no street address, nothing. I simply had to wait to see if he would show up at our planned meeting point.

I'd flown halfway around the world for this meeting. But I had no backup plan if he didn't show up. I felt exposed.

This is what it takes for me to do my job as a journalist in a world where my location can be tracked remotely through my cell phone. That means I must meet some of my sensitive sources in person, without the aid of digital technology.

And so I stood awkwardly under the clock that for decades has been a meeting point for people in Berlin. Everyone around me was checking his or her phone. I imagined them texting their friends with those reassuring exchanges—"Where r u?" "On my way"—that are the privilege of the digital age. I had no such digital reassurance.

I glanced at a long-haired man locking up his bicycle. Was that Jake? It occurred to me that I had only seen his picture on the Internet—and for all I know, he could be shielding his identity by using an outdated or inaccurate photo. But the bicyclist pulled out a cell phone to make a call, so I decided it wasn't him. A few minutes later, my gaze landed on a man with wire-rim glasses who was not staring into a phone. Maybe it was him? But he didn't glance at me, and a few minutes later he waved to a man across the plaza.

Finally, without warning, Jake appeared right at my side. He looked exactly as I expected. Since my photo is easily findable online, he recognized me immediately. I sighed with relief as we walked to a nearby coffee shop to talk.

Eventually, I confessed that my cell phone was in my purse. I knew I shouldn't have brought it, but at the last minute I threw it in my bag. I was in a strange city and I was afraid that somehow I would need it.

"I turned it off," I said, apologetically.

"Ha!" Jake laughed. "How do you know it's off?" he said. "Did you remove the battery? Spyware could have been installed on your phone to force it to continue to transmit information even when it appears to be off."

At the time, I thought that Jake was being slightly paranoid. As a WikiLeaks volunteer who is often detained at the U.S. border, Jake is far more attuned to surveillance threats than most people. But in this case he was right. About a year after our meeting, Ira "Gus" Hunt, the chief technology officer for the Central Intelligence Agency, gave a speech bragging about the CIA's capability to track mobile devices. "You are aware of the fact that somebody can know where you are at all times, because you carry a mobile device, even if that mobile device is turned off," Hunt said in a speech titled "The CIA's 'Grand Challenges' with Big Data." "You know this, I hope? Yes? Well, you should."

It's still not clear exactly what tracking technology Hunt was referring to. But in 2006, the FBI sought and obtained a court order to install a "roving bug" on the phone of a mobster that allowed agents to eavesdrop even when his phone was off. Hunt was confirming what Jake and others already knew: our cell phones are the world's most effective tracking devices, even when they are turned off.

✦

In spycraft, there is a term of art called "pocket litter." It used to mean, literally, the scraps of paper and other items that can be found in a person's pocket. These items often contain information about the person's associations—phone numbers, addresses, an account number—that can further an investigation.

Today, our pockets contain the ultimate litter: cell phones that are miniature computers. In them can be found our entire address book, nearly all of our written communications, our photos, our music, and even the games we like to play.

Even worse, our electronic pocket litter can sometimes be viewed remotely. In the old days, law enforcement agents had to arrest a suspect before they could search his pockets. Now, commercial and governmental dragnet operators can view the location and some of the contents of our phones from afar—by demanding information from cell phone carriers.

The most outrageous example of cell phone monitoring is, of course, the program exposed by the former NSA contractor Edward Snowden, in which for seven years the phone companies have been turning over every single record of calls made in the United States. President Obama described the program as simply collecting "call pairs." He gave a very innocuous description: "You have my telephone number connecting with your telephone number. There are no names, there's no content in that database. All it is, is the number pairs, when those calls took place, how long they took place."

The vast majority of local police departments also track cell phone usage by submitting secret requests to cell phone companies, often without obtaining a search warrant. In 2011, the top U.S. wireless carriers responded to 1.3 million law enforcement demands for subscriber information, including caller location. For instance, AT&T said it responded to about seven hundred requests a day—approximately three times the number it received in 2007.

As warrantless cell phone tracking has increased, some judges have started questioning its legality. Since 2005, more than a dozen magistrate judges have written opinions denying applications for court orders to track cell phones. The revolt started in 2005 when Stephen Smith, a magistrate judge in the Southern District of Texas, turned down a government request for real-time cell phone location data. Smith challenged the government's "creative" legal theory to justify not needing a search warrant. After Smith's decision, magistrate judges across the country began turning down warrantless requests for cell phone location data.

Higher courts have split on the issue of access to historical cell phone location data. In 2010, the Third Circuit Court of Appeals ruled that magistrate judges have the discretion to require a search warrant for historical cell phone records, even though "we are stymied by the failure of Congress to make its intention clear." But in 2013, the Fifth Circuit Court of Appeals overturned a 2010 decision by Judge Smith to deny historical cell phone location records to the government without a warrant. "We understand that cell phone users may reasonably want their location information to remain private . . . ," Judge Edith Brown Clement wrote. "But the recourse for these desires is in the market or the political process."

Until the Supreme Court or Congress sorts it out, cell phone dragnets are the law of the land.

✦

How important is pocket litter? Whom we call and when we call can be just as revealing as what we say.

Spies who cannot read the contents of their enemies' messages have long relied on what is known as "traffic analysis"—studying the patterns of the sender, the receiver, the time, and the length of messages. During World War I, the French had difficulty deciphering the German code—known as the ADFGVX cipher. But they knew that the cipher was used to communicate orders and directions for an advance, so they were able to predict the approximate time of German offensives during the spring and summer of 1918. Even when the Germans changed radio call signs—the characters that identified the broadcaster—the French traffic analysts could identify the calls by other patterns. "Several days prior to an operation the volume of messages which were intercepted always increased noticeably above the normal," U.S. Army Lieutenant J. R. Childs wrote in *German Military Ciphers from February to November 1918.*

During World War II, the Japanese outsmarted the United States in part by creating deceptive radio traffic. Prior to the attack on Pearl Harbor, the Japanese transferred their aircraft radio operators ashore, which persuaded Americans that the Japanese fleet was still in port.

The United States learned its lesson. In 1942, it set up a traffic analysis group devoted to studying the Japanese messages in the Pacific. Although it didn't break the Japanese codes until 1943, the traffic analysis unit was able to "identify troop locations, chain of command and order of battle."

During the 1950s, the National Security Agency moved traffic analysis from punch cards to computers. The goal of a traffic analyst was to "draw a picture of his communications target," according to a 1982 NSA study. "Once he knows what his target's normal behavior is, then he is in a position to detect variations, and report them to intelligence consumers."

Those "anomalies" can divulge a lot of information. In 2004, Hezbollah in Lebanon captured what some estimates place at one hundred spies—which may have included some CIA operatives—by identifying cell phones that were rarely used or used only from specific locations for a short period of time.

✛

The more I learned about cell phone dragnets, the more impossible it seemed that I would be able to escape them.

The obvious solution was to leave the phone at home but, as a mother of small children, I felt it would be irresponsible not to be reachable on my cell phone at any time of day or night—and my husband agreed. So I decided that the next best thing would be to buy a "burner." Burners are a slang term for prepaid phones that are used for a short time and then ditched.

Burners are not a perfect option—with enough effort, investigators can tie a burner to your identity based on your calling patterns or location. But buying one anonymously means that, at the very least, when your data are sold or collected by the government, it will take investigators some time to tie the information to your actual identity.

So I figured I would give it a try. As I researched phones, I decided I needed an Android phone because there were more privacy-protecting apps available for Android phones than for the iPhone. Choosing a carrier was more difficult. None of them offer a zero-data storage option. According to a law enforcement document obtained by the American Civil Liberties Union, most cell phone providers store call detail records for about two years, and AT&T stores them for five to seven years. In the end, I decided they were basically all equivalent, except AT&T, so I chose a cheap prepaid plan from Virgin Mobile.

The best practice when buying a burner phone is to pay cash and buy it at a store far from home. So I withdrew $200 in cash and went to a store in midtown Manhattan—which seemed suitably anonymous—to buy the phone. The checkout clerk insisted that I click through a few screens on the credit card swipe machine, even though I was paying cash. Then she offered me a discounted warranty if I would enter my personal information onto the machine. Then she offered me a discount on the phone, as well, if I would enter the information. I respectfully declined, but being forced to repeatedly decline to identify myself made me feel like a criminal. By the time I left the store, with my phone in a bag, I felt like I was carrying contraband. I looked up to see if I could spot surveillance cameras near the door. I wished I had worn a baseball cap.

My next stop should have been to buy a prepaid monthly service card with cash from a different store. But I knew I would eventually miss a monthly deadline if I relied on cash. I went home and used my Ida Tarbell credit card to sign up for a monthly prepaid service from Virgin Mobile.

After all, my goal is not to be perfectly anonymous: it's just to make the trackers work a little harder.

✦

I didn't give out the phone number for the burner. Instead, I gave my husband, my babysitter, and a few friends the MaskMe phone number that I had purchased from Abine. I set it up so that all calls to the masked number forwarded to my burner.

But the problem was that I couldn't make outgoing calls or send texts using the masked number. I could receive text messages through the masked number, but my text message replies would reveal my burner number.

I was veering close to a gray area of the law. It is illegal to "spoof" your phone number with an intent to defraud. In 2010, President Obama signed into law the Truth in Caller ID Act, which made it illegal to "knowingly transmit misleading or inaccurate caller identification information with the intent to defraud, cause harm, or wrongfully obtain anything of value."

Of course, I was not planning to use the spoofed number to defraud or cause harm, but even if I successfully spoofed my number, my calls were likely to reveal my identity. Looking through my calling log on my regular phone, I realized that my calling patterns are highly predictable (and rather boring). Every day I call my husband at around six p.m. Every other day or so, I speak to a rotating cast comprised of my mom, my brother, and a few friends. All of my other calls slip into the contours of that larger outline.

So I decided I would use the burner only for work calls. I took it on a business trip to Washington, D.C., and used it exclusively for three days of meetings and interviews. I brought my personal iPhone as well and kept it in the hotel room, turned off, vowing to use it only for personal calls.

But, ultimately, it was difficult to keep the two phones separate. I was stuck in traffic in a cab and wanted to call home, so I used the burner. And when I was back at the hotel room, I forgot to turn off the burner so as to keep a separation between the locations of the two phones.

I started to understand what Mike Perry, the self-proclaimed "surveillance vegan," was talking about when he said that his practice of using different phones for different social networks had hurt his ability to have close relationships.

✦

I also loaded up my burner with privacy-protecting apps. Almost immediately, I hated them.

To navigate the Web, I had installed anonymizing software that would bounce my Internet traffic through computers around the world. That way, websites I visited on my phone wouldn't know where I was coming from. (Of course, my cell phone provider still knew where I was, or at least where Ida Tarbell was.)

I had thought that the anonymizing software—Tor—was slow when I used it to set up Ida's online accounts on my laptop computer. But on my phone it was far worse. It was glacially slow and it wore down my battery. I took out a stopwatch and found that it took fourteen seconds to activate the worldwide routing through the Tor network, and then it took another six seconds to launch the Web browser that routes through Tor, and finally a simple Web search for "weather NYC" took forty-three seconds. In total, that meant it took more than a minute to search for the weather.

By comparison, launching Google's Web browser, Chrome, and searching for "weather NYC" on my iPhone took nine seconds.

Harlo Holmes, head of metadata at the Guardian Project, which makes the official Tor software for Android, told me that browsing the Web using Tor takes longer because it makes more "hops" between my phone and the website I'm visiting. "There is definitely a trade-off between speed and anonymity when using Tor," she told me.

Eventually, I gave up on Tor and installed DuckDuckGo's app on my phone. Launching DuckDuckGo and searching for "weather NYC" took only fifteen seconds—still slower than Google but not as interminable as Tor.

Even so, I realized I was avoiding conducting Web searches at all. One evening, when I met my friend for a drink, we decided we would like to get something to eat. But where? As people do today, we each pulled out our phones. I searched on DuckDuckGo for restaurant recommendations, but since it doesn't know where I am located it takes a while to get the coordinates right. By the time I had typed in "Mexican restaurants Madison Square Park New York City," my friend had already found a restaurant nearby.

Depressed, I called Moxie Marlinspike, the developer who built the secure texting and calling apps that I was using (which were actually fairly easy to use). Marlinspike is one of the most thoughtful and talented cell phone hackers out there. I asked him why it was so difficult to use all these anonymizing tools.

"There is not really a market for consumer privacy software," Marlinspike told me. He and other privacy-oriented cell phone developers—such as the Guardian Project—are funded largely through grants.

Marlinspike said he has been trying to attract talented programmers who might otherwise go to work at Silicon Valley start-ups. He used his latest grant to fly a team of developers to Hawaii for a week of programming at the beach. But Marlinspike is working on a small scale. His apps—RedPhone and TextSecure—work only on Android and most of my friends are on iPhone, so I can't encrypt our communications with his apps.

He laughed when I told him about my struggles with Tor. "Whenever I'm using Tor and it's fast, I get nervous that I've misconfigured it," he said. "All this stuff is unusable. All the tools we have are awful. We have to acknowledge that."

✦

Meanwhile the cell phone tracking industry has been building ever more sophisticated tools for location tracking.

The private sector race to map the location of every device in the world started with a practice called "wardriving." I first went wardriving in Denver in 2002 with some cable company technicians who were showing me how it worked. We drove around in a car, while the technician in the passenger seat kept a laptop open. On his computer was software that would scan the surrounding areas for Wi-Fi networks. When we found an unencrypted Wi-Fi hot spot, we would stop and watch the Internet traffic streaming through his computer screen. We didn't read any of it, but we could have.

In 2003, a Boston company called Skyhook made wardriving into a business. Skyhook deployed cars that scanned the names and signal strengths of Wi-Fi hot spots. Skyhook didn't read any of the Wi-Fi traffic, it was just mapping the location of Wi-Fi hot spots around the world. "For the first four or five years, people thought we were nuts," said Skyhook's founder, Ted Morgan.

But Skyhook's bet paid off. It turned out that Wi-Fi hot spots were dense enough that they could often provide accurate location information. The way it works: a cell phone notices the Wi-Fi networks around it, locates them in Skyhook's database, and uses that information to estimate the phone's location.

Finding a location via Wi-Fi was often an improvement over previous methods—by triangulating between either cell phone towers or Global Positioning System satellites, whose signals can be blocked by buildings or other obstructions.

Soon, Skyhook had competition. In 2007, Google began using its Street View cars to wardrive and build its own Wi-Fi database. After its cars were caught sweeping up e-mail passwords and other personal information via this process, Google stopped wardriving and started using its Android phones to collect information about Wi-Fi signals.

In 2010, Apple also started building its own Wi-Fi database, using its iPhones to collect Wi-Fi information. In essence, Google and Apple were using their customers' phones to do their wardriving. (Shall we call it "war-phoning"?)

Meanwhile, cell phone apps and advertisers were war-phoning, too. In 2010, the privacy investigative team I led at the *Wall Street Journal* tested 101 smartphone apps and found that 47 of them transmitted the phone's location to outside companies. Forty-five of the apps didn't provide privacy policies that stated what they might do with the information.

Start-ups raced to build equipment that could pull Wi-Fi signals from users' phones as they walked by a location. Some companies placed the equipment in shopping malls to track visitors. One London marketing company, Renew, even installed smartphone trackers in London recycling bins to monitor people as they walked by. (The company stopped after the financial district requested the collection be stopped.)

Kaveh Memari, the CEO of Renew, said that the system worked because 80 percent of Londoners leave their Wi-Fi on when they leave their home or office. "The chances are, if we don't see you on the first, second, or third day, we'll eventually capture you," he said. "We just need you to have it on once."

Suddenly, the wireless carriers no longer had a monopoly on the location of cell phone users. There was no reason for them not to sell the data, too.

In 2012, Verizon launched a business called Precision Market Insights to sell data about its cell phone users' "age range, gender and zip codes for where they live, work, shop and more," as well as information about mobile-device habits "including URL visits, app downloads and usage, browsing trends and more." In 2013, AT&T said it would also begin selling information about its users' locations and website browsing habits. Tracking people's location via their cell phones became a hot business opportunity, spawning conferences such as Location Intelligence in Washington, D.C., the Geoweb Summit in New York City, and Location Business Summit USA in San Jose, California.

At the Signal conference in Chicago in 2012, a location analysis company called JiWire described the insights it had gleaned from its profiling the behavior of more than seven hundred million devices. "Where you are says more about you than any other point of data," JiWire's president, David Staas, said.

✦

Of course, all the location tracking companies say the data they collect are anonymous. All they gather is a bunch of numbers that are the equivalent of a serial number for your phone.

"We cannot and never will receive any information relating to names, addresses, phone numbers, emails, etc.," wrote Will Smith, the CEO of the location company Euclid in a letter to Senator Al Franken of Minnesota, who has introduced legislation that would require companies to seek permission before tracking people's location.

Euclid helps retailers to identify shoppers via the Wi-Fi signals emitted by their cell phones and the phones' MAC (media access control) addresses, which are unique identifiers assigned to a phone, sort of like a serial number. Since its launch in 2011, Euclid says it has counted fifty million devices in its clients' stores.

Smith said that by collecting only anonymous information, Euclid seeks to "safeguard consumer privacy." But the truth is that location is one of the most revealing pieces of data about a person. In 2013, researchers at the Massachusetts Institute of Technology and the Université catholique de Louvain in Belgium studied fifteen months of location data for 1.5 million people. They found that four instances of a person's location at a given point in time were enough to uniquely identify 95 percent of the individuals in the study. "Human mobility traces are highly unique," the researchers wrote. "Mobility data is among the most sensitive data currently being collected."

Location is also predictive. Researchers at Microsoft found that location data can be used to predict fairly accurately where people will be located in the future. Using data from more than three hundred volunteers, they found that they could predict where people would be located in the future. Wednesdays were the easiest to predict, and weekends the hardest. "While your location in the distant future is in general highly independent of your recent location," the researchers wrote, "it is likely to be a good predictor of your location exactly one week from now."

This seemed pretty far afield from anonymity. Not only do they know who I am and where I've been, but they know where I am going to be next week.

✦

To limit location tracking, I turned off Wi-Fi on my cell phones (regular and burner) and vowed never to turn it on again. I disabled location services on both phones as well. I even changed the name of my home Wi-Fi router, adding _nomap to the end of the name, in order to opt out of Google's Location Service database.

I also identified fifty-eight companies that appeared to be in the mobile location tracking business—ranging from advertisers, to the folks tracking phones from recycling bins, to wireless carriers. Of those, only eleven offered opt-outs—which I completed.

I still wasn't very far out of the location tracking net. I decided to start turning my cell phone off more often, so that my location wouldn't be continuously tracked. I considered putting it in airplane mode, but then (once again) I didn't want to bother with constantly fiddling with the settings.

I decided it would be easier to put my cell phone in a bag that blocked the signal. Such bags are called "Faraday cages" after the English scientist Michael Faraday, who discovered that lining a room with metal can block electromagnetic radiation. Since then, Faraday cages have been used in health care, the military, and other places where people want to prevent electromagnetic interference with their instruments.

When I told John Strauchs, the former CIA agent, that I wanted a Faraday cage for my phone, he laughed and told me a simple trick that can be used in a pinch. "You can just use aluminum foil!" he told me.

Sure enough, it worked. I wrapped my burner phone in tinfoil and tried calling it. It didn't ring. So I threw the aluminum foil–wrapped burner in my purse and went out for a full day of meetings in New York.

I kept it in my purse and unwrapped it only between meetings when no one was looking. It took a few minutes for it to connect to the tower and download any texts, e-mails, and missed calls. Satisfied, I wrapped it up again and threw it in my purse.

By the end of the day, the tinfoil was a mess. It was crinkly and was torn in a few places. Rewrapping the phone completely was becoming more difficult as I tried to patch up the holes. My colleague Jeremy Singer-Vine was mock horrified when he saw my tinfoil contraption. "I have a Faraday bag that I'm not using," he told me. "Do you want it?"

A few days later, Jeremy brought me a lovely silver bag with a Velcro closure. My phone fit perfectly in the bag—and calls didn't get through. I loved it.

The tinfoil made me seem like a crazy person. The Faraday bag made me cool; all my friends wanted one.

✦

Of course, I was curious about the inventor of my Faraday bag. So Jeremy introduced me to Adam Harvey.

Adam and I met for coffee in midtown. Tall and lanky, Adam told me that he got interested in the convergence of fashion and countersurveillance when he was in a graduate program at New York University in 2009.

His first so-called stealth wear was an "anti-paparazzi clutch." It is a purse that responds to a camera flash by firing a bright light that ruins the photo being taken. "I believed that people being photographed by paparazzi should have a way to flash back," he told me. The clutch didn't take off, but it got him thinking about other ways to protect privacy in public. For his master's thesis, he created a series of hair and makeup styles that could thwart face detection software. However, the system wasn't very practical: many of the styles involved wearing hair over your face or painting parts of your face black.

Eventually, he stumbled on the idea of building Faraday cages for cell phones. At first, he tried creating a pair of pants that contained a pocket made of cotton and silver threads, which would block the cell phone signal. But he soon realized that it was unrealistic to build it into the pants. So he started working on a cell phone sleeve—which he calls an OFF Pocket.

The one that I had in my purse, he said, was a prototype. It would reduce the signal strength of a cell-tower signal by 80 decibels. "What you want for full protection is over 95 decibels," he said. The new one he was launching would be more than 100 decibels. "My vision is that privacy won't be given to you as a law completely," he told me. "You have to commercialize it so people can speak with their money."

✦

Even by throwing money at the problem, I hadn't gotten very far. My masked phone number and burner phone were fun, but neither protected my location or calling network.

Putting my cell phone in the Faraday cage worked. But it was almost as bad as leaving my phone at home; I wasn't reachable until I took it out of the bag.

My experiments with cell phone privacy were my biggest failure by far.

11
OPTING OUT

When I told my brother that I was going to take down my profile on LinkedIn, he told me I was crazy. "It's how you get recruited for your next job."

I could hardly afford to pass up my next job. My industry—newspapers—was basically in free fall. Even if I didn't need my next job this year, it definitely wouldn't be long before I did.

But I really couldn't justify staying on LinkedIn, given how much it exposed my social network. LinkedIn's privacy settings allowed me to prevent others from seeing my "connections," but its privacy policy states "people will always be able to see shared connections."

That means that if you and I share a LinkedIn connection, we will both see that friendship displayed. That sounds innocuous, but it really isn't much different from the NSA's database of telephone calls. It's a giant dragnet of associations.

There was also this disturbing line in LinkedIn's privacy policy: "We do not rent or sell personal information that you have not posted on LinkedIn." Um, I guess they are selling all the information I *have* posted on LinkedIn? LinkedIn says that it doesn't sell personal information to third parties, but it does sell services that allow recruiters to search members' information and contact them.

And I was exposing all this in exchange for what? I rarely use LinkedIn.

I had 220 connections, 27 unread messages, and 570 invitations awaiting me. Even if a recruiter tried to reach me through LinkedIn, I probably wouldn't notice.

But I was seduced by the idea that I *might* use LinkedIn one day, that it *might* help me get a new job when I was in a bind. This is what the behavioral economist Dan Ariely calls our "irrational compulsion to keep doors open."

Ariely describes an experiment he conducted, in which students played a video game where they were shown three doors—red, blue, and green. Each door opened to a virtual room where players could earn a certain amount of money per click. The goal of the game was to make the most money with a fixed number of clicks.

Once the game began, it became evident that those players who picked a room and stayed in it would have the best economic outcome. Even when the economics were explained clearly, however, players persisted in keeping all the doors open. "They still could not stand to see a door close," Ariely wrote. "They still had the same irrational excitement about keeping their options open."

The problem is that humans hate to experience a loss, even if the loss is of something inconsequential. That perfectly described my feeling about leaving LinkedIn. I obsessed about it for months. I consulted two experts in search-engine optimization to ask whether quitting would hurt my search results. (It wouldn't.) I talked to friends and family about whether I should pull the plug.

All this for a website I hadn't logged in to in nearly two years. A website whose passwords had been hacked and revealed to be not properly "salted." A website that sent me an annoying amount of e-mail. A website I didn't need to describe my job accomplishments because I had a full bio on my own website. Talk about an irrational fear of loss.

Finally, I took the plunge and closed my account. LinkedIn said that after closing my account, it would de-personalize any logs related to my account within thirty days.

In a culture where people judge each other as much by their digital footprints as by their real-life personalities, it's an act of faith to opt out of sharing your data. Now I would simply have to trust that future employers would find me some other way.

✦

Opting out of the personal data marketplace is a trust exercise.

In the digital world, our profiles on sites like LinkedIn and Facebook help us establish trust with people we've never met. The strength of social networks is that your "connections" or "friends" serve as an implied endorsement of your trustworthiness. "A public display of connections is an implicit verification of identity," the researchers Judith Donath and Danah Boyd wrote in their 2004 paper on social networks.

It's easier to verify trust when you meet someone in person. Scientists have found that people make surprisingly accurate judgments about each other within thirty seconds, but that additional time spent doesn't usually improve the accuracy of their assessments. Online, people have fewer tools with which to assess trust. Online photos are notoriously misleading, birthdays can be faked, and e-mails arrive that look like they are from your bank but are really from a criminal.

Donath, who is a fellow at Harvard's Berkman Center for Internet and Society, has done fascinating work comparing online trust issues to the problems that animals have in sorting out honest signals from deceptive signals. For example, consider the "femme fatale" Photuris firefly, which mimics the behavior of a female Photinus firefly. It then lures the male Photinus, attacks him, and eats him. This is an example of a deceptive signal.

On the other hand, consider big horns on a stag deer. An animal cannot support massive horns without being big and strong. "Potential rivals or mates need not directly test the stag's strength; they can simply look at the size of the horns," she writes. This is an example of an honest signal.

Donath says that online friendships are viewed as honest signals. If an unknown person is a friend of my friend, then he may be worth a bit of my trust. But the pressure to create online identities is creating tension between "privacy and reliability." Public histories of a person's behavior are helpful for creating reliability, she said, "but if everything has to be done in your real name, then you have the chilling effect or you make people very vulnerable."

Donath is working on ways to design systems that will add reliability to pseudonyms. "If I am going to rate underarm deodorant, I don't need to share my real name with the online world," she said. "Pseudonymity is key to our online privacy."

In honor of Donath, I created a LinkedIn profile for my online pseudonym, Ida Tarbell. Ida has no "connections," but she does allow me to log in to LinkedIn and see what is going on there. And her presence assuaged my irrational feeling of loss about quitting LinkedIn.

✦

As I prepared to unplug from Facebook, I consulted a recent college graduate, Gaebriella Todesco, for advice.

Todesco deleted her Facebook account during Christmas break of her senior year at Cal Poly, San Luis Obispo. She was studying to become a high school teacher and she didn't want a future employer to see her college photos. "There are pictures out there—especially with the red cups—those are really dangerous," she told me. "It just really scared me, so I just deleted all of it."

Gaeby's relationship with Facebook was complicated. During her freshman year, she and her friends logged on to Facebook all the time and uploaded photos from parties where they were holding red plastic cups.

Stuck in their dorm rooms without a car, she and her three freshman roommates had what she called a "strange addiction" to Facebook. "There was nothing to do but go on Facebook or upload pictures or stalk people," she said.

Like a true addict, Gaeby also regularly quit Facebook. For the first three years of college, she gave up Facebook for Lent. If there was too much "drama" with a boyfriend, she and her friends would cut each other off from Facebook for a few weeks. "You change my password and when I decide to go back on it, you give me the password," Gaeby would instruct a friend, to force herself to go cold turkey.

Gaeby knew her way around Facebook's privacy settings and she never allowed her profile to be completely open. She restricted access to her pictures and her "wall." Before a breakup, she took down her "relationship status" so it wouldn't be too public when it happened. And she deleted albums and tagged pictures of herself that she didn't want her friends to see.

Still, she wasn't sure it was enough. In the fall of her senior year, as she started planning to pursue her teaching career, she began censoring her posts and she asked her roommates to get permission before uploading photos of her to Facebook. "We go through it together and say 'don't put up this one,'" Gaeby said. "It's good teamwork."

By December, she realized that it would just be easier to quit Facebook than to police it. After reading an article about a teacher who lost her job because of a picture she posted on Facebook, she decided to pull the plug.

On December 24, 2010, she downloaded all her photos and deleted her account. She missed it at first. "In the beginning, I felt like I wanted to relapse a little bit," she told me. But she soon began to appreciate all the time she had reclaimed, now that she wasn't checking Facebook every day and every night.

When I checked in with her a year later, she had landed her dream job and was glad she had quit Facebook. She was happy her students couldn't locate her there.

Of course, there were moments she missed on Facebook. When one of her high school classmates passed away unexpectedly, she didn't hear about the funeral service until it was too late to attend. "I realized that if I had been on Facebook, I'm sure I would have known when the ceremony was," she said. "I felt out of the loop."

On the other hand, not having Facebook was intriguing to some potential dates. "It makes me a little unique and mysterious," she said.

✦

When I joined Facebook on June 26, 2006, simply having an account indicated that you were connected to an elite university. At that time, membership was available only to people with e-mail addresses from universities and some high schools. In fact, I signed up for an alumni address from my college just for the purpose of joining Facebook.

My motivation was primarily journalistic: I was researching a book about the social network MySpace and needed to understand the social networking landscape. But I also enjoyed stumbling across the high school math teacher who inspired me, or the girl who stole my college boyfriend. I liked keeping up with the Pakistani journalist who once visited my office on a fellowship.

But Facebook has also repeatedly abused users' trust. I've lost track of the number of times the company has changed its privacy settings and forced me to dig deep in its menus to reclaim control of my data. But it's worth taking a closer look at just one of Facebook's privacy snafus, in order to understand how it views its users as objects to be sold rather than as customers. Facebook's position is somewhat understandable, since users don't pay for the service, but that doesn't make its approach any more appealing to me.

In 2007, Facebook launched a service called Beacon that aimed to help people "share" their online shopping activity with their friends. As a result, when Sean Lane bought a diamond ring for his wife on Overstock .com as a surprise gift for Christmas, he was shocked to find that his purchase was automatically posted to all 720 of his friends, including his wife. In 2009, Facebook agreed to pay $9.5 million to settle a class action lawsuit over Beacon and to shut down the service.

Instead of dropping the idea of turning its users into free product advertisements, however, Facebook revived it in 2011 with a product called Sponsored Stories that allowed advertisers to buy the rights to republish a user's post and display it to that user's friends as an advertisement. In 2013, Facebook agreed to pay $20 million to settle a class action lawsuit over Sponsored Stories. But rather than do away with the product, Facebook simply added new language to its privacy policy to make it clear to users that Facebook has the right to use its customers' images and posts in advertisements. In other words, Facebook has been waging a six-year war to be able to turn its users' conversations into ads that it can sell. (Google has since joined the fray, launching a similar program called "shared endorsements" that will turn users' reviews, ratings, and comments into advertisements.)

My breaking point with Facebook came in December 2009 when Facebook suddenly made changes to its privacy policy that included exposing the names of my friends to the public, when they had previously been private. As a journalist, I need to protect my sources. And as a human being, I prefer not to have a hidden audience keeping tabs on me as I get in touch with friends.

Outraged, I wrote a column for the *Wall Street Journal* declaring that Facebook had betrayed the confidential nature of friending and that I was going to treat it as a public forum like Twitter. I opened up my profile entirely; I began accepting all friend requests, even really creepy ones, and scrubbed my profile clean of any personal details. (Facebook later agreed to settle charges brought by the Federal Trade Commission, which alleged that Facebook's actions were unfair and deceptive. But that settlement came two years after the changes were implemented—too late to make a difference to me.)

The technical name for my approach to Facebook was "privacy by obscurity." By burying good data (my actual relationships) amid bad data (people I didn't know), I hoped that my real relationships could hide in plain sight among the fake ones.

But I found myself sanitizing all my posts as I tried to address a wildly diverse audience that included my boss, my sources, the parents of my kids' friends, and strangers I had friended on a trip to Brazil. I found I had less and less to say to such a broad range of people. In 2012, my updates petered out to exactly zero. I realized that my approach had erased my ability to have a real relationship with anyone on Facebook.

Still, I wasn't ready to leave Facebook entirely. I still wanted to be able to find people and to be found by others.

I considered trimming my friends list to a small and manageable list of close friends, but I realized that I don't actually keep up with my closest friends and family on Facebook (we use e-mail, texting, and phone). And when I considered keeping a wider list of acquaintances, I was tripped up by Facebook's continued exposure of the friends list.

I dug around in Facebook's privacy settings and found that it still didn't allow you to completely protect your list of friends. It stated: "People on Facebook may be able to see mutual friends, even if they cannot see your entire list of friends."

For a journalist, even that amount of disclosure is too much. Imagine a low-level employee of an institution who befriends a journalist to share information. If an official spokesman for that same organization notices that he or she shares a "mutual friend" with a journalist, that disclosure could expose the employee as a source. So that argued against reducing my list of friends to people with whom I actually have a relationship.

I considered just deleting my profile. But, again, I was irrationally reluctant to close off my options.

I was going to miss three things about Facebook: (1) I liked being able to send private messages to people through Facebook when I didn't have their latest contact information; (2) I liked being notified when I was tagged in a photo or in a post (usually so I could request being untagged); and (3) as a journalist and author, I like being "found" by people who wanted to read my writing.

So I decided to unfriend all of my Facebook friends—more than six hundred—and keep a bare-bones profile for the simple purposes of messaging, untagging, and being found by people who might want to find me.

It turned out that unfriending was hard. I felt awful when I tried to unfriend a former calculus student or the page for my upcoming high school reunion.

I ended up having to pay my researcher Courtney Schley to hit the "unfriend" button for me.

It took her seven hours. But after it was over, I felt as if a huge burden had been lifted.

✦

I soon found an unexpected upside to living without Facebook: people no longer expected me to know what was going on with their lives.

I was at dinner with a friend I hadn't seen in nearly ten years. He started talking about his vacation in Italy as if I already knew the details, then paused and stopped himself. "Oh yeah, you don't do Facebook," he said. He rewound and started from the beginning (which, by the way, started with his baby being born—something I also had missed).

It was a huge relief to have an excuse for not keeping up with people's Facebook updates. When I first joined Facebook, I found the stream of updates provided a comforting sense of intimacy with far-flung friends. But when I dug deeper, I realized that this sense of intimacy could be misleading.

I learned that lesson the hard way when I was on a business trip to Chicago in 2009, where I met up with an acquaintance from college.

I hadn't seen him in seventeen years, but I had been keeping up with his life through his Facebook and Twitter updates. I knew that he had recently lost his job and had moved into a new apartment. I even knew about his struggles to get DSL installed in his new apartment. So when we met in person, I didn't ask him, "How are you?" Instead, I assumed a level of intimacy and asked, "So how is your job search going?"

We had a lovely conversation, but after we parted I felt like something was missing. So I called him up and asked him what I hadn't asked the first time: "How are you, really?"

It turned out that he'd been through a harder time than I realized. He had been in the midst of buying a condo when he lost his job, causing his mortgage to fall through. He had already committed to leaving his apartment, so he had to scramble to find a place to live. He admitted that his updates about the situation had been "oblique" and that he didn't want to burden people with too much information.

I felt foolish and naive for being lulled into a sense of complacency by digital small talk. I vowed from then on to ask my online friends, "How are you, really?"

Now that I had no more Facebook friends, I was even less likely to succumb to the false intimacy of social media.

✦

Removing my information from commercial data brokers was a different kind of trust exercise: the kind of trust you place in a mob enforcer. You hand over the bribe, but you're never quite sure if it will get results.

Many data brokers required me to submit sensitive information, such as my driver's license or social security number, to complete the opt-out. One site even asked for a credit card number. So in each case, I had to make a calculation: Did I trust this site not to abuse my information? Or was it safer to leave my data in their hands and not give them additional information?

I had created a list of 212 data brokers during my audit. Of those, only 92 allowed opt-outs. Two sites demanded a fee to opt out—Mugshots .com asked for $399 to remove a listing and SearchBug.com said it would cost $27.95 to remove a listing from its "premium records" compiled from online public records. I decided to skip those.

The vast majority of the rest, sixty-five, required me to submit some kind of personal information in order to process the opt-out. Thirty-five required submitting a form of ID, social security number, or credit card in order to opt out. Ten required submitting a phone number and twenty-four required sending my home address. Twenty-four sites required the opt-out forms to be sent by mail or fax.

Overwhelmed by the magnitude of the task, I decided to turn to my "pay for performance" guiding principle. I would buy some help.

For the big data brokers, who sell information to the people-search websites and others, I turned to TrustedID Catalog Choice—a company that got its start fighting junk mail. For $35, Catalog Choice promised to opt me out of nine of the biggest U.S. data brokers, such as Acxiom and Experian.

For the lookup sites, I signed up for a $209 two-year service called DeleteMe, from Abine, the Boston privacy start-up that created the masked phone numbers, e-mail accounts, and credit cards I was using. DeleteMe said it would opt me out of the seventeen biggest people lookup websites, such as Intelius and Spokeo.

After a few weeks, it appeared that my data had mostly vanished from the lookup websites. When I searched for my name on Spokeo, I saw that the only results were in Idaho, Wyoming, and Utah—three states where I have never lived. On WhitePages.com, there were no results for Julia Angwin.

But after two months, my data were still showing up on the largest lookup sites—Intelius, US Search, and ZabaSearch. I called Jim Adler, the chief privacy officer at Intelius, one of the few data broker executives who attended privacy conferences and took calls from privacy advocates. (He has since left Intelius to join a "big data" start-up.)

He investigated and found out that Intelius hadn't received an opt-out request on my behalf from Abine. When I contacted Abine, I was told that the company's failure to send my opt-outs was due to a "bug" in the process.

Suspicious, I double-checked to see if my other Abine opt-outs had worked. Sure enough, my data were still showing up on another site Abine said it had opted me out of, USA People Search. It turned out that USA People Search doesn't accept opt-outs from Abine or anyone other than the individual.

Abine attorney Sarah Downey apologized and refunded my money. But she said that the data brokers make it deliberately difficult to submit opt-outs. "That's one of the reasons why I've always pushed so hard for legislative fixes to the data broker problem: it's a legal issue, and services addressing that issue can only go so far," she said. "We do what we can, but it's not always enough."

It was more difficult to verify whether Catalog Choice had performed its opt-outs. The commercial data brokers don't display the data they have. So I contacted each of them and asked if I had been opted out of their databases.

The results were shocking. Catalog Choice had failed to process more than half of the opt-outs it promised to conduct on my behalf. It failed to submit my opt-outs to LexisNexis and Datalogix. It sent my opt-out to

Epsilon, but it was processed for only one of two databases there. And it submitted opt-outs to two data brokers, I-Behavior and KBM Group, that told me that they do not accept opt-outs from Catalog Choice.

A spokeswoman for Catalog Choice said the problems at Lexis-Nexis and Datalogix were due to "a technological issue" on the day that my order was processed. When I asked for a refund, she agreed to provide one.

I had just learned the hard way that you can't always buy privacy. Privacy is an ephemeral good that is difficult to verify. Unfortunately, it's all too easy for companies to exploit that ambiguity for profit.

✦

Throwing money at the problem hadn't worked. And I still had more than fifty opt-outs to go.

I decided to skip the shadier-looking sites that asked for extremely personal information to process the opt-out. I didn't feel comfortable giving my name, e-mail address, and cell phone number to FreePhoneTracer.com in order to opt out of its service, which offered "reverse lookup and trace any phone number."

Similarly, I decided not to send my credit card number to MyLife.com, which suggested that it needed the number for me to "claim my profile." It stated: "Following verification of profile ownership, we will try to comply with your suppression or removal request as soon as reasonably practicable."

But, for the rest, I dutifully sent in my driver's license and filled out the online forms. I spent nearly sixty hours submitting opt-outs and chasing down whether my data had truly been opted out. Courtney, my researcher, spent another sixty hours putting together the spreadsheet of more than two hundred data brokers.

But one website—PeopleSmart.com—stumped me. I thought I had opted out, but Courtney said I had not. I was in New York and she was in Japan, where she was working for a few months while her husband completed a fellowship.

We e-mailed back and forth—and finally realized that we were seeing different things on our computer screens. In Japan, Courtney was seeing my data appear on PeopleSmart. In New York, my data appeared to be suppressed. It appeared that PeopleSmart had opted me out of search results only in the United States but kept my results in international search results. "That is SO sneaky!" Courtney e-mailed me.

It seemed particularly underhanded for a company that claimed to be in the business of "privacy innovation." On a section of its website called "How we're different," PeopleSmart listed its "free and easy opt-out" as the top difference between itself and other people-search websites where it claimed, "Some don't fully remove personal information, even when requested."

A bit of Web sleuthing led me to the surprising conclusion that this company was actually a hot Silicon Valley start-up called Inflection. Its website describes the company as a "Big Data start-up" and advertises employee perks like sailing trips, meditation, yoga, and hiking retreats. I fired off an angry e-mail demanding an explanation.

To his credit, the company's CEO, Matthew Monahan, replied almost immediately, promising to look into it. One day later, he sent a detailed response explaining that the company used different data sources for its international site and had failed to opt me out of that data set as well. "There's no mal-intent here," he told me on the phone a week later. "We don't make any money from international users. We don't even have any international payment options. For us, it was kind of a comedy of errors."

Monahan told me that he and his younger brother Brian had founded Inflection in 2006 with only a slight idea of what it would become. Matthew Monahan had dropped out of the University of Southern California to run a start-up that sold e-books offering tips on how to get into college. (This was before e-readers, so they were just downloadable PDF files.) Brian was studying at Harvard. Their ideas were a bit vague: "We decided we would move out to California, right next to Facebook, and tackle an inefficient industry," Matthew told me. They decided that their first goal would be to digitize public records.

They took the money that Matthew had made from the sale of his e-book venture and invested it in building technology to digitize court records and people's public records. Their first product was something called CallerID that would let you enter a cell phone number and find the owner of a phone.

"We were pretty unsophisticated," Matthew recalled. And soon after they launched, reverse cell phone lookups faced a public backlash. In 2008,

Intelius launched a mobile phone lookup service that let people search for cell phone numbers by user name. Intelius claimed to include ninety million cell phone numbers. A few months later, Intelius shut down the service, under pressure from Verizon and privacy advocates.

The brothers decided to switch gears to focus on historical public records. In 2009, they launched GenealogyArchives.com, which later became Archives.com, to provide access to digitized historical records. In 2012, Ancestry.com bought Archives.com for $100 million.

After their windfall, the brothers could have retired. But instead they decided to refocus on their people lookup services. They revamped PeopleSmart.com, launched an employment-screening site called Good-Hire.com, and began working on a new service, called Identity.com, that would help people manage their personal information across the Web. "I just feel like our work is not done," said Matthew. "I wouldn't feel right about anything else other than to keep working on the products right now."

Matthew told me that they tried to make their opt-out particularly easy. PeopleSmart's opt-out is an online form, unlike the opt-out at other sites that force you to send in a driver's license or send opt-outs by mail. "We think that's just an intentionally burdensome process," Matthew told me.

Matthew said he was disappointed when he got my e-mail stating that the opt-out hadn't worked. "We spent so much time getting this to work," he said.

The problem, he said, was with their matching algorithm. Their computers failed to match the Julia Angwin who was opted out in the United States with the Julia Angwin whose records were stored in a secondary database for international usage.

One reason the match didn't work: "We didn't ask you for your social security number," he said. "We're not using that to match data sets. So we have to use combinations of other things." (Monahan later told me that the company had improved the opt-out process so this mistake wouldn't happen again.)

It may have been inadvertent but I couldn't help thinking that, in the personal data marketplace, being a bad actor pays off. If I opt out of all the databases that are available, that only makes my data rarer and more valuable for those who hang on to it.

✦

In the end, I felt that I had lost more than I gained in the opt-out process. I experienced a feeling of loss when I closed my accounts. I worried that I had shut off possible future job options. And I had reduced my "authenticity"—I was less verifiable in the personal data economy.

And for all that loss, I had not even fully succeeded in opting out. My data were still on file with the worst actors—the ones who made it difficult for me to opt out. And even those who let me opt out didn't promise to delete my files, only to "suppress" them.

Of all the dragnets I had confronted, this one was the most misleading in its promise of offering users a choice about their data.

12

THE HALL OF MIRRORS

When Rayne Puertos started a new job at a computer retailer in Tampa, Florida, she was not trying to hide her sexual orientation, but neither was she hoping to advertise it to her new colleagues. But her cover was blown when she checked her Facebook profile on the shared computer in the communal break room. One of her colleagues leaned over and said, "Look—all the ads on your page are all gay ads. Why is that?"

To her dismay, Facebook's customized ads had outed her.

"I'm very out and very gay," she told me. "But when I'm at work I'm not there to talk about my personal life." After that incident, she started checking her Facebook profile on her phone rather than on the shared work computer.

Rayne was outed by one of the most supposedly innocent types of dragnets—the Hall of Mirrors that advertisers create from personal data they sweep up across the Internet.

✦

The online ad-tracking industry has created one of the most comprehensive dragnets in the world.

Most websites invite dozens of ad-tracking companies to spy on their visitors and to follow them across the Web. In 2013, there were 328 separate companies tracking visitors to the top fifty content Web sites, according to a study by Krux Digital, a company that monitors digital tracking technology. That's nearly double the 167 companies that Krux found stalking visitors on the top fifty sites in 2011.

The information collected by ad-tracking companies is extremely detailed. Ashley Hayes-Beaty was shocked when she learned that an ad-tracking company had placed a file on her computer containing a single code—4c812db292272995e5416a323e79bd37—that secretly identified her as a twenty-six-year-old female in Nashville, Tennessee. In addition, the company had compiled a list of her favorite movies, including *The Princess Bride*, *50 First Dates*, and *10 Things I Hate About You*. "Well, I like to think I have some mystery left to me, but apparently not!" she said when I told her what her profile contained. "The profile is eerily correct."

Seventeen-year-old Cate Reid didn't know why she saw only weight-loss ads online, until my *Wall Street Journal* colleague Emily Steel showed her that Yahoo!'s advertising network had pegged her as a thirteen- to eighteen-year-old female interested in weight loss.

And Google accurately identified a dozen of ten-year-old Jenna Maas's likes, including pets, photography, "virtual worlds," and online goodies such as animated graphics. "I don't like everyone knowing what I'm doing and stuff," Jenna told my *Wall Street Journal* colleague Steve Stecklow, when he showed her what Google knew about her.

The online tracking companies say that the information they obtain is anonymous, and thus innocuous. A typical response: a Google spokesman said its tracking of Jenna was "based on anonymous browser activity. We don't know if it's one user or four using a particular browser, or who those users are."

But there is increasing evidence that information about people's Web habits can uniquely identify them. In 2006, the *New York Times* combed through anonymous search query records released by AOL and managed to identify the searches conducted by a sixty-two-year-old woman named Thelma Arnold. In 2008, researchers at the University of Texas combed through anonymous movie rental records released by Netflix and found that "an adversary who knows only a little bit about an individual can easily identify this subscriber's record in the dataset."

In addition, many websites inadvertently share their visitors' names with ad-tracking companies. In 2012, my *Wall Street Journal* team logged in to roughly seventy popular websites and found that more than a quarter of the time, the sites transmitted a user's real name, e-mail address, or other personal details (such as username) to third-party companies. One major dating site even sent a person's self-reported sexual orientation and drug-use habits to advertising companies.

And all of those Facebook "Like" buttons and "Tweet this story" links can identify users by name—even if users don't click on the buttons. In 2012, my team at the *Wall Street Journal* found that 75 percent of the top one thousand websites included code from social networks that could match people's names with their Web-browsing habits.

Of course, the companies also say this identified tracking is anonymous. "We will serve ads to you based on your identity," said Erin Egan, the chief privacy officer at Facebook, "but that doesn't mean you're identifiable."

That's a pretty thin line. After all, does Rayne really care whether Facebook "identified" her before outing her?

✦

The Hall of Mirrors that advertisers create with all these tracking data is still rather crude. Gay people see gay ads. People who are interested in cruises see cruise ads. When my husband and I were remodeling our house, I shopped for bathtubs online and was followed around by bathtub ads for a month.

It all seems rather innocuous, the occasional outing notwithstanding.

But Professor Ryan Calo of the University of Washington paints a disturbing picture of how the Hall of Mirrors is likely to evolve. He points to a Stanford University study showing that an individual will respond more positively to a politician whose picture is subtly blended with his or her own photo. The change in the photo is undetectable, but it makes the viewer more receptive to the politician's message.

"It turns out we like people more who look like us," Calo concluded. "Now imagine if a social network were to offer a comparable service, permitting advertisers to blend their spokesperson with the user's own profile picture." Calo doesn't know of anyone using this technique. But he speculates that it is not a far leap from our current state of bathtub ads following us around.

After all, if food engineers can design junk food to specifically target our taste buds in a way that makes us consume more and gambling companies can build slot machines that encourage us to play more, why won't marketers design their online presence to manipulate us in new ways?

Already, my privacy team had uncovered companies changing their prices based on a user's location. And Calo speculates that companies will soon find ways to tailor prices based on when people are the most vulnerable—perhaps after a long day at work.

People may also be manipulated into giving up more data than they want to. Companies can use that data to find out more about how to target that person. In one experiment, researchers at Carnegie Mellon University found that people could be manipulated to give out more personal data on a social network if they were given greater "perceived control" over their data.

Calo says that market manipulation is essentially "nudging for profit." Marketers are likely to use all available means to nudge us toward more expensive products or to make ill-advised purchases. And they can do it using the information we leave behind for them to analyze: our online data trail.

And there are real profits at stake. Benjamin Reed Shiller, an economics professor at Brandeis University, analyzed data about a large panel of computer users and found that Netflix could raise profits by 1.4 percent if it adopted individually tailored prices based on customers' Web-browsing histories. He found that Web-browsing data were more predictive than standard demographic data of users' willingness to pay high prices for a Netflix subscription. "This suggests that 1st degree price discrimination might evolve from merely theoretical to practical and widely employed," he concluded.

✦

I wanted to block ad tracking. But first I had to sort through all the misinformation about how to block tracking.

Many people believe that they can use Google Chrome's "Incognito" mode or Microsoft Internet Explorer's "InPrivate Browsing" mode to avoid being monitored online. But that is not true.

Incognito mode is privacy protection against one threat: the person with whom you share a computer. It simply wipes away the tracking cookies that were generated during a Web-browsing session, once the session is completed. However, the websites that you visited while in Incognito mode still receive information from you—and so do the trackers on those sites.

Not to put too fine a point on it, but Incognito mode is built for one thing: browsing porn. It removes the cookies with porn names from your computer so your spouse won't see. The website and its advertisers on those sites still know you were there.

That is not my threat model. So I needed to look further.

My next stop was the advertising industry's own opt-out tool. But it would have required me to install cookies on my computer to alert the tracking companies that I didn't want to be tracked. This seemed vaguely Orwellian: I had to allow myself to be tracked in order *not* to be tracked.

Even then, the industry's list of tracking companies included only ninety-six companies, while the latest studies showed more than three hundred tracking companies in the market. The ad industry says the companies on its list account for the vast majority of ad tracking, but I wanted comprehensive blocking of all companies that compile dossiers. So I decided to skip the ad industry opt-outs.

Then I turned on the "Do Not Track" button on my Web browser, which broadcasts a signal to tracking companies that I do not want to be monitored. But since the ad industry has not agreed to stop tracking users who send that signal, turning it on was simply a political protest.

Finally, I decided to go nuclear. One night, after the kids went to bed, I sat down at my computer and installed the two most popular anti-tracking software extensions onto my Firefox Web browser.

The first, Adblock Plus, blocked advertisements from displaying—thus preventing advertisers from the opportunity of dropping tracking cookies on my machine in the first place. Since my profession, journalism, derives much of its revenue from advertising, I'm not in favor of blocking ads, but I figured I'd give it a shot in the name of protecting myself from being watched.

The second, NoScript, blocked a type of computer code called Java-Script, as well as some other software such as Flash, from loading on Web pages without my permission. JavaScript can be used to load all sorts of tracking technology, including cookies, and can even be used to monitor how you move your mouse on the page. But it also has a lot of legitimate uses.

Immediately, Firefox sputtered and stalled. When I clicked on Apple's page to set up a Genius bar appointment, nothing worked. I had to set up an exception on NoScript to allow Apple's JavaScript.

The same thing happened at Amazon.com. At first, I thought that everything I was trying to order was out of stock, but then I realized that I had to set up an exception for Amazon's JavaScript, as well.

Within two days, I was ready to quit. Every Web page I visited required a huge set of decisions about which scripts to allow. My daughter would stand next to me and laugh while I tried to load a page and navigate through all the permissions. And to top it all off, Adblock was conflicting with my password manager, 1Password. I eventually had to uninstall Adblock in order to get 1Password to work.

But I stuck with NoScript. And once I got the hang of it, I started to get angry. Why did my online grocery, FreshDirect, want to load scripts from five separate companies onto my computer while I shopped? I spend a lot of money with them, and so I don't expect them to be providing peepholes to companies that want to watch me shop.

The companies that FreshDirect was allowing to monitor me were:

- Google's online advertising company DoubleClick;
- AddThis, a company that boasts that it tracks 1.3 billion users per month;
- ConvergeTrack, which describes itself as "one of the most advanced tracking and reporting technologies";
- Bazaarvoice, which says it "connects hundreds of millions of consumers to each other and to the brands they buy"; and
- IBM's Coremetrics, which offers customers the ability to "automatically generate personalized product recommendations based on each customer's current and historical shopping interests."

Talk about a recipe for financial manipulation. I imagine it won't be long before IBM will run the numbers and advise FreshDirect to charge me more when I shop late at night because I'm tired, or that I seem willing to tolerate higher prices on peanut butter than on steak.

I asked FreshDirect about the relationships, but a company spokeswoman refused to answer my questions. "Hi Julia—We're not going to be participating in this story but appreciate you reaching out," she e-mailed me with false cheerfulness.

Reading FreshDirect's privacy policy didn't make me feel any better. It stated, "We share demographic information with our partners and advertisers on an anonymous and aggregate basis. This type of data is not readily linked to any personally identifiable information." However, it did offer me the option of opting out of data sharing by e-mailing FreshDirect, so I did.

The experience made me mad. In real life, a supermarket would not invite a half dozen other companies into the store to watch people as they shopped. Why was it okay in the digital world?

✦

If it's any consolation, the guy who invented ad tracking feels bad about the vast extent of tracking in today's world.

In 1995, Daniel Jaye, a Harvard graduate, was looking for a way to get in on the Internet mania. At the time, he was running the massive back-end databases at Fidelity, a job as dull as it was important.

He wanted to do more exciting work. So he joined the founding team of a Boston start-up called Engage Technologies, which was trying to bring the tactics of direct marketing to the Internet—by developing "lists" of potential buyers of products such as textbooks.

His problem: how to identify potential buyers? He doubted that people would fill out online forms indicating their interests. "Very quickly, I came to the conclusion that a great source of information would be people's interests as evidenced by their browsing behaviors," he told me.

So Dan began using small text files called "cookies" to identify the computers of people who had browsed a particular Web site. Previously, cookies were used by websites to store data such as a user's log-in or password. His idea was that cookies could also be used to compile information about a user's browsing habits.

The beauty of his technique was that it was anonymous. A Web user would be identified only by a cookie ID number, a long string of numbers assigned to her computer. Dan believed his method was an improvement over traditional direct marketing, where advertisers bought and sold lists of people's names and addresses.

But Dan's timing was off. The Internet was brand-new, and the few advertisers buying ads were not worried about targeting—anonymous or not. Most Internet ad buyers were other dot-coms trying to generate buzz for their initial public offerings.

Meanwhile, Engage Technologies was at the center of the dot-com hurricane that was about to make landfall. Engage was part of a conglomerate of Internet companies—ranging from search engines AltaVista and Lycos to websites Shopping.com and Furniture.com—that resulted from a buying spree by the entrepreneur David Wetherell. In the fall of 1999, Wetherell appeared on the cover of *BusinessWeek* under the headline "Internet Evangelist." His conglomerate, CMGI, was a poster child for the dot-com boom, with a massive stock market value of $10 billion, despite the fact that it was losing $127 million a year on revenues of just $176 million.

By 2001, the dot-com stock market bubble had burst. CMGI's losses had reached $1 billion a quarter and its stock plummeted to less than $1. Dan quit the company, which eventually folded. But the idea of using cookies to track users survived.

Meanwhile, Dan figured that privacy would be the next big thing. In 2001, he launched a privacy software company called Permissus. His idea was to sell technology to businesses that could help them track their customers' data as it traveled through their computer systems.

But businesses had no incentive to crack down on their own internal use of data. After a few years, the company folded and Dan returned to his roots: the online advertising business. It was 2007 and the Internet market was just starting to emerge from the dot-com bust. He joined a start-up called TACODA (which stood for Targeted Coordinated Data), which aimed to build the same type of profiles that Engage had sought to create. "We started thinking about behavioral targeting—this person spends 30 percent of his time on international news and 20 percent on gadgets and 20 percent on football tickets," Dan told me.

To get a bird's-eye view of people's behavior, however, TACODA needed to track a wide swath of the Web. So TACODA started paying websites that agreed to place its cookies on their visitors' computers.

This was a huge change in the market. Previously, websites had tracked visitors only on behalf of their existing advertisers. Now they were essentially selling their visitor data to anybody. It was wildly popular: websites were struggling to sell ads, and TACODA seemed to be offering free money.

Soon, online tracking was the new hot business. In 2007, TACODA sold itself to AOL for $275 million, Google paid $3.1 billion for Double-Click, and Microsoft paid $6 billion for the online advertising company aQuantive.

But widespread tracking arguably hurt big publishers like the *Wall Street Journal* and the *New York Times*. Advertisers no longer had to pay a premium to reach their readers on their websites; instead, advertisers could track those readers onto another website and buy cheaper ads on that site.

Data about readers became a commodity. Online auction houses such as BlueKai sprang up to broker real-time auctions of data. Each day, BlueKai sells eighteen million pieces of information about specific individuals' browsing habits, for as little as a tenth of a cent apiece.

The auctions can happen instantly: when you arrive on a website, your attributes are sold at auction to the highest bidder. The winner then displays a customized advertisement to you. But the data rush spurred some companies to use invasive tracking techniques.

By 2010, Dan was worried about the implications of the Wild West environment that he had helped create. He was particularly worried about the growing trend of matching online Web-browsing data with people's real identities and off-line shopping habits. The way it works is as follows. A user logs in to a website that requires a name, e-mail address, or other identifier; a company on that website, such as Acxiom, pulls up its file on that individual and drops a cookie on the user's machine containing that individual's segments—information pulled from voting records, address, income, mortgage, vehicle ownership, and so forth. The data are still technically anonymous, but once again the line becomes rather thin. If an advertiser knows everything about you except your name, does the name really matter?

Online–off-line matching is why Linda Twombly, a sixty-seven-year-old resident of Nashua, New Hampshire, was peppered with online ads for Republican candidates during the 2010 elections. A company called Rapleaf had used this technique to identify her as a conservative who was interested in Republican politics, had an interest in the Bible, and contributed to political and environmental causes.

"Holy smokes," Linda said after my *Wall Street Journal* colleague Emily Steel decoded the information in Rapleaf's file on her. "It is like a watchdog is watching me, and it is not good."

Dan worried that this development was destroying the anonymity he had tried to build into the system initially. "When you're in the business of slinging data left and right, there's no real way to control it," Dan told me.

In 2011, he launched a company called Korrelate, which he hoped would introduce privacy back into Web tracking. Korrelate's goal is to help companies prove that their Web advertising translated into sales without tossing the customer's name and information around. In virtual "clean rooms," his team uses sophisticated math techniques to try to anonymize the data that they are using to match users' online and off-line behaviors. The goal is to let a Honda dealer know which of its online ads led to a purchase without breaching the anonymity of the individual's Web behavior.

In Dan's mind, pervasive tracking was inevitable. His goal was simply to make sure it wasn't identifiable.

✦

In some ways, the people battling over tracking cookies are fighting the last war. As people have become aware of cookie tracking, marketers have started looking for new tracking technologies. Google is said to be developing a new form of cookie-less tracking that would assign a unique ID to each Web browser.

Other marketers are moving toward "fingerprinting" techniques that allow them to identify a user's device even if she tried to block tracking through other programs. "If you don't want anybody to know anything you've done online, don't go online," the CEO of one fingerprinting company said.

Even more disturbing: the next cookie is your face. As facial recognition improves, it is becoming increasingly likely that the Hall of Mirrors will not just be a Web phenomenon. When you enter a store, the sales associates will likely be able to identify you and pull up the same "segment" data that websites are currently accessing.

A company called FaceFirst is offering technology that retailers can install in their store to photograph and identify customers as they walk in the door. "Instantly, when a person in your FaceFirst database steps into one of your stores, you are sent an email, text, or SMS alert that includes their picture and all biographical information of the known individual," the company states in a marketing brochure.

A retail executive who requested anonymity described how he is using the technology to *LP Magazine,* a trade publication for the loss-prevention industry. This retail executive, who was given the pseudonym "Tom Smith, vice president of loss prevention at Store-Mart," said that his retail chain, which was given the pseudonym "Store-Mart," is using it to identify known shoplifters.

It works like this: a shoplifter is detained at a Store-Mart branch. He is photographed and asked to sign a notice agreeing not to return to the store. If the shoplifter shows up again at a Store-Mart, the cameras will have captured his photo and identified him within five seconds. An alert is sent to a store employee who approaches the shoplifter and asks him to leave the store.

Of course, there is the problem of making the wrong match and alienating a customer. "That's a scary part for me," Smith told the magazine, "the false alert; the boy who cried wolf. But so far it's low enough— about six out of a hundred alerts—that it hasn't gotten to that stage."

FaceFirst is already envisioning a future in which retailers could use the technology for marketing. The company's marketing brochure states: "Build a database of good customers, recognize them when they come through the door, and make them feel more welcome." Left unsaid is how retailers will treat customers they don't like as much, people who shop only sales and discounts, or those who try on a lot of clothes but don't buy anything.

I am pretty sure that this facial-recognition-based Hall of Mirrors will not benefit me. Once retailers figure out that I am a harried working mom who values convenience over thrift, I will likely be steered toward more expensive products.

And there was not much I could do about it. I tried to remove most pictures of myself from the Web, in an effort to not contribute to any facial recognition databases being built. I paid an artist to draw a stencil of my photograph that I began using on Twitter and Facebook. And I hired a photographer to shoot a photo of me that I hoped I could use to promote my writing but would obscure my features enough that it wouldn't be usable for facial recognition purposes.

But I drew the line at donning stealth wear. I wasn't going to wear a baseball cap with LED lights on it to foil cameras, or an anti-drone hoodie that thwarts thermal imaging, which was created by Adam Harvey, the designer who made the Faraday bag for my cell phone.

+

Still, I kept fighting the last war. After a month of using NoScript, I wanted to test its effectiveness. So I called Ashkan Soltani, the leading technical expert on ad-tracking technology.

I first met Ashkan when he had just graduated from the master's program at the University of California at Berkeley's School of Information. There he had led a comprehensive study of different types of Web tracking being conducted by advertisers. After graduation, I convinced him to conduct a similar study for me at the *Journal*, and he soon became a technical adviser on many of our privacy investigations. Since then, Ashkan had testified twice about online privacy in Congress (wearing his one and only suit) and had become the definitive technical source on ad tracking.

Ashkan agreed to check if my techniques were effective at blocking tracking. Following his instructions, I changed a few settings in my Web browser, and *poof*, all my Internet traffic was funneled through his computer in Washington, D.C.

"Okay, go to a website," he said. I clicked on to my employer's website, WSJ.com.

Ashkan started reading off the names of the tracking companies that he saw in the traffic. "Twitter, BlueKai, DoubleClick."

"What?!" I said. I thought I had blocked all that.

Ashkan explained: WSJ.com was sending my information to BlueKai, an online ad auction company, which was sending it to Google and Yahoo!. Even though NoScript was blocking JavaScript, it couldn't prevent backend coordination among tracking companies.

As for Twitter, I had forgotten that I had previously logged in to the Twitter site, which allowed it to set a cookie. That allowed Twitter to see that I had visited WSJ.com.

That's the problem with Web tracking: if you let someone into the tent once, they often get a free pass for future tracking.

"This is much worse than I thought," I said.

Ashkan laughed. "That's exactly what you said to me three years ago when we first talked."

Ashkan showed me the setting—buried deep in Firefox's "custom history" section—that let me turn off third-party cookies, such as Twitter, from tracking me on other sites just because I had once logged in to their site. But there was no setting to block the *Journal*'s behind-the-scenes sharing.

So then we tried Adblock Plus, but BlueKai was still making it through those filters. After all, Adblock Plus is designed to block ads, not to block tracking. BlueKai isn't an advertiser, it's just a company that scoops up user data and sells it at auction. Similarly, a bunch of analytics companies, such as Omniture, were now getting through. They don't sell ads, but they do build user profiles.

This was a threat model problem. Adblock Plus was built for people who view advertisements as the threat. NoScript was built for people who view a certain technology—JavaScript—as the threat.

But my view of the threat was different: I wanted to block tracking, whether or not it was related to ads or a certain technology. So that led me to a different kind of blocking technology: companies that compile lists of trackers.

Ashkan and I tried a few companies that manage lists of trackers. Surprisingly, we found the best results from a tracker-blocker called Ghostery.

I'd always been a bit skeptical of Ghostery, ever since it was purchased by a company that is a consultant to the advertising industry. Also, Ghostery allows tracking by default. But once I found the setting to turn off all tracking, I realized it was more powerful than any of the others.

Ashkan watched my traffic as I cruised from WSJ.com to HuffingtonPost.com to Gawker.com. No analytics companies appeared. No BlueKai appeared. In fact, I soon realized that only a few ads were appearing. "This is the cleanest I've seen so far," Ashkan said. "But nothing will protect you totally."

✦

I was intrigued by Ghostery. Why would the advertising industry provide me with the best way to protect myself against itself?

In 2009, an entrepreneur named David Cancel founded Ghostery as a bit of free software to show people the trackers on each site. In 2010, he sold it to an advertising services company that is now called Evidon, which promised to keep the service free and the data private and not to use it for advertising purposes. Evidon kept its promise, but it did begin selling analysis of the data gathered by Ghostery to websites and advertisers. To its credit, Evidon asked users to opt in to its anonymous Ghostery usage panel rather than turn it on by default. About eight million people joined. (I did not.)

Andy Kahl, the director of data analysis at Evidon, told me that buyers of the data were often tracking companies that wanted to keep tabs on their competitors. In effect, Evidon had built a clearinghouse for trackers to track each other.

This game of competitive intelligence benefited me. By the time I started using it, Ghostery had compiled one of the most comprehensive lists of tracking technologies used by more than sixteen hundred companies. During the first month that I began using it, Ghostery added one hundred new trackers to the list.

But Ghostery's pro-tracking bias also hurt me. Ghostery was set to allow tracking by default, which meant I had to fiddle with the settings to block all tracking. And after a month of using Ghostery, I noticed that some tracking was still getting through. Kahl explained to me that Ghostery does not automatically block new trackers that are added to the list. He showed me the setting that allowed me to force Ghostery to block new trackers as well. It seemed a little bit sneaky to me, but Kahl assured me it was just part of Ghostery's attempt to put me in control. "We are incentivized to make sure we are doing right by our users, because only if we are really doing our job can we collect the data that the industry is interested in," he told me.

But I still felt a bit uneasy about Ghostery's motives. It was run for the benefit of the tracking industry, not the people using it.

✦

A tracking blocker with better motives was software called Disconnect— founded by a defector from the world of tracking.

Brian Kennish, an engineer at Google, built his first tracking blocker after reading an article by my colleague Emily Steel in the *Wall Street Journal* in 2010 that detailed how Facebook had inadvertently sent its users' names to ad-tracking companies. Kennish couldn't believe that Facebook had violated the anonymity promised by Web tracking companies. He had worked on Google's advertising side for nearly six years—and he knew that Google was committed to keep Web tracking data anonymous.

At that time, Ghostery did not block tracking from social networks such as Facebook. So that evening, Kennish went home and wrote a small program called Facebook Disconnect that would disable Facebook from tracking users across the Web. Within two weeks, his free software had caused a minor sensation in the technology community and had been downloaded fifty thousand times.

But as his software became more popular, he started thinking about Google's own tracking. "Your search history on Google, Yahoo!, and Bing says as much about you as your browsing history," Kennish told me. "I realized I would have to leave Google to address that."

He left Google in November 2010. In December, he launched a free program called Disconnect, which blocked Google from collecting search queries when a user was logged in to Gmail or other Google services and also blocked tracking by social networks such as Facebook, Twitter, Google, Yahoo!, and Digg.

Disconnect was immediately popular. But Kennish wasn't sure it was a business. All the other tracker blockers were free, so he couldn't charge a subscription fee. But it was an arms race trying to keep up with all the new tracking techniques. He needed funds for the arms race.

At first, he worked at home and lived off of his savings. In October 2011, he raised $600,000 from investors (including Ghostery founder David Cancel) and got serious about the business.

I went to visit Kennish in August 2012. He and his team of four engineers were crammed in a small conference room in Silicon Valley, in the offices of one of their financial backers, Highland Capital. The shades were drawn and the only light came from the computer screens. They had a basketball hoop on the wall, but it had fallen down and only the tape was left. They had a bunch of snacks from Costco piled up on a table. And they had a dashboard of statistics about usage of their software, which they said was a necessary prop in case a financial backer stopped by for an update.

Kennish doesn't drive, so I drove him in my rental car to the house he had rented with a few colleagues. It was the ugliest house on a very nice block. Inside, it was clean but spare, decorated with a single table and a couch.

"I only have five things," he warned me before opening the door to his bedroom. Inside was a twin futon mattress on the floor. In the closet were three pairs of pants, four pairs of shoes, and a few shirts stacked on the floor. Other than his computer, this was all he owned.

"I think that might be why I'm into data," he told me. "I don't have anything. All I have is data."

Over lunch in Palo Alto, I told Brian that I found his motives confusing. Living like a monk was something that entrepreneurs did when they were betting on future riches. But was he really expecting to cash in on the measly market for privacy-protecting software?

He said that he still had hope for the market for privacy. First, he said, users will "disconnect" from the trackers. Then, he said, users can get paid to "reconnect" with select businesses. Eventually, he said, there will be money to be made.

"I'm a capitalist," he told me. "And I want to change the world."

I wanted to support Brian's approach. It fit with my guiding principle of pay for performance. But his tracker blocked only social networks and I wanted to block everything. By the time Ashkan and I ran our tests, Ghostery was blocking social networks, too, so there was no need for Disconnect.

Finally, in April 2013, Kennish's new software came out. The list of trackers it blocked was longer than Ghostery's. It was a bit buggy. When I tried to buy groceries online from FreshDirect, Disconnect blocked all the trackers but also blocked the "order" button from appearing on the checkout page.

Still, I switched to Disconnect and made a donation using my masked disposable credit card number.

I decided that in the arms race on tracking, I needed to fund the insurgents. Otherwise, without competition, benevolent services like Ghostery provided by the tracking industry weren't likely to remain on my side for very long.

The choice reminded me of the early days of the organic food movement. Often, the organic aisles of the supermarket were filled with shriveled, spotted produce. But slowly, over time, as more people bought the organic apples, quality improved. Now, organic vegetables are often just as good-looking or better than the conventional produce.

For me, using Disconnect was similar to buying organic produce in the early days. I was choosing to support the privacy-software market—even if its product wasn't always as shiny as the competition's.

13

LONELY CODES

Three days before my birthday dinner party, I realized that nobody was going to show up if I kept trying to communicate with my guests in code.

A month before the party, I mailed each of my guests a book, *Secret New York: An Unusual Guide*. A week later, I mailed them a "key" that described how to locate words and characters in the book. For example (12,2,3,1) meant Page #12, Line #2, Word #3, Character #1.

Running out of time, I sent the final invitation, written in code, via e-mail. It said:

> (377,23,7) (197,136)
> (61,4,3) (29,27,4,1) (23,3,8,1) (23,4,10,1)
> (87,26,25) (25,27,3) (25,27,4)
> (393,1,2) (123,2)
> (95,30,11) (389,26,12) (159,41,4) (179,16,13) (113, 14,14)

Decoded, the invitations said:

> Privacy Dinner
> Day 9/26
> Time 6 o'clock

Place 41½ 2nd Avenue
Purchase subway ticket in cash

A week before the party, I started getting nervous. I had invited a half dozen of my closest girlfriends. But so far only one friend had mentioned to me that she had decoded the invitation. I started to doubt that my other friends had even tried to decode it.

I tried gently probing another friend: "So what are you doing next week?" "Oh, I'm on a business trip," she said. If she had known she was missing my party, she would have mentioned it. I knew then that she hadn't decoded the invitation.

Unfortunately, codes don't lend themselves to the constant calendar syncing that is a precursor to dinner parties these days.

Another friend, who has a PhD and MD, finally confessed that she had tried to decode it and failed. "Darling, I am terribly fond of you. . . . [Of] this I am not," she wrote. "I just don't have the sufficient patience or native intelligence to make it to your party!"

Three days before the party, I realized that nobody was going to show up except one friend who had called to tell me she had decoded the message. So I canceled my restaurant reservation—under Ida's name, of course—and called my friend to let her know it was canceled.

The date came and went. None of my other guests mentioned the privacy dinner party. Two weeks later, I arranged another dinner party using regular noncoded e-mail, and it was quite a success.

But the lesson of the privacy dinner party was to hold true throughout my experiments with code: communicating in code was often a lonely business.

✦

I couldn't blame my friends for failing the encryption challenge.

The book cipher I sent them was difficult for two reasons: (1) the invitation arrived separately from the codebook, requiring them to keep track of both; and (2) using the codebook to decrypt the code was not trivial.

Modern computerized encryption was supposed to solve both problems.

Today, computers magically do all the encrypting and decrypting. And even more amazingly, there are no more codebooks. I have a key stored on my computer that is secret and known only to me. And I have a public key that I post on my website for anyone to download. Together, those two keys allow me to encrypt and decrypt messages without consulting a codebook.

But I had just as difficult a time recruiting people to use e-mail encryption. Even many of my hacker friends declined to use encryption with me—some claimed it was because they didn't trust me to do encryption correctly, and some said they didn't trust themselves to use the extremely complicated system.

Consider what it took for me to set up my e-mail encryption system.

First, I downloaded free encryption software from GNU Privacy Guard to help me manage my keys. To generate a key, I had to move my mouse around to help the random number generator develop my key. Once I had a key, I uploaded it to the public key server so people could search for me.

Then I downloaded a program called Enigmail, which was supposed to work with Postbox, the software I use to manage my e-mail. (GPG is designed to run with e-mail software that you install on your computer, not e-mail you access on the Web.)

But I couldn't get Postbox and Enigmail to work together. The Postbox support page said to contact Enigmail with any issues. The Enigmail support forums said Postbox had created its own version of Enigmail that wasn't supported by Enigmail.

I was trapped in the gap between two pieces of software that were supposed to work together but weren't cooperating. I was left feeling vaguely nauseous. I went downstairs and poured myself a glass of wine and thought about why I struggle with debugging tech problems. I have no problem writing and rewriting, which should be similar. But debugging has always made me feel ill. I remember spending hours in the computer lab in college, trying to debug my programs—and feeling the same sense of nausea and the same desperate need to escape.

I decided that the problem was the uncertainty. I read a lot, so I know the landscape of writing. When I revise my writing, I often refer to techniques used by other authors. But with tech debugging, I don't know the landscape as well. As a result, I feel like I am stumbling around in the dark without any reference points.

Of course, there are tech instruction manuals out there. I had eagerly downloaded the CryptoParty handbook, which contained helpful step-by-step illustrations for installing e-mail encryption. But the instructions were for the e-mail program Thunderbird, not the Postbox program I was using. In a world of rapidly changing tech tools, it is hard for manuals to stay up to date.

After a glass of wine and some reflection, I steeled myself and went back upstairs to try again. But I still couldn't do it. After another round of attempts, I gave up. Eventually, I convinced a more technically savvy colleague to help. Within an hour, she found the instructions (there were some) and got the two pieces of software to play nicely with each other.

Now I just needed to find some people with whom to exchange encrypted e-mail. I could find lots of people listed on the GPG keyserver, but it wasn't always clear if the person listed was the same person that I knew in real life.

For instance, after the Snowden revelations, I found three public keys listed for Edward Snowden on the GPG public keyserver. One was for a Lavabit e-mail address. One was a Booz Allen e-mail address. And one was for the e-mail address ItAllGoesToTheSamePlaceAnyway@anydomain.com. Presumably, the third one was somebody's idea of a joke. But whether the first two were authentic are anybody's guess (although it turned out that Snowden apparently used the Lavabit address to reach out to Russian human rights workers). That's why some people have "key signing" parties, where they get together and verify each other's identities before downloading that person's keys.

But key signing seemed a bit too much like Facebook friending for me. The whole point of cryptography is to be secret, so why would I establish yet another publicly viewable list of people with whom I communicate and how much I trust them? Instead, I posted my key "fingerprint"—a forty-digit string of letters and numbers—on my website for anyone who wanted proof that it was me.

Once I had my system up and running, it was fun to exchange encrypted e-mails with a few colleagues and tech-savvy friends. Messages showed up in my inbox looking like huge long blocks of random numbers, letters, and symbols. But once I entered my password, the random text magically transformed into plaintext e-mail.

I was just starting to enjoy my encrypted e-mail existence when I ran into the ACLU technologist Christopher Soghoian at a conference. The first of the Snowden revelations had just come out and we were discussing the need for encrypted e-mail.

"I really dislike using GPG," Soghoian told me. "It is so complex that there is a good chance someone is going to mess up when using it. My fear is that users will be lulled into a false sense of security, and put something in writing that could get them into trouble."

He told me that he keeps his master key on an encrypted hard drive in a locked drawer in his office. He keeps his subkeys, which last for one year, on a smart card in his wallet. To read or write encrypted e-mail, he inserts the smart card into a smart card reader attached to his laptop and then enters an additional password.

I was immediately deflated. I didn't have a master key or a subkey, nor did I even know I needed a master key and subkey. My key wasn't in a locked drawer or on a smart card; it was on my laptop computer.

Later, at a conference after-party, I lamented my GPG incompetence to David Robinson, a law and technology consultant who helped found Princeton University's Center for Information Technology Policy. Robinson showed me a website that made me feel better. It was the personal website of Karl Fogel, a leading software developer. It displayed his public key and this disclaimer: "I don't trust my ability to use GnuPG. . . . Guarding against [possible attacks on GPG] would require constant vigilance, and I'm not up to the task. Therefore, if it's important that your message to me be truly secret, please contact me before you send it, and we'll work something out."

✦

The fatal flaw of public key encryption is that it relies on individuals to protect their keys.

Back in the days of physical codebooks, specially trained messengers ferried codebooks between spies and military operatives. But now we must guard the private keys stored on our computers as effectively as those operatives guarded their codebooks.

That is basically an impossible task. Our computers and smartphones are promiscuous, spewing data as they connect to the Internet. And our codebooks can also be intercepted at the border, where the government regularly seizes computing devices and copies their entire contents without a warrant. In 2010, Immigration and Customs Enforcement investigators set up an alert for future travel by David House, a supporter of Bradley Manning, the army private who passed U.S. government communications to WikiLeaks. When House returned from a trip to Mexico, he was pulled aside for questioning and his devices were seized. (House sued the Department of Homeland Security and eventually reached a legal settlement, in which the government agreed to destroy the data it obtained from his electronics.)

The more I learned about border searches, the more worried I was that my data—my contacts, my codes, and my passwords—were at risk. So I decided to start carrying zero data across borders. On a business trip to Europe, I brought my husband's old laptop and no phone. The laptop contained no files or e-mail. Instead, I accessed my files from my SpiderOak encrypted cloud and retrieved my e-mail from the Web.

But my keys were a problem. I wanted to use encryption while abroad. So I brought my secret key on a thumb drive and planned to destroy the thumb drive before returning to the United States. But I hadn't planned how to destroy the drive, and when it came time to depart I didn't have the heart to start smashing the thumb drive with a lamp in my hotel room. Instead, I deleted the contents of the thumb drive and hoped for the best. Luckily, when I arrived in New York, I breezed through customs without any problems.

Traveling without data was surprisingly relaxing. I logged in to e-mail each evening at the hotel and, voilà, I hadn't missed anything. And I was much more able to focus on my work without the distraction of the phone and its siren song of constant communication.

I decided that zero data border crossings not only were good for privacy but they were also good for my mental health.

✦

But I was still at risk of having my codebook compromised by malicious software on my computer—which is the cutting edge of cyber espionage.

Consider the story of Husain Abdulla, a U.S. citizen who is director of the Americans for Democracy and Human Rights in Bahrain. In April 2012, he was walking to a meeting on Capitol Hill to discuss the brutal crackdown on pro-democracy protesters in Bahrain. As he walked, he clicked on an e-mail from a journalist on his BlackBerry titled "Existence of a new dialogue—Al-Wefaq & Government authority," referring to the Al-Wefaq political party in Bahrain that had been supportive of the protest movements. Husain tried to download the e-mail attachment but it didn't work. Suspicious, he and other Bahraini activists who received similar attachments turned over these e-mails to an intrepid reporter at Bloomberg News, who arranged for computer security researchers to analyze the files.

After months of painstaking examination, the researchers found that the attachments contained malicious software that, once opened, could log all of the activists' keystrokes, take screen shots, turn on their cameras and microphones, and listen in on their calls. The software—created by UK-based Gamma Group—appeared to send the information back to computers in Bahrain. Gamma told Bloomberg that it didn't sell the software to Bahrain and that possibly its software had been stolen.

Gamma is a leader in the fast-growing world of cyber-espionage. These companies make software that circumvents encryption. Their tools can turn on a microphone in your pocket and capture each word as you type.

In October 2011, my colleague Jennifer Valentino-DeVries and I went to Washington, D.C., to visit ISS World, a conference where governments from around the world buy cyber-espionage tools from companies like Gamma. It is sometimes called the Wiretapper's Ball.

Not surprisingly, we couldn't get in, but Jennifer managed to obtain more than two hundred marketing documents for thirty-six companies, including Gamma. The brochures advertised hacking tools that enable governments to break into people's computers and cell phones, and "massive intercept" gear that can gather all Internet communications in a country. We published much of the literature online in a database called "The Surveillance Catalog: Where governments get their tools."

The brochure for Gamma Group's FinSpy, the tool used to monitor the Bahraini activists, touted its capability of "monitoring of encrypted communications." The brochure also stated that it had been used in an Internet café to monitor Skype communications, and even to take pictures of people as they use Skype. "FinSpy is a field-proven Remote Monitoring Solution that enables Governments to face the current challenges of monitoring Mobile and Security-Aware Targets that regularly change location, use encrypted and anonymous communication channels and reside in foreign countries," the brochure stated.

"Monitor a hundred thousand targets," was the headline for the brochure from an Italian company called Hacking Team. "Remote Control System can monitor from a few up to hundreds of thousands of targets."

Jerry Lucas, the organizer of the Wiretapper's Ball, told us that the off-the-shelf surveillance market had grown from "nearly zero" before the 2001 terrorist attacks to about $5 billion a year.

"We don't really get into asking, 'Is this in the public interest?'" Lucas said.

✦

I hoped I didn't need to worry about the U.S. government installing monitoring software on my computer or phone.

After all, in the United States, law enforcement agents appear to have obtained a search warrant to install monitoring software on a suspect's computer or phone. In June 2007, for instance, the FBI obtained a search warrant that allowed it to send spyware to the MySpace account of a person sending bomb threats to a high school near Olympia, Washington. (In a separate case, Judge Stephen Smith, the Texas magistrate judge who initially rejected a cell phone location surveillance order, turned down a search warrant request to install spyware because, in part, he believed it was closer to video surveillance than a traditional search. Like wiretaps, video surveillance can require additional justification to the court.)

However, I did worry about my encrypted communications ending up in the National Security Agency's dragnets. The NSA has established taps at domestic telecommunications companies that have the capacity to pull in roughly 75 percent of U.S. Internet traffic, according to reporting by my colleagues Siobhan Gorman and Jennifer Valentino-DeVries.

The NSA is supposed to destroy purely domestic communications that it pulls in through its dragnets. But the NSA appears to have carved out an exception for encrypted communications. In a 2009 memo revealed by Edward Snowden, the NSA said that it retains "all communications that are enciphered or reasonably believed to contain secret meaning"—even if they are entirely domestic communications.

That means that by using encryption I am likely raising a red flag that sweeps me into the NSA dragnet.

I had been warned. Even before Snowden's revelations came out, the NSA whistle-blower Bill Binney told me that encryption, or "crypto," was a red flag. "I don't trust any crypto in the public realm. If they can't break it, they'll come across the Net and get it," he told me. Binney said he sent all his e-mail unencrypted, knowing it would be monitored. "I send everything in the clear because I want them to know everything," he told me. "I call them the Gestapo and White House brown shirts."

One night I met the three NSA whistle-blowers Binney, Kirk Wiebe, and Thomas Drake for dinner at a Bethesda diner. Wiebe advised me to use GMRS (General Mobile Radio Service) walkie-talkie radios. Binney suggested returning to actual codebooks, distributed through the postal mail.

Drake told me that he learned that lesson back in his days when he was a supervisor on an airplane specially designed to intercept and jam enemy communications. During exercises in Nevada, his team was able to evade an F-15 fighter jet by executing maneuvers that broke the lock on the F-15's pulse-doppler radars, allowing them to fly to a very low altitude and merge into the ground clutter.

"That's how you defeat high-tech," Drake told me, "with low-tech."

✦

I still wanted a technological solution. And the one that most of my hacker friends used was an encrypted instant messaging protocol known as Off-the-Record Messaging.

Off-the-Record was created in 2004 by Nikita Borisov and Ian Goldberg, under the guidance of Eric Brewer, a professor of computer science at the University of California at Berkeley. It is a free encryption protocol that can be used on top of existing instant messaging programs.

Off-the-Record helps solve the problem of users needing to guard their keys by automatically making new keys frequently throughout a chat. That means a person monitoring the conversation would have to seize the keys during the conversation.

Theoretically, that makes Off-the-Record more secure than encrypted e-mail. But it certainly wasn't much easier to use.

To use Off-the-Record, I had to download three different software programs and then convince them to cooperate with one another. First, I used Tor's anonymizing software to connect to the Internet. Then I signed up for a Jabber instant messaging account. Then I downloaded an instant messaging program called Adium that contains the

Off-the-Record messaging protocol. Then I configured Adium to work with Tor and Jabber.

The only reason I was able to do any of this is because the computer security researcher Jacob Appelbaum walked me through each step and told me where to click and what to type in the settings.

And yet this cobbled-together mash of free software was actually the state of the art for encrypted communications. I found that many of my sensitive journalistic sources would talk to me only over the combination of Tor, Jabber, and Off-the-Record messaging. For the most sensitive sources, actually, I sometimes used Tor, Jabber, and Off-the-Record on a clean computer that I had booted using a thumb drive containing The Amnesic Incognito Live System (Tails) operating system. Tails is free, open source software that was surprisingly easy to use once a hacker friend installed it on a thumb drive for me. The amazing thing about Tails is that it is designed from the ground up for privacy, so there are no settings to jiggle or opt-outs required. Using Tails was my only and best glimpse into an alternate universe where privacy could be the default.

At his military court proceedings, Bradley Manning, the U.S. Army private who leaked documents to WikiLeaks, described how he connected with WikiLeaks using Tor and Jabber for encrypted chats. "The anonymity provided by TOR and the Jabber client and the WLO's [WikiLeaks Organization's] policy allowed me to feel I could just be myself, free of the concerns of social labeling and perceptions that are often placed upon me in real life," Manning said in his statement to the court.

Of course, encryption ultimately didn't save Manning. He was betrayed by a friend—a hacker named Adrian Lamo, who turned Manning in to the FBI. Government investigators later found traces of Manning's correspondence on his computer; Julian Assange was on Manning's "buddy list" in Jabber.

And so, even this ungainly setup that is designed to conceal can reveal too much. And the trio of services working together is extremely delicate. Any change in one service can domino into the others. For example, a year after I set it up, Tor changed its proxy settings, and it took weeks for me to figure out why Jabber had stopped working.

I couldn't blame the software developers. Tor is the only one among them that has any paid staff. Jabber is run by volunteers who struggle to defend it against repeated hack attacks while running on donated computers. Off-the-Record is a volunteer project led by founder Ian Gold-berg, who is now a professor at the University of Waterloo.

Adium is an open source project led by Evan Schoenberg. There wasn't much information about him on the website, so I called him up. It turned out he was an ophthalmologist finishing his fourth year of medical residency. He started Adium in college and had been trying to keep it up. "I thought when I went to medical school I was going to make the transition—I would hand the reins over to someone else," Schoenberg told me. (He had time to talk because it was a quiet day at the hospital.) "But there was never anyone with programming experience who seemed to want to get involved in leadership." And so Adium languished. "I simply haven't had time and a lot of our core development team has moved on to jobs that pay," Schoenberg told me.

On this fragile foundation rested my most robust hope of encryption.

✦

This is not how it was supposed to turn out.

When the antinuclear activist Philip Zimmermann released the first mass-market encryption program called Pretty Good Privacy in 1991, it seemed for a brief time that encryption could liberate humanity from oppression.

PGP was the first program to offer access to military-grade encryption to ordinary people. Until then, powerful computerized encryption was available only to the government and to large companies willing to pay huge licensing fees. (The software I was using for encryption, GPG, is a free software version of PGP.)

The widespread availability of powerful encryption helped spur a movement called Cypherpunks. On March 9, 1993, Eric Hughes published *A Cypherpunk's Manifesto.* "Privacy is the power to selectively reveal one-self to the world," Hughes wrote. "When I purchase a magazine at a store and hand cash to the clerk, there is no need to know who I am. . . . When my identity is revealed by the underlying mechanism of the transaction, I have no privacy. I cannot here selectively reveal myself; I must *always* reveal myself." He called on the Cypherpunks to build systems that allow people to remain anonymous. "We must defend our own privacy if we expect to have any," he wrote. "People have been defending their own privacy for centuries with whispers, darkness, envelopes, closed doors, secret handshakes, and couriers. The technologies of the past did not allow for strong privacy, but electronic technologies do."

Not surprisingly, the U.S. government was not thrilled with the Cypherpunk uprising. The U.S. Customs Service began investigating whether Zimmermann had violated arms trafficking laws, since high-powered encryption was considered a munition subject to export restrictions. In 1996, however, the government dropped the investigation without pressing any charges. And in 1999, the United States dropped the ban on exporting encryption products.

The National Security Agency attempted to co-opt the movement in a different way. It developed the "Clipper chip" to encrypt voice transmissions. The catch: copies of the encryption keys would be stored with the government, meaning that the government could potentially decrypt everything.

In 1994, Matt Blaze at AT&T Bell Labs revealed a basic flaw in the Clipper chip that the spymasters overlooked—it was possible to send a spoofed useless key to the government and then continue using encryption. Embarrassed, the NSA sidelined the project soon after, giving the Cypherpunks a big win. Flush with victory, a leading Cypherpunk, Bruce Schneier, wrote in his book *Applied Cryptography* in 1996: "It is insufficient to protect ourselves with laws; we need to protect ourselves with mathematics."

But it turned out that cryptography could not protect against the law. The Cypherpunks built "remailers"—services that would let users send encrypted anonymous messages, back in the day when disposable e-mail accounts were not as easy to come by as they are today. But in 1996, the largest remailer, based in Finland, shut down rather than comply with a court order to unmask the identity of a user who had used the remailer to distribute material critical of the Church of Scientology.

Nor could cryptography overcome the challenges of bad passwords, insecure computers, and sloppy computer programming.

By 2000, Bruce Schneier issued a correction to his earlier enthusiasm. In his book *Secrets & Lies*, he declared that he had been wrong to lead readers to believe that "cryptography was a kind of magic security dust that they could sprinkle over their software and make it secure." Schneier wrote that he had come to believe the problem wasn't cryptography; it was the people using it. "Mathematics is logical; people are erratic, capricious and barely comprehensible," he concluded.

The National Security Agency has long exploited the capriciousness of humans to circumvent cryptography. In 2013, documents revealed by Edward Snowden outlined the NSA's "aggressive, multipronged effort to break widely used Internet encryption technologies" by persuading technology companies to provide access to the NSA, using malicious software in targeted attacks, and using its influence to weaken encryption standards.

Yet lost in the hue and cry about the NSA's attacks on encryption was the fact that the NSA's use of circumvention tactics seemed to imply that the agency has still not cracked the mathematical formulas that underpin public key cryptography.

Schneier, who reviewed the Snowden documents for the *Guardian*, declared: "Trust the math. Encryption is your friend. Use it well, and do your best to ensure that nothing can compromise it. That's how you can remain secure even in the face of the NSA."

✦

In some ways, the Cypherpunk movement is coming back to life.

Julian Assange, a longtime Cypherpunk, transformed the relationship between journalists and their sources with his 2006 launch of the WikiLeaks encrypted drop box that promised complete anonymity to people who wanted to leak information.

Other Cypherpunks focused on building "liberation technology" to help liberate people from oppressive regimes. Moxie Marlinspike in San Francisco built encryption apps—RedPhone and TextSecure—for Android phones. Nathan Freitas and the Guardian Project in New York built apps to bring encrypted calls and Tor to cell phones.

The U.S. government funded some projects, such as Tor, in the name of Internet freedom, while at the same time the Justice Department was investigating Tor developer Jacob Appelbaum for his involvement in WikiLeaks.

And Phil Zimmermann, the founder of Pretty Good Privacy, went the capitalist route. He sold PGP to Network Associates in 1997 for $36 million. And in 2012, he joined with the cryptographer Jon Callas and the former navy SEAL Mike Janke to build a paid cryptography service called Silent Circle, which sold apps for encrypted texts and phone calls.

✦

Silent Circle was the easiest encryption program I had ever used. All I had to do was download two apps onto my iPhone, Silent Text and Silent Phone, and, presto, I was encrypted.

But I needed someone to talk to. The service cost $9.95 a month, and I had a hard time finding anyone willing to sign up.

Eventually, I convinced a sensitive source to install Silent Text and Silent Phone as well. We sat at a bar and spent an hour installing the apps on our phones and making sure they worked. I set myself up as Ida and my source set up a fake name.

We successfully texted a few times, and even had a long phone call on Silent Phone. The call was painful—with three-second delays between speech and transmission, but it mostly worked. Silent Circle CEO and cofounder Mike Janke told me that the delays were because I was using it on the cell phone network instead of Wi-Fi. (I had turned off Wi-Fi to evade commercial location tracking.) In addition, he pointed out that my source and I had not pressed the "verify" button at the start of the call, an omission that can also cause interference on a call.

But when my source and I tried to arrange an in-person meeting, I suddenly stopped receiving replies to my Silent Texts. All I saw was a message that said "Establishing keys."

Later, when I asked Silent Circle about this mishap, chief technologist Jon Callas explained to me that with every text, Silent Text exchanged a new set of keys. This meant passing key information back and forth at least three times before the texting was initiated. This allowed Silent Circle to dispose of my keys after each session, in a similar fashion as Off-the-Record instant messaging.

But both parties needed to be online at the same time for the dynamic key exchange to work. I found that if I or my Silent Text partner were in an elevator or in a zone without cell signals, the key exchange might not be completed.

In this case, one of us—either my source or myself—had dropped a key in the midst of our exchange. As a result, our texts weren't going through. We were supposed to meet in the evening, but we hadn't yet specified a time and location.

As the day wore on, I became increasingly desperate. I texted my source in the morning to ask where and when we should meet. I got no reply. By the afternoon, I was starting to worry.

At 3:13 p.m., I wrote, "Feel free to call or to text a place to meet. Hope we can make it work!" Still no reply. I was starting to worry that my source had gotten cold feet.

At 5:07 p.m., I tried again: "Hmm—I got a notification of a text but no text." Still no reply.

Finally, at 6:24 p.m., my source called me on my cell phone to check in. So much for encryption. We were back in the dragnet.

This is the conundrum of using encryption in today's world. When it works, it's magical. When it doesn't work, it's the worst kind of false promise, the kind that can betray sensitive relationships.

✦

I kept using Silent Circle. For all its flaws, it was much less painful than the other encryption programs I was using.

I persuaded a few people to join me on Silent Circle: a close friend who was living in Paris; my book researcher, who was living in Japan; and a professional colleague.

And I learned to live with dropped keys. My friend in Paris—whose Silent Circle name was Hedy Lamarr—and I dropped keys so often that we set up a weekly phone call during which we would both press "reset key" at the same time over and over until our keys finally reset.

Eventually, we both came to view Silent Text as closer to instant messaging than to texting. We both had to be online at the same time. If one of us was off-line, our keys would often drop and our messages would disappear in the ether.

Silent Text also brought out Hedy's inner pyromaniac. She fell in love with a feature that let her set her messages to "burn." They would dissolve before my eyes twenty-four hours after I received them. Occasionally, her messages burned before I even got to read them. I complained that I needed to document our exchanges for my book research, but that just spurred her to burn more.

During one of her visits to New York, Hedy told me that she finally had begun to have doubts about burning all of the messages. "I read one of your messages and you had a very witty reply," she told me. "But I had already burned my message so I couldn't remember what you were wittily replying to."

She briefly considered not burning the messages but ultimately decided to keep tossing our data into the virtual flames.

"It's bittersweet," she said. "But that's life."

14

FIGHTING FEAR

My job is to surveil my children. It is a nonstop occupation—every waking and sleeping minute of my life I am supposed to know where my children are, what they are doing, and how they are staying safe.

As every parent knows, it is an exhausting job. Not only is it physically exhausting to chase little children around, but it is also mentally taxing to know that you are on the hook for anything that happens—whether or not it is your fault. If I happen to be looking at my cell phone while one of my kids runs out into the street and gets hit by a car (God forbid), not only would I blame myself, but every single person in the world would blame me, too.

It's the kind of pressure that can drive a person to take extreme measures: to put children on leashes, or to secretly monitor children using spyware, or to set up nanny cams to watch a babysitter.

And, in fact, much of the expert advice about protecting kids' privacy boils down to "surveil your kids."

• The American Academy of Pediatrics recommends that parents supervise their kids whenever they use a computer, use software to track which websites their kids visit, and consider using censorship software to block access to objectionable websites.

• The FBI recommends that parents use blocking software and "always

maintain access to your child's on-line account and randomly check his/
her e-mail."

• The Department of Homeland Security suggests using software to
monitor websites that kids visit. "Monitoring tools can be used with or
without a kid's knowledge."

I can understand why many parents follow this advice. After all, it
comes from legitimate sources. Parents are scared of a terrifying world.
And they hope surveillance will help them prevent a catastrophe.

I imagine that same parental feeling motivates the executives at the
National Security Agency. Their job is to protect the nation, and they
know they will be blamed if there is a terrorist event. So they decide to
monitor everything—just in case.

But I couldn't justify setting up dragnets to snare my children's every
move while trying to evade dragnet surveillance of myself. If nothing
else, it was entirely hypocritical.

✦

Why not succumb? Why not just embed a GPS chip in my children's back-
packs? Why not install spyware on their computers monitoring their
every mouse click? Wouldn't my kids be safer?

Maybe. But it's worth remembering that my kids are pretty safe already.
Crime has plummeted in the United States during the past twenty
years. The rate of violent crime declined by about 40 percent from 1990
to 2009. Property crimes are down nearly 40 percent. Auto thefts have
fallen by more than 50 percent.

In New York City, where I live, the numbers are even more dramatic.
Murders are down 83 percent since 1993. Robberies are down 78 percent.
Burglary is down 83 percent. The city had the second-lowest murder rate
among large cities, with a rate of 5.05 homicides per 100,000 people in
2012. Only San Diego's rate was lower among cities with more than a
million residents, with a homicide rate of 3.51 per 100,000 people.

Crimes against children are also down. Sexual abuse of children plummeted in the United States between 1992 and 2010, according to a compilation of studies analyzed by the Crimes Against Children Research
Center. Other studies show that bullying is on the decline, although the
rates are still higher than they should be. Teen suicide and teen preg-

nancy rates have declined in the past twenty years. And research consistently shows that crimes against children are mostly perpetrated by people they know.

So why is there this perception that our digitally saturated world is so dangerous that kids need to be monitored? David Finkelhor, the director of the Crimes Against Children Research Center, calls the paranoia about children and the Internet "juvenoia." He speculates that juvenoia results from the fact that modern parents feel they are pitted against popular culture. In the past, families lived in smaller societies and tribes where they shared values with other families. Today, modern parents often feel that they are holding back a tide of popular culture with its celebration of sexuality, junk food, violence, and consumerism. "It is ironic, but parents in the most elite environments in America feel as desperate as everyone else to shield their children from much mainstream cultural influence," Finkelhor writes.

And so it is not only crime that parents are afraid of, it is also the influence of corrupting ideas from outside the home. Is that enough of a reason to conduct surveillance?

It's a particularly poignant question now that I understand the psychological effects of surveillance. Research shows that covert surveillance can cause anxiety and self-repression in adults. In children, surveillance appears to do something particularly depressing: it undermines their enthusiasm to learn.

A landmark 1975 study concluded that adult surveillance of children had the effect of "turning play into work," dampening the children's enthusiasm for playing with an interesting puzzle. In the study, children were left alone in a room with a camera pointed at them and told that an adult would be watching them through the camera as they played with the puzzle. The next time the surveilled children were presented with the puzzle in a normal classroom setting, they had far less interest in playing with it than the control group. "The knowledge that one's performance at a task is being observed and evaluated by someone else . . . appears sufficient to decrease later interest in the task," wrote the study's authors, Mark R. Lepper and David Greene.

The children's enthusiasm for the puzzle declined even further when they were given explicit rewards for playing with the puzzle. Children were shown enticing toys and told that they could play with them if they did a good job on the puzzles. The next time that they were presented with the puzzle in a normal classroom setting, their interest in the puzzle fell even further. Lepper and Greene concluded that the best way to interest children in an activity is to "employ the minimal amount of pressure sufficient to elicit or maintain the desired behavior."

✦

Even before I got interested in privacy, I had decided that it wasn't fair to post any pictures of my children online. I didn't think it was fair for me to build a digital trail for them that they would later have to manage.

Ever since our kids were born, my husband and I have always shared pictures of the kids privately. At first, we used the now-defunct website Kodak Gallery to send our family and friends links to slide shows. For the grandparents, we regularly printed out pictures and sent them hard copies. But we stopped using Kodak Gallery when it began threatening to delete our photos if we didn't buy photos often enough.

After leaving Kodak Gallery, we briefly used another photo-sharing service, Shutterfly. But eventually we realized that we weren't that into "sharing." Only a few people really wanted to see endless baby photos. So we just started e-mailing photos to the grandparents and a few other close relatives.

Even so, we've had a few lapses where a photo escapes into the public domain. When my son was born, in 2008, I was so exhausted and had so many people to notify that I posted a picture of him on Facebook. That photo is still there—and it bothers me. I've deleted it, but it's still in the data I downloaded from Facebook.

My husband once mistakenly uploaded family photos onto Google+ when he thought he was just logging in to his Gmail account. He was able to delete them, but it took a while for them to disappear from Google search results.

Another time, my mother posted a photo of my daughter and me in our pajamas (!) on her blog without asking. My daughter noticed it and told Grandma to take down the photo. Grandma took it down and, once again, it took a while to disappear from search results. But now it's gone.

But policing my children's digital images is not easy. Every summer camp and after-school activity comes with a form asking me to allow them to take pictures of my children and use them for whatever purpose they like. I decline to sign, but I dislike being an annoying parent who causes problems.

I know that it's a losing battle. Just as I can't prevent myself from being photographed in public, I can't prevent my children from living in a world that is saturated with cameras. But it seems unfair that I have no rights over images of my kids. If someone were to videotape my kids in public and post the video online, I would have no legal right to have it removed. But if that video contained copyrighted music, the copyright owner would be able to get it taken down in a flash.

I briefly—and mostly in jest—asked a few lawyers if I could copyright my kids' images. They said I couldn't.

And so I continue to try to keep their images off-line, knowing that I will eventually fail.

✦

There are two laws that are supposed to protect children's privacy: the Children's Online Privacy Protection Act and the Family Educational Rights and Privacy Act. However, neither of them is particularly effective.

In fact, before even starting my privacy experiments, I had already violated the Children's Online Privacy Protection Act of 1998. The law required websites to get parental permission before collecting personal information from children under the age of thirteen. In 2013, the law was updated to expand the type of information that requires parental consent to include online behavioral tracking, photos, videos, and location.

The goal of COPPA is to prevent websites from exploiting kids. But, unfortunately, the law also discourages companies from building websites aimed at kids under thirteen, because once they have "actual knowledge" that kids are using their site, they need to find a way to get parental permission.

As a result, COPPA encourages lying. I set up my daughter with a Gmail account when she was seven years old—even though Gmail requires users to be thirteen. We wanted her to be able to send e-mails to her grandparents who live in India.

In my defense, I am not the only parent lying about my kids' age online. In 2011, researchers led by Microsoft's Danah Boyd surveyed more than one thousand parents of kids aged ten to fourteen and found that one-third of them reported that their kids had Facebook accounts before age thirteen and that two-thirds of the parents helped their kids set up the Facebook accounts. The researchers concluded that the law's age restrictions are "neither a solution to privacy and online safety concerns nor a way of empowering parents."

The Family Educational Rights and Privacy Act of 1974 was designed to give parents the right to access their children's education records and to require parental consent before those records are turned over to a third party. However, FERPA is filled with loopholes. Schools can hand over records to "school officials" or to "organizations conducting studies on behalf of the school" without parental consent. And information about a student's name, address, e-mail address, telephone, weight, height, and photograph are considered "directory information" that can also be disclosed without parental permission.

In New York, where I live, the public schools send student data to an outside data storage center, inBloom, which says it aims to help schools develop technology that promotes "personalized learning." Apparently, personalized learning will let "teachers take on the role of coaches, students learn at their own pace, technology tracks student progress, and schools are judged based on the outcomes they produce." For this dream, New York could start paying $2 to $5 per kid to inBloom in 2015.

I would rather they spent that money on salaries and textbooks instead of donating my children's data to a Hall of Mirrors database of dubious, unproven value. But I can't remove my children's information from the database. There is no opt-out provision in FERPA if a school wants to share data with "organizations conducting studies," although school districts can establish their own opt-outs if they wish. InBloom, which is a nonprofit, says it doesn't view, use, analyze, or sell kids' data.

Sadly, I must conclude that neither of the two children's privacy laws is serving me very well.

✦

Conventional wisdom states that kids don't care about privacy. Adults are constantly telling me that privacy is a generational issue and that kids are perfectly happy living a completely public life.

And it's true that kids have made terrible mistakes in posting dumb things online—sometimes with severe consequences.

Consider, as just one extreme example, eighteen-year-old Justin Carter of Texas, who was arrested for writing a sarcastic comment on his Facebook page. Carter and a friend were arguing about an online video game League of Legends, and Carter's friend called him crazy. Carter wrote back: "I think I'ma [sic] shoot up a kindergarten and watch the blood of the innocent rain down and eat the beating heart of one of them." He was arrested and charged with making a terroristic threat. Carter was jailed from February to July 2013 before an anonymous donor posted the $500,000 bail that his family could not afford.

But it's worth remembering that adults write just as many stupid things online, which have resulted in outsize consequences. Consider these two stories.

• In January 2012, two British tourists were detained for twelve hours and denied entry to the United States after one of them tweeted about the upcoming trip: "Free this week, for quick gossip/prep before I go and destroy America," in a reference to "partying" in the United States.

• On September 9, 2009, Joe Lipari had a bad experience at an Apple Store in New York. When he got home, he paraphrased a *Fight Club* quote on his Facebook wall. It read, "Joe Lipari might walk into an Apple store on Fifth Avenue with an Armalite AR-10 gas powered semi-automatic weapon and pump round after round into one of those smug, fruity little concierges." Less than two hours later, New York Police Department officers were at his door. They searched his house for explosives, arrested him, and charged him with making terroristic threats. He fought the charges for one year, refusing to take a plea bargain, until finally the charges were dropped.

Research shows that kids do care about privacy. A 2012 survey of teens who used apps on their smartphones found that 46 percent of them had turned off location tracking features on their phones, and 26 percent had uninstalled an app because of privacy concerns. The study also found that 70 percent of teens had sought advice on how to manage their online privacy.

Even kids who don't appear to care about their privacy often engage in tricks to protect themselves on social networks, according to interviews with 163 teens analyzed by Microsoft researchers Danah Boyd and Alice Marwick. The researchers describe a ploy used by a seventeen-year-old girl named Carmen who struggled to communicate with her friends on Facebook, even though her mother was also a Facebook friend.

Carmen was sad over a breakup, so she posted song lyrics on Facebook from "Always Look on the Bright Side of Life." Carmen's mother took the lyrics literally, and commented that Carmen seemed to be doing really well. But Carmen's friends understood the hidden meaning of the song lyrics: the song appeared in the Monty Python movie *Life of Brian* as the main character faced crucifixion.

Carmen's hidden messages resonated with me. Back in my high school years, we didn't have Facebook. Our Facebook "wall" was the yearbook. At the end of the year, each senior got to decorate a page in the yearbook. My page—and many others' pages—was a mixture of inside jokes and lyrics designed to be obscure.

I dug up my yearbook page and inspected my messages. I couldn't decode most of them. Why did I shout out "Liquid Paper" to my friend Heidi? And what did I mean by telling my friend Suzy to "take a walk on the mild side"? What happened on "Aug. 15" that I wanted to recall with my friend Sheryl? It is all lost in the sands of time.

At the time, however, the hidden messages were effective. My friends knew what I meant, and my parents were most likely just as mystified as I am now.

In fact, I had always cared about privacy, even as a teenager. As a kid, I was concerned about parental surveillance. Now I am concerned about corporate and governmental surveillance.

Over time, my threat model had simply changed.

◆

When I started my privacy experiments, my children saw privacy as a challenge to be overcome.

I nicknamed my daughter Harriet the Spy because she was so good at spying on me. Once, I was working at home and my daughter was home from school with pink eye. I was in my room on the phone with a girlfriend complaining about how I couldn't get my Mac laptop to work with my Hewlett-Packard monitor when this e-mail arrived in my in-box:

> I've been hearing every word you said about how your mac doesn't go with the HP you have. Heard over 10 curse words and most of them were the F word.

I opened the door to my bedroom and there was my daughter, holding the iPad and giggling at her successful eavesdropping. She also loved to sneak up on me as I was typing in passwords.

My kids also thought I was mean for not letting them post videos to YouTube. My daughter is nine; my son is five. They love the Internet, particularly YouTube. My daughter taught herself to play piano by watching YouTube. My son fell in love with Woody Guthrie's music when he found it on YouTube. (He would like me to call him Woody in this book, so I will.)

Harriet and Woody dream of posting their own videos to YouTube. After all, in the world of YouTube, that's how you have a conversation. One person posts a video, and then another person posts a video that builds on the first, or responds to it. My kids are right that this is how art evolves, through artists sharing their work. YouTube is the Paris coffeehouse of their time. And I feel terrible about denying them the pleasure of such creative exchanges.

But I can't promise them that those videos—or some other online activity—won't end up coming back to haunt them someday. It could be used to deny them a job or a passport or simply to deny them the right to shape the way they are viewed by the world.

When I think of my own childhood, I feel blessed that my life was barely documented. Without digital footprints, I was able to reinvent myself completely whenever I wanted. In junior high school, for example, I wore only pink and turquoise. But when I moved across town for high school, I changed my wardrobe entirely and wore only preppy clothes with penny loafers. Nobody knew about my transformation because there was no trail, except for a few dusty photographs in a shoe box in my parents' closet.

I want my children to have the same freedom to reinvent themselves. But I realize that saying no all the time was only causing them to hate privacy and try to circumvent me.

✦

I decided to take a new approach. Taking a page from the study about turning "play into work," I would attempt to turn privacy into play.

I decided to treat privacy tools as attractive toys that my kids had an opportunity to play with, without any explicit rewards or surveillance of their actions.

The password business was a great start. My daughter loved all the money she was making rolling dice and selling strong passwords. And she loved that it was a grown-up activity; adults were impressed when she told them about the password business, and adults were her biggest customers.

As an added bonus for me, after Harriet started her password business, she stopped trying to sneak peeks at my passwords. She knew that they were either stored in 1Password or salted versions of the passwords she had made for me. The game had changed for her: now the game was to build better passwords, not to break mine.

Harriet soon became curious about my other privacy experiments. She loved my fake identity of Ida Tarbell. Harriet decided she would use her fake name for her online accounts as well. Neither kid is old enough for a social media profile, but Harriet changed her e-mail address to her fake name. After all, her friends and family would still know it was she. It was an innocuous bit of social steganography.

I also realized that there was no reason not to get Harriet into encryption. So I set up a Silent Circle account for her on the iPad. Soon, Harriet and Ida were exchanging encrypted texts and phone calls.

Harriet also got interested in my attempts to block online tracking. She stood by my computer and laughed with me while I tried to browse the Web using the cumbersome NoScript, which made it difficult for my pages to load correctly. She cheered when I switched to Ghostery and fewer pages were breaking. She particularly liked Ghostery's logo—a cute little blue ghost that sits at the top right corner of the Web browser. Soon, she wanted to use Ghostery, too.

So I installed Ghostery on her computer, an old netbook that we got for free when setting up our high-speed Internet connection. She began to view Ghostery as a video game, with the goal being to find websites with the most trackers. "Mommy, I found one with forty-one trackers!" she told me, running into my room with her computer.

Harriet even started to like DuckDuckGo, with its cheerful duck in a bow tie. I set it up as her default search engine and she enjoyed showing off the duck to her friends.

But she complained that the Ghostery app—which uses DuckDuck-Go's search engine—on the iPad was too slow. After a month of complaints, I finally got out a stopwatch and we timed it. Searching for the "Grammy awards" on the Ghostery app took 6.7 seconds. The same search of Apple's Safari Web browser took 1.7 seconds. She was right. The Ghostery app was too slow on the iPad.

So we gave up on Ghostery on the iPad. Together, we installed Disconnect Kids, an iPad app from Brian Kennish, the Google engineer who launched Disconnect in 2010. Disconnect Kids was basically the same technology that I had used when I allowed Ashkan Soltani to route my Web traffic through his computers to check for trackers. Disconnect Kids did the same thing—it captured all the traffic leaving the iPad and blocked any contact with a list of known mobile tracking companies.

I thought it was quite clever. But Harriet was disappointed that there was no video game aspect. She couldn't *see* how many trackers were being blocked because its work was invisible.

After she had used it for a while, and none of her apps broke, I decided to install Disconnect Kids on my iPhone. After all, I had been struggling to find a way to block ad tracking on my phone—and it was the best solution I'd seen so far.

Now, whenever I glance at Disconnect Kids' dancing green robot on my phone, I am reminded that my kids and I face the same challenges in protecting ourselves from dragnets.

There is really no need for a distinction between "kids" and "adult" privacy-protecting software when we are all being swept up indiscriminately.

15

AN UNFAIRNESS DOCTRINE

A t the end of my year of trying to evade surveillance, I felt surprisingly hopeful.

On one level, my efforts to evade the dragnets were not very successful. I hadn't found a way to use my cell phone—or my burner phone—in a way that protected my location and calling patterns, short of leaving the phone at home or putting it in a metal-shielded cage, rendering it useless. I hadn't extricated myself entirely from the clutches of Google and Facebook. My name and address were still on file at more than one hundred data brokers that didn't provide me with a way to opt out. And I wasn't going to be able to avoid facial recognition cameras.

But, on another level, I had exceeded my expectations.

I had avoided the vast majority of online ad tracking. My passwords—made by my daughter by rolling dice and picking words out of a dictionary—were pretty good. My fake identity as Ida Tarbell had allowed me to disassociate my true identity from sensitive purchases and some phone calls and in-person meetings. And I had managed to convince some of my friends and sources to exchange encrypted texts, instant messages, and e-mails.

My biggest success, surprisingly, was with my kids. They started out thinking that privacy was another word for "no." But over time, they came to embrace privacy-protecting technology, from blocking online tracking to encryption. I even wondered if I had gone too far when my daughter reprimanded me for entering her social security number on a school form.

Of course, my successes were only temporary. New technology will make it easier to break my new twenty-character passwords. The more that my kids and I use fake identities, the easier it will be to link those identities back to us. My encrypted conversations are likely being stored by the NSA for later analysis. And the online ad trackers are already developing new technology to circumvent my blocking techniques.

But I realized there was value in trying. My opt-outs were one more bit of evidence to undermine the data brokers' argument that few people care enough about privacy to opt out. My use of encryption and anonymizing software put the NSA and Internet companies on notice that I didn't want them to read my messages, and I had encouraged some of my friends and associates to join me in embracing cryptography. My use of fake identities had encouraged my kids to develop their own pseudonym strategies, which we hoped would serve them well in their teenage years.

In short, I came to believe that my actions were likely more effective at changing the conversation about privacy than at countering surveillance. They reminded me of the lunch-counter sit-ins of the 1960s, when black students in Greensboro, North Carolina, sat at a "whites only" lunch counter in an F. W. Woolworth store, in order to protest the company's policy of racial segregation. The sit-ins did not immediately destroy segregation, but they led to a national conversation that ultimately unraveled it.

My hope is that if enough people join me in refusing to consent to ubiquitous indiscriminate surveillance, we might also prompt a conversation that could unravel it.

✦

However, I wasn't happy with the toll that my countersurveillance techniques had taken on my psyche. The more I learned about who was watching me, the more paranoid I became. By the end of my experiment, I was refusing to have digital conversations with my close friends without encryption. I began using my fake name for increasingly trivial transactions; a friend was shocked when we took a yoga class together and I casually registered as Ida Tarbell.

I didn't want to live in the world that I was building—a world of sub-terfuge and disinformation and covert actions. It was a world based on fear. It was a world devoid of trust. It was not a world that I wanted leave to my children.

I remember my parents expressing the same feeling about the two big threats of their generation—environmental damage and the prolif-eration of nuclear weapons. They didn't want to leave their children a world that was destroyed by those threats. Of course, we have not totally solved either one of those problems, but we have contained the threat of nuclear weapons through international treaties, and we have mitigated pollution through laws and social pressure.

The lessons of the environmental cleanup are particularly relevant to the problem of privacy. Of course, there is more to do, but it's worth remem-bering how polluted the United States was not that long ago. In 1969, a chocolate-brown oil slick on the Cuyahoga River in Cleveland, Ohio, caught fire. It was not the first time that debris on the heavily polluted river near the city's steel mills had caught fire, nor was it even the worst fire on the river. But *Time* magazine's coverage of the 1969 river fire (com-plete with a dramatic and misleading picture from a much more devastat-ing 1952 river fire) was a wake-up call for the nation. We spent the next decades reconsidering the unfairness of asking the public to clean up after industrial polluters.

By almost any measure, our rebalancing of the burden of pollution has been a success. The air is cleaner. The water is cleaner. Endangered species have been saved. The Cuyahoga River had no fish in the late 1960s. Now there are more than forty fish species in the river, and even a few freshwa-ter mussels, which are a sign of improving water quality. (Of course, we did overlook a big environmental problem—the accumulation of carbon dioxide and other greenhouse gases in the atmosphere and the subse-quent warming of the earth—that hopefully we will address soon.)

Privacy and pollution are similar problems. Both cause harm that is invisible and pervasive. Both result from exploitation of a resource—whether it is land, water, or information. Both suffer from difficult attri-bution. It is not easy to identify a single pollutant or a single piece of data that caused harm. Rather, the harm often comes from an accumulation of pollutants, or an assemblage of data. And the harm of both pollution and privacy is collective. No one person bears the burden of pollution; all of society suffers when the air is dirty and the water undrinkable. Similarly, we all suffer when we live in fear that our data will be used against us by companies trying to exploit us or police officers sweeping us into a lineup.

To understand the links between privacy and pollution, I called Dennis Hirsch, a professor of environmental law at the Capital University Law School in Ohio, who has been studying privacy and environmental law for a decade. Hirsch compared institutions that mine individuals' personal data to ranchers who overgraze their cattle on commonly owned grasslands, as portrayed in Garrett Hardin's seminal 1968 essay in *Science* magazine, "Tragedy of the Commons." Hardin described how each rancher seeks to increase profits by adding cattle to his herd, even though too many cattle will overgraze and ruin the pasture for all. "Freedom in a commons brings ruin to all," Hardin wrote.

Hirsch described excessive data mining as a similar tragedy of the commons. Like the cattle herders, he said, companies that mine data have an incentive to use more and more data to gain a competitive advantage. But each time they do so, they undermine users' trust that their data will be appropriately cared for and protected. Eventually, he said, individuals will no longer trust companies to protect their data and will no longer disclose it. "The risk here is that eventually our trust will be so abused that we will pull back from the Web," he told me.

That was certainly a good description of my own behavior. In my investigation of dragnets, I had lost my trust in the institutions that stored my data. I had become a data survivalist, pulling my data back from the Web and stockpiling it at home. I had also become a disinformation specialist, overcoming my fear of lying to spread lies about my habits and myself.

By fighting to protect my data, I had polluted the public square and sowed distrust. There had to be a better way to fight back against unfair dragnets.

✦

One way to even the playing field would be for everyone to be in the surveillance business.

This is the argument put forth by some technologists, including David Brin, the author who described the inevitable rise of ubiquitous surveillance in his book *The Transparent Society*. Brin argues that the only thing that will blunt the rise of the surveillance state is the rise of what he calls "sousveillance," in which citizens monitor the government from below as aggressively as the government monitors them from above.

Certainly, the fact that every citizen is now carrying a cell phone camera has made the police more accountable for their actions. For instance, a police officer who pepper-sprayed nonviolent student protesters at the University of California at Davis in 2011 was fired after a video of his actions was made public.

Sousveillance has also become an antiwar activity. In 2010, the actor George Clooney and the human rights activist John Prendergast launched a satellite surveillance program to monitor the civil war in Sudan. In May 2013, Clooney and Prendergast's Satellite Sentinel Project released evidence that Sudan and South Sudan had failed to meet their obligations to withdraw troops from the demilitarized zone along the border.

But, unfortunately, there is much government action that citizens can't police with cameras or satellites. We might never have known about the NSA's dragnets of innocent Americans if Edward Snowden hadn't exposed them. Nor would we likely have known how much taxpayer money was being spent to fund those dragnets without Snowden's revelations of the intelligence agencies' "black budget."

We may not have seen the chilling video of U.S. soldiers shooting innocent journalists and children from their aircraft in Baghdad if Private Bradley Manning hadn't exposed it. Nor would we likely have received an accurate count of the civilians killed in the Iraq and Afghanistan wars if Manning had not revealed hundreds of thousands of war records.

The revelations by Snowden and Manning, however, were also indiscriminate. Both obtained troves of documents that, in total, painted a more comprehensive picture than any one document might have. In a sense, they were conducting "sousveillance" of the government using their own information dragnets.

But it turns out the government doesn't like being caught in dragnets any more than I do. The Obama administration has thrown the book at both Manning and Snowden, charging them with a range of crimes including espionage. In 2013, Manning was sentenced to thirty-five years in prison, and Snowden obtained temporary political asylum in Russia.

And it's not just Snowden and Manning whose efforts to unmask government behavior are being prosecuted. Traditional journalists—who are the front lines of surveilling the government—are increasingly being targeted in criminal investigations. In 2013, the Justice Department informed the Associated Press—after the fact—that it had obtained two months' worth of phone records of several AP journalists, as part of an investigation into a leak of information about a CIA operation in Yemen. Gary Pruitt, the AP's president and chief executive, protested the intrusion, saying, "We regard this action by the Department of Justice as a serious interference with AP's constitutional rights to gather and report the news."

And the Department of Justice is pushing for the *New York Times* reporter James Risen to reveal his sources for a book that exposed a botched CIA operation to provide Iranian scientists with error-ridden blueprints for a nuclear device. Risen has said that he will go to prison rather than testify about his sources.

Mutual surveillance is not likely to level the playing field if the government uses its power to prosecute those who seek to hold the government accountable for its actions.

✦

Another possible way to make dragnet operators more accountable for their actions is simply to charge them for access to our personal data.

This idea is seductive in its simplicity. I would reclaim my personal data, store it in a virtual locker, and sell some of it on the open market— rather than having it "taken" from me. A few start-ups have popped up in the hopes of privatizing the personal data market. And in 2011, the World Economic Forum declared that personal data was emerging as a "New Asset Class."

But so far, personal data are an underperforming asset. The reason is simple supply and demand: I don't have the only copy of my data, since there is no law requiring data brokers to give it back to me. Therefore, no one is going to pay me much to use my copy of the data when they can get it somewhere else cheaper.

An analysis by the *Financial Times* found that the ubiquity of personal data has driven prices down so that an average person's age, gender, and location is worth only a fraction of a cent. And the sum total of information about most people sells for less than a dollar. I entered my information into the *Financial Times*'s data calculator and found that my information was worth only 28 cents.

Laws that give people ownership—or partial ownership—of their data might help boost the price for data. But it would also get complicated really fast. After all, how do I share ownership of my phone calling data with AT&T? And how do I prevent the government from taking my partially owned data from AT&T?

And I'm not sure that selling data would end up limiting the chilling effects of surveillance. Before we had a minimum wage and limited work hours, people were willing to "sell" their labor at extremely low prices for very long hours.

Carnegie Mellon professor Alessandro Acquisti, who studies the economics of privacy, has found that people are less willing to pay for privacy when they don't already have it. In one experiment, Acquisti and his fellow researchers offered one group of people a free $10 Visa gift card and told them their spending would be anonymous. They offered another group a $12 gift card and told them that their spending would be identified. Then they offered members of each group the opportunity to trade their card for the other group's card. Fifty-two percent of the $10 cardholders kept their card—in effect agreeing to pay $2 to keep their privacy. But over 90 percent of the $12 cardholders refused to trade—meaning that they refused to give up $2 to protect their privacy. "What this tells us is that people value some things more when they have them than when they do not have them," Acquisti told me.

In essence, when you don't have privacy, you feel less pain from losing it. Instead, you feel the pain of having to "buy back" privacy. This inability to accurately assign value to our data is one reason that most products that are sold to protect privacy fail. And it's one reason that turning personal data into a currency—without any enabling legislation to make personal data scarce, and thus more valuable—could just enable and legitimize ubiquitous surveillance.

✦

And so I return, reluctantly, to laws to limit dragnet surveillance. My reluctance is due to the fact that privacy laws have a poor track record in the United States. Unlike most Western nations, the United States has no comprehensive privacy law requiring all data collectors to meet some minimum standards. Instead, there are privacy laws covering certain sectors—health, finance, children, and government records. Most of those sectoral laws require the data collectors to disclose their data practices and to seek user consent to the use of their personal information. It sounds like a good idea. But in practice, notice and consent turn out to be easy to circumvent.

The Children's Online Privacy Protection Act is a good example. Rather than get parental consent for collecting children's e-mail addresses, companies prefer to remain ignorant that there are any children on their websites.

Or consider the Health Insurance Portability and Accountability Act of 1996, which is supposed to give people access to their medical records, allowing them to bring records to their next provider. It also prohibits the sale of identifiable health data for marketing purposes, but "de-identified" data is largely exempt from the restrictions. As a result, many pharmacies do a lucrative business selling de-identified prescription records to giant national databases. (Vermont tried to ban the sale of pharmacy records, but the Supreme Court struck down its law, stating that its restrictions on pharmaceutical manufacturers' ability to conduct marketing violated the First Amendment.)

Or consider the Federal Privacy Act, which is supposed to force federal agencies to obtain consent before sharing a citizen's information with other agencies for purposes that aren't "compatible" with the reason the data were originally collected. But, instead of seeking consent, agencies simply describe their interagency data sharing as a "routine use," which is exempted under the act. As a result, the Privacy Act failed to prevent the National Counterterrorism Center from downloading entire databases of citizen files from other government agencies to look for terrorism clues.

Privacy laws based on consent inevitably seem to end up creating manufactured consent.

◆

Privacy laws that give people the right to see the data that is used against them, however, seem like a good idea.

Consider the injustice of the terrorist watch list. In 2009, Gulet Mohamed, a U.S. citizen who was born in Somalia and had immigrated to the United States when he was three years old, went to visit relatives in Somalia for several months and then moved to Kuwait to study Arabic and live with an uncle.

On December 20, 2010, Mohamed went to the Kuwait airport to renew his visa, as he had done every three months since his arrival. While he was at the airport, two men approached him, handcuffed him, blindfolded him, and drove him to an undisclosed location. Mohamed, who was only eighteen years old at the time, says he was tortured for more than a week, whipped with sticks, and forced to stand for long periods; at one time his arms were tied to a ceiling beam until he passed out. He was questioned about the militant leader Anwar al-Awlaki.

On December 28, he was transferred to a deportation facility, where he was visited by FBI agents. He refused to answer questions without a lawyer, and they said he would be detained indefinitely if he didn't answer questions. On January 12, he was again visited by the FBI and again he refused to answer their questions. Finally, on January 16, 2011, Kuwaiti officials took him to the airport and gave him an airline ticket to the United States, which his family had purchased. However, Mohamed was not allowed onto the plane because he was on the no-fly list. Eventually, he was allowed to fly home on January 21. But he has not been able to fly since then.

Mohamed's ordeal was likely triggered by some piece of personal data gathered about him. But he has not been allowed to see that data. Instead, the government argues that he should seek redress by filing a claim with the Department of Homeland Security's Traveler Redress Inquiry Program (TRIP). Travelers who are denied boarding can submit their information to the department, which will assess whether they have been improperly targeted because they share a name with someone on the watch list or because of some other misunderstanding. However, the department is not required to offer individuals who are on the watch list an opportunity to challenge their inclusion; in fact, the department does not ever confirm or deny if they are on the list. Mohamed claims that by denying him a "constitutionally sufficient legal mechanism" to challenge his inclusion on the no-fly list, he is being denied his constitutional right to due process of law.

This is the worst kind of abuse of personal data: Mohamed was tortured and to this day cannot board an airplane, for reasons that he does not know, and he is told that he cannot challenge those reasons in a court of law. Not all data abuses are as dreadful as in Mohamed's case, but his plight reminds me how important it is to have a mechanism to allow people to see the data that are used against them.

There is already a growing movement to hold companies accountable for the data they hold about individuals. The European Union requires companies to provide citizens access to the data that are held about them. In 2011, Senators John McCain and John Kerry proposed commercial privacy legislation that would have required data collectors to provide individuals with access to their data, a chance to opt out, and an opportunity to decline having their data shared with some third parties. However, the legislation was opposed by both privacy advocates and data brokers and failed to make progress. In 2012, the Obama administration declared that it wouldn't wait for Congress to act on privacy, and instead launched an effort to get the commercial data industry to develop voluntary compliance with a set of privacy standards, including offering individuals access to their data.

One of the most successful methods of holding data brokers accountable is the Fair Credit Reporting Act, which allows people to access, correct, and dispute the commercial data that are used to evaluate them for financial decisions. As a result, even though my credit report contained inaccuracies, it was easy for me to fix them. The law also requires anyone who uses my credit report to deny me a loan, insurance, or employment to notify me of the underlying reason for the rejection and give me an opportunity to dispute the information.

Of course, the credit-reporting law has its flaws. It can be too difficult to dispute the data contained in credit reports. It covers only certain kinds of financial decisions. And it's too easy for big data brokers that have detailed dossiers about individuals to claim their data is not covered by the law. The credit-scoring company eBureau, which pegged me as a high school dropout, for instance, says its scores are used to "evaluate" people for marketing purposes, but not to approve people for credit, loans, or insurance—which could mean that its scores are not covered by the law.

Federal Trade commissioner Julie Brill has advocated for the law to be expanded to cover a wider swath of data usage, particularly if personal data are used to decide "whether we are too risky to do business with or aren't right for certain clubs, dating services, schools or other programs." She has asked data brokers to voluntarily give individuals access to their data, an opportunity to correct their data, and to opt out of its use for marketing. But since the Federal Trade Commission is not empowered to easily write rules—unlike the Environmental Protection Agency—all Brill can do is encourage the data industry to regulate itself, unless the industry's activities cross the line and violate more general laws, such as the FTC's ban on "unfair and deceptive" practices.

In an information economy, we probably need an Information Protection Agency that is empowered to police the information economy, with a particular focus on bringing transparency and accountability to data handling and usage.

✦

But just creating an Information Protection Agency is not going to be enough to police government surveillance or to remedy the plight of people like Gulet Mohamed.

When it comes to government surveillance, we have tended to allow dragnets when the benefits to society appear to outweigh the intrusiveness of the search. We tolerate surprise workplace visits from government inspectors. We allow police to set up dragnet roadblocks to search for drunk drivers. We endure drug testing in certain workplaces.

But we don't accept dragnets that are too intrusive for their purpose. We rejected airport body scanners that revealed the contours of individuals' naked bodies. We do not embed tracking microchips under our children's skin, the way that we do with pet dogs. We do not place surveillance cameras in bathroom stalls.

And we demand that government dragnets not be racially discriminatory. In 2013, Judge Shira Scheindlin of the federal district court ruled that the New York Police Department's "stop and frisk" dragnet violated the Constitution by targeting otherwise suspicionless young black and Hispanic men. "No one should live in fear of being stopped whenever he leaves his home to go about the activities of daily life," she wrote.

Of course, sometimes, in the heat of wartime, we have allowed government dragnets to go too far. In 1944, the Supreme Court ruled that the detention of more than one hundred thousand Japanese Americans during World War II was lawful because "it was impossible to bring about an immediate segregation of the disloyal from the loyal." In an impassioned dissent, Justice Frank Murphy wrote that the ruling "goes over 'the very brink of constitutional power' and falls into the ugly abyss of racism."

Still, despite its missteps, in recent years the court seems to have set out a compelling set of questions to ask when judging the fairness of a dragnet:

- Is the dragnet too intrusive for its purpose?
- Does it benefit society?
- Does it fall into the ugly abyss of racism (or other prejudices)?

These admittedly fuzzy criteria reminded me of the publicity test that I had used to evaluate whether I could justify lying about my identity. In that situation, I decided that a reasonable person would support my lies because they were limited in scope, not intended to harm, and were my attempt to remedy an unfair situation. Now, in the wake of Edward Snowden's revelations, the public was evaluating whether the NSA's dragnets passed the publicity test.

The publicity test is also reminiscent of one of the most effective tactics of the environmental movement. Every year, the Environmental Protection Agency publishes a list of the companies that store the most toxic pollutants in its Toxics Release Inventory. The publicity of the list caused companies to compete to hold fewer toxins, which then resulted in fewer spills. "Everybody wants to avoid being high on that list," said Lisa Heinzerling, a Georgetown University environmental law professor. "That's been a big success story."

I wondered if maybe the solution for government dragnets was a similar push for transparency. This is the essence of an argument raised by Christopher Slobogin, a Vanderbilt University law professor who has extensively studied government dragnets. He suggests that courts should ban government dragnets that are not specifically authorized by legislatures. "While leaving courts in control of search and seizure law in individual cases, it reinforces democratic values . . . when the search or seizure is of a group," he wrote. In addition, he suggests that courts could still curb dragnets if they are too intrusive or biased against a particular group.

In short, he argues that the government dragnets must not be covert. They must be scrutinized by either a legislative body or a court.

✦

Surveillance dragnets are inherently unfair. By definition, they capture the innocent and the guilty indiscriminately. In doing so, they create a culture of fear—in which people like Sharon Gill and Bilal Ahmed are afraid to talk online about their mental issues, in which Yasir Afifi cuts off his friendship with his friend who says dumb things online.

Okay, so life is unfair. The question becomes: How unfair is acceptable?

We tolerate a lot of unfairness in society. Some people are rich; some are poor. Some children go to good public schools; some children go to terrible public schools. Some people live near nice parks and greenery; other people live in places with no green space.

But there is some unfairness we don't tolerate. We don't tolerate people stealing and getting away with it. We don't tolerate bribery. We don't tolerate companies that sell goods that injure people.

Our sense of fairness changes over time. We used to think it was fair for children to work long hours on assembly lines. Then we didn't. We used to think it was fair for companies to pollute our rivers and skies. Then we didn't. We used to think it was fair to leave our dog's poop on the sidewalk. Then we didn't.

As citizens of a democracy, we get to make these decisions.

For data dragnets, we have already seen that transparency and account-ability work with credit reports. And we have witnessed the criteria that judges use to assess dragnets. Putting those together with the publicity test, I believe that we can assemble a list of six questions that should be asked of every dragnet:

- Does the dragnet provide individuals with legal right to access, correct, and dispute the data?
- Are the dragnet operators held accountable for the way the data are used?

- Is the dragnet too intrusive for its purpose?
- Does it benefit society?
- Does it fall into the ugly abyss of racism (or other prejudices)?
- Can it withstand public scrutiny?

By asking these questions of every dragnet, I hope that we can distinguish the intolerably unfair dragnets from those that we can tolerate.

Some of today's technological dragnets would not survive the test. Consider online and retail tracking. By following our every click online or tracking our cell phones in a shopping mall, they are too intrusive for their frivolous purpose of marketing. Nor do they provide any opportunity for redress.

Or consider the NSA's dragnets. The agency has yet to provide convincing evidence that its dragnets of innocent Americans have benefited society enough to overcome their intrusiveness. Individuals have no access to their data, and the legality of the sweeping dragnets is judged by a secret court.

Or consider the New York City Police Department's infiltration of Muslim mosques and community groups, a racially targeted dragnet that appears to have fallen into the ugly abyss of racism.

But other dragnets might survive the test. Police use of surveillance and license plate cameras might be beneficial enough to society to justify their intrusiveness, particularly if alleged criminals have an opportunity to challenge the footage in court. Data brokers that are accountable for their data—the same way that credit-rating agencies are—could also pass the test.

Even Freestylers such as Google and Facebook could perhaps pass the fairness test if they limited the intrusiveness of their tracking, provided more meaningful and real access to their data, and were held accountable for data they shared with others.

My unfairness checklist is almost certainly not perfect. But it is an attempt to carve a middle path between those who ask us to hand over all our data and "get over it," and those who suggest that we throw our body on the tracks in front of the speeding train that is our data economy. Nobody, including me, wants to give up on all the benefits of our information economy—with its magical maps and facts at our fingerprints and the ability to connect with anyone in the world in an instant. But nor should any of us simply give up all of our data without any assurances that it will not come back to bite us.

We didn't shut down the industrial economy to stop pollution. We simply asked the polluters to be more accountable for their actions. We passed laws and created a new governmental agency and forced polluters to be transparent. Similarly, we don't need to shut down the data economy. We just need to make the data handlers let us see what they have about us and be accountable for any harm caused by their use of our data.

If we succeed at finding this middle path, we might find ourselves in a shiny new world where privacy is not a goal in and of itself. We might find that privacy was just a shield we had been holding up to protect ourselves from harm. If the harm is contained, we might be able to lower the shield enough that my children could post their own videos on YouTube, Sharon and Bilal could renew their conversations on the PatientsLikeMe medical forum, and Yasir and Khaled could reclaim their childhood friendship.

That would be a world I would want to leave to my children.

AFTERWORD

When it comes to privacy, the world can be divided into two epochs: the time before Edward Snowden's revelations and the time after.

Privacy was a niche issue before Snowden revealed the scope of the U.S. government's mass spying operations. Sure, some people were alarmed by Facebook's repeated changes to its privacy settings or by Google's pervasive online tracking infrastructure. But many more were enthralled enough by the benefits of the technology to ignore the occasional privacy hiccup. Now, not a day goes by without dozens of news stories about privacy. Software and services that claim to protect users' privacy pop up every day.

I wrote this book in a strange time that straddled those two worlds. I was two-thirds finished with my draft of the manuscript when *The Guardian* published its first story based on Snowden's revelations, about the National Security Agency's bulk collection of domestic telephone calling records.

I remember exactly where I was when I heard the news. It was the afternoon of June 5, 2013, and I was talking with two technologists in a public park near the San Francisco waterfront. I was feeling quite proud of myself for being able to hold up my end of a fairly technical conversation about various countersurveillance techniques. Suddenly, one of the technologists, Christopher Soghoian, broke into the conversation to show me his cell phone screen displaying the *Guardian* article.

I was shocked. I considered myself to be on the far end of the privacy paranoia curve, but even I had not read such boundlessness into Senator Ron Wyden's cryptic warnings in 2011 about surveillance: "When the American people find out how their government has secretly interpreted the Patriot Act, they will be stunned and they will be angry."

Wyden's warning prompted me, along with several other journalists, to try to figure out what the senator was referring to. Piecing together various clues that indicated he was talking about phone surveillance, I theorized that the NSA had been testing a program to track individuals' locations via cell phone. But I always imagined it as a small-scale program targeted at people located near a terrorist suspect. I never imagined that he was referring to a program that tracked every single American's phone calls.

In other words, I had been under-paranoid.

It would not be the first time I found myself in that position. As the Snowden revelations unfolded in a steady drip of news over the coming year, I would continually find myself surprised. I had not envisioned that the NSA would infiltrate links to the data centers of Google and Yahoo!, or that it would seek to undermine cryptographic standards, or that it had eavesdropped on prominent Muslim Americans, including one staunch Republican Muslim official who had served in the George W. Bush administration.

After Snowden, another whistle-blower emerged. A former State Department section chief named John Napier Tye went public in the summer of 2014 with allegations that a presidential executive order authorizing the NSA to conduct foreign intelligence also allows the NSA to collect the domestic communications of nearly every American, because American communications are often stored or transit overseas. In an editorial in *The Washington Post*, Tye wrote: "Based in part on classified facts that I am prohibited by law from publishing, I believe that Americans should be even more concerned about the collection and storage of their communications under Executive Order 12333 than under Section 215," the law that authorized the NSA's phone dragnet. The agency acknowledges that its dragnets sweep up "incidental" domestic communications, but says that those communications are not usually searched or analyzed.

Even now, as I write, more Snowden-fueled news continues to trickle out every few weeks, making it difficult to assess the full magnitude of his revelations.

And yet it is already clear that the conversation about privacy has irrevocably changed. Before Snowden, it seemed paranoid to imagine that democratic, free societies were exploiting every possible vulnerability in the Internet's infrastructure to conduct mass surveillance. Now it seems naive to believe otherwise.

The Snowden revelations also coincided with increased aggressiveness on the part of commercial data gatherers—perhaps because public attention was focused on the National Security Agency. The online tracking industry ramped up its resistance to a standard "Do Not Track" setting that users could enable in their Web browser to block tracking with a single click. As of this writing, the large online ad tracking networks Google, Yahoo!, and Facebook ignore the Do Not Track button in most cases, and the industry-wide effort to build consensus on Do Not Track appears to be dead.

At the same time, online trackers have instituted more intrusive techniques to identify users by name. Facebook said it would begin tracking its users across the Web using widgets including the "Like" button— which would allow Facebook to keep tabs on its members by name as they browse the Internet—and did not offer users an opt-out in its privacy settings. Other tracking companies also began using the technique, often called "onboarding," that identifies users when they log into a Web site, thus allowing Internet tracking companies to match users' online and offline identities.

Some trackers began using a persistent, difficult-to-block tracking technique called "canvas fingerprinting," which instructs the visitor's Web browser to draw a hidden image. Because each computer draws the image slightly differently, the images can be used to assign each user's device a number that uniquely identifies it. As of this writing, the only Web browser that can block canvas fingerprinting without the installation of additional software is the Tor Web browser.

In other words, commercial data gatherers are also racing to exploit every possible vulnerability in the Internet's infrastructure to conduct mass surveillance.

At first glance, it appears that there hasn't been much of a response to the rising tide of surveillance. There have been a few protests, but not many. President Obama made a speech promising a few modest reforms to NSA surveillance and commissioned a study of the privacy effects of big data. Congress has considered—but not yet passed—legislation that would end the NSA's phone dragnet but would leave intact the NSA's worldwide eavesdropping apparatus. There has been no political movement on legislation that would curb commercial data gathering.

But beneath the surface, the ocean is roiling. In 2013 and 2014, Oregon, Montana, Illinois, Idaho, Indiana, Iowa, Tennessee, Texas, Wisconsin, and Florida enacted laws requiring law enforcement officers, in most cases, to get a search warrant before conducting surveillance using drone aircraft. During that time, California enacted two forward-looking privacy laws: a requirement that Web sites disclose whether they honor users' Do Not Track requests; and a so-called "eraser" bill that would allow a minor to remove content that he or she had posted on a Web site.

Meanwhile, in 2014, the European Court of Justice ruled that Google must comply with the European data protection laws, which allow individuals to request that data gatherers remove information about them that harms their fundamental right to privacy and is not in the public interest. The case was triggered by a Spanish man's request for removal of links to a sixteen-year-old newspaper article about proceedings related to the recovery of his social security debts. The court ruled that he had a right to have links to the newspaper article removed from Google's search results for his name. Since then, Google has processed requests for removal of links from tens of thousands of European residents. When Google approves a request, it removes the offending link from the search results that are returned upon a search of that user's name. However, the links remain online and can still show up in search results for other queries.

Web users also appear to be taking increased action to protect their own privacy. The search engine DuckDuckGo, which I discuss in chapter 8, has seen its traffic more than double since the Snowden revelations. The number of people using online ad-blocking tools is estimated to have almost tripled after the Snowden revelations—to 144 million in June 2014, up from just 54 million a year earlier, according to a study by a company that sells tools to help Web sites prevent ad blocking.

A small but growing market for privacy services also seems to have emerged. Most notably, in the fall of 2014, Apple began touting its commitment to privacy as part of the campaign for its new iPhone 6. And nearly every day I receive e-mail from start-ups that are offering privacy-protecting services, and many of them are charging fees for their services. The Blackphone, a $629 Android-based smartphone that is installed with privacy-protecting software that allows users to send encrypted texts and make encrypted calls, says it has sold thousands of units. And a New York entrepreneur named Adam Harvey sold out his first run of the OFF Pocket—an $80 cell phone case that blocks signals to and from the phone.

Add it all up and it's not quite a revolution. But it's an evolution. We are still a dragnet nation—in fact, a dragnet world—but there has been movement toward establishing technological and legal limits on the dragnets.

So, what kind of limits are we going to set?

It would be unfortunate if we set only technological limits, which would mean that privacy would largely be available just to people like myself, who have the money, time, and technological expertise to implement countersurveillance tools. In the course of reporting this book, I spent nearly $2,500 and countless hours on privacy-protecting technology. Some of the most expensive items on my list: $200 for encrypted cloud storage, $640 for a cell phone and service under another name, $125 for encryption software, and $70 for password-management software. At those prices, privacy is well on its way to becoming a luxury good.

And even after paying through the nose, I am likely to be outspent and outgunned by government and commercial data gatherers with better tools.

A better option would be that we all agree to set some legal limits on the dragnets. I like to draw a comparison to automobiles. Driving a car is extremely dangerous, but most of us do it every day. The reason: we know that cars must meet some baseline safety standards before they can be sold. It seems to me that we ought to set similar baseline limits for surveillance.

Of course, the intelligence agencies and the commercial data gatherers all say that they have set their own limits, and that they are judiciously self-policing their data gathering practices. But should we trust the watchers to watch themselves?

I heard a compelling answer to that question the day after the first Snowden revelations. It came from the lunchtime keynote speaker at a Privacy Law Scholars Conference in Berkeley, California.

The speaker was Magistrate Judge Stephen Smith of Houston, Texas, who has written several defining opinions challenging the constitutionality of law enforcement using cell phone surveillance without a search warrant. I expected him to talk about his decade-long legal battles on this topic. But he did not.

Instead, he opened with the usual self-deprecatory remark about how he had at first thought that the invitation to speak was sent to him by mistake. Then he turned to the topic of mistakes in general: "Government officials—myself included—don't like to admit mistakes. Often they—we—are blissfully unaware of those mistakes. So we need to keep an eye on what government does to be able to discover and correct those mistakes."

Smith then traced the history of judicial openness, arguing that public proceedings have conferred legitimacy on courts. In 1581, the great jurist of the Elizabethan era, Sir Edward Coke, wrote of a judge that rules from his chambers, "offendeth he the law." In 1676, the early American colonists in the province of West New Jersey wrote that courts must be open to the public and that "justice may not be done in any corner." And in 2006, Judge Frank Easterbrook of the U.S. Court of Appeals for the Seventh Circuit wrote that what happens in federal court "is presumptively open" to public scrutiny.

"Are secret courts really courts at all? I rather doubt it," Smith concluded.

Smith described a rising tide of secrecy in the courts, particularly with regard to surveillance. In 1978, the U.S. Foreign Intelligence Surveillance Court was established—its hearings and decisions are secret and rarely declassified. Smith estimates that he and his fellow magistrate judges issued more than thirty thousand secret electronic surveillance orders in 2006—and likely issued even more in the years since then.

"Without transparency, we are at the mercy of judges," he concluded. "And trust me, judges should not be trusted."

It's not just government that wants us to trust our data to their secret courts. In June 2014, Facebook revealed that as part of a research study two years earlier, it had manipulated the news feeds of seven hundred thousand users for one week. Some users saw a reduction in updates from friends that included happy and positive words. Other users saw a decrease in updates from friends that included negative and unhappy words.

The study was meant to demonstrate the existence of "emotional contagion" on the social network—users posted happier updates when they saw happy updates in their feed. But the study also demonstrated something else: that Facebook seemed to think that it didn't need any public oversight in deciding to manipulate the emotions of its users.

If the Facebook study had been conducted at a university, academic ethics would require informed consent from its participants. But Facebook is not subject to the ethical rules of academia. And, of course, the fine print in its privacy policy covers all sorts of data usage for internal research purposes.

When the results of the test were released in the *Proceedings of the National Academy of Sciences,* a huge outcry erupted. Scholars decried the fact that Facebook operated outside the boundaries of typical ethical constraints on research. Facebook users were shocked that their news feeds had been manipulated without their consent. The journal subsequently published an "Editorial Expression of Concern," admitting that it was "a matter of concern that the collection of the data by Facebook may have involved practices that were not fully consistent with the principles of obtaining informed consent and allowing participants to opt out."

Facebook's response? Four months after the study was revealed, Facebook announced that it had "taken to heart the comments and criticism," and announced it would set up an internal review board—comprised of Facebook employees—to review future research projects based on internal guidelines that it did not disclose.

In other words: Trust us. We are a secret court, but we have your best interests at heart.

That appears to be a view shared by most Silicon Valley companies. Consider the reaction of the dating Web site OKCupid to the Facebook study. Christian Rudder, one of the site's founders, wrote a blog post defending Facebook's actions and describing several experiments that OKCupid had conducted on its users, including telling users that they were compatible when they were not.

"But guess what, everybody: if you use the Internet, you're the subject of hundreds of experiments at any given time, on every site," Rudder wrote. "That's how Web sites work."

I hope that readers of my book will have learned some tools and tactics to navigate the dragnets that aim to manipulate our emotions and determine our futures. But if I were to write it over again, I would add a heavier emphasis on the need for collective action to rein in surveillance.

In the post-Snowden era, the central question we face is no longer *if* we are being spied on, but *who* gets to decide how our data is used. Who watches the watchers? Will it be a secret court? Or will the public oversee the watchers? As citizens of a democracy, we hold the answer in our hands.

NOTES

1. HACKED

1 *Sharon is a forty-two-year-old single mother*: Sharon Gill, in discussion with author, July 12, 2013.

2 *Bilal Ahmed, thirty-six years old*: Bilal Ahmed, in discussion with author, January 27, 2013.

2 *"I live in a small town"*: Sharon Gill, in discussion with author, July 12, 2013.

2 *On May 7, 2010, PatientsLikeMe noticed*: Julia Angwin and Steve Stecklow, "'Scrapers' Dig Deep for Data on Web," *Wall Street Journal*, October 12, 2010, http://online.wsj.com/article/SB10001424052748703358504575544381288117888 .html.

2 *The website was also selling data*: Ben Heywood, "Transparency, Openness and Privacy," *The Value of Openness Blog*, May 20, 2010, http://blog.patientslikeme.com/2010 /05/20/bentransparencymessage/.

2 *"I felt totally violated"*: Angwin and Stecklow, "'Scrapers' Dig Deep."

2 *Nielsen was operating in a gray area*: Kim Zetter, "Prosecutors Drop Plans to Appeal Lori Drew Case," *Wired, Threat Level* (blog), November 20, 2009, http://www.wired .com/threatlevel/2009/11/lori-drew-appeal/.

3 *Privacy is often defined*: Merriam-Webster Online, accessed June 5, 2013, http://www .merriam-webster.com/dictionary/privacy.

3 *Dragnets that indiscriminately sweep*: For an in-depth look at the gap between legal and socially acceptable tracking, please consult: Helen Nissenbaum, *Privacy in Context: Technology, Policy, and the Integrity of Social Life* (Stanford, Calif.: Stanford Law School, 2010).

3 *We are living in a Dragnet Nation*: For a deeper discussion of why indiscriminate tracking is so problematic: Susan Freiwald, "First Principles of Communications Privacy," *Stanford Technology Law Review* 3 (2007), http://stlr.stanford.edu/pdf /freiwald-first-principles.pdf; and Christopher Slobogin, "Government Dragnets,"

Vanderbilt Law and Economics Research Paper No. 10–25 (2010), http://ssrn.com/abstract=1640108.

3 *Computer processing power has doubled*: "Moore's Law at 40: Happy Birthday," *Economist*, March 23, 2005, http://www.economist.com/node/3798505.

3 *recently, the cost to store data*: Julia Angwin and Jennifer Valentino-DeVries, "New Tracking Frontier: Your License Plates," *Wall Street Journal*, September 29, 2012, http://online.wsj.com/article/SB10000872396390443995604578004723603576296.html.

4 *In addition to its scooping up vast amounts of foreign communications*: "NSA Inspector General Report on Email and Internet Data Collection Under Stellar Wind—Full Document," *Guardian*, June 27, 2013, http://www.theguardian.com/world/interactive/2013/jun/27/nsa-inspector-general-report-document-data-collection.

4 *But the NSA is not alone*: "Which Governments Are in the Market," *The Surveillance Catalog* (blog), *Wall Street Journal*, February 7, 2012, http://projects.wsj.com/surveillance-catalog/attendees/.

4 *ranging from "massive intercept" equipment*: Jennifer Valentino-Devries, Julia Angwin, and Steve Stecklow, "Document Trove Exposes Surveillance Methods," *Wall Street Journal*, November 19, 2011, http;//online.wsj.com/article/SB10001424052970203611404577044192607407780.html.

4 *Even local and state governments*: Andy Pasztor and John Emshwiller, "Drone Use Takes Off on the Home Front," *Wall Street Journal*, April 21, 2012, http://online.wsj.com/article/SB10001424052702304331204577354331959335276.html.

4 *to automated license plate readers*: Angwin and Valentino-DeVries, "New Tracking Frontier: Your License Plates."

4 *Local police are increasingly*: Julia Angwin and Scott Thurm, "Judges Weigh Phone Tracking," *Wall Street Journal*, November 9, 2011, http://online.wsj.com/article/SB10001424052970203733504577024092345458210.html.

4 *AT&T and Verizon are selling*: Mike Dano, "The Sale of (Anonymous) Wireless Users' Location and Behavior Is Already Big Business," *FierceWireless* (online newsletter), May 23, 2013, www.fiercewireless.com/story/sale-anonymous-wireless-users-location-and-behavior-already-big-business/2013-05-23.

4 *Mall owners have started*: Euclid Analytics, "Euclid Analytics—How It Works," accessed March 2, 2013, http://euclidanalytics.com/product/how; and Stephanie Clifford and Quentin Hardy, "Attention, Shoppers: Store Is Tracking Your Cell," *New York Times*, July 14, 2013, http://www.nytimes.com/2013/07/15/business/attention-shopper-stores-are-tracking-your-cell.html?hp.

4 *Retailers such as Whole Foods*: Pam Dixon, "Privacy Implications of the New Digital Signage Networks," World Privacy Forum, January 27, 2010, http://www.ftc.gov/os/comments/privacyroundtable/544506-00112.pdf.

4 *Some car dealerships*: Jennifer Valentino-DeVries and Jeremy Singer-Vine, "They Know What You're Shopping For," *Wall Street Journal*, December 7, 2012, http://online.wsj.com/article/SB10001424127887324784404578143144132736214.html.

4 *Searching for a bra*: Julia Angwin, "The Web's New Gold Mine: Your Secrets," *Wall Street Journal*, July 30, 2010, http://online.wsj.com/article/SB10001424052748703940904575395073512989404.html.

4 *companies are building facial recognition technology into phones and cameras*: Emily Steel and Julia Angwin, "Device Raises Fear of Facial Profiling," *Wall Street Journal*, July 13, 2011, http://online.wsj.com/article/SB10001424052702303678704576440253307985070.html.

5 *technology to monitor your location*: Keith Barry, "Insurance Company Telematics Trade Perks for Privacy," *Wired*, August 19, 2011, http://www.wired.com/autopia /2011/08/insurance-company-telematics-trade-perks-for-privacy/.

5 *wireless "smart" meters*: Jim Marston and Joshua Hart, "Should Consumers Participate in Their Utility's Smart-Meter Program?," *Wall Street Journal*, April 12, 2013, http://online.wsj.com/article/SB10001424127887323415304578368683701371280 .html.

5 *Google has developed Glass*: "Glass," Google Inc., accessed July 22, 2013, http://www .google.com/glass/start/.

5 *The confidentiality of personal information*: "Protecting Your Answers," United States Census, 2010, https://www.census.gov/2010census/about/protect.php.

5 *During World War I*: William Seltzer and Margo Anderson, "Government Statistics and Individual Safety: Revisiting the Historical Record of Disclosure, Harm, and Risk." Paper prepared for presentation at a workshop, "Access to Research Data: Assessing Risks and Opportunities," organized by the Panel on Confidential Data Access for Research Purposes, Committee on National Statistics (CNSTAT), the National Academies, Washington, D.C., October 16–17, 2003, https://pantherfile.uwm .edu/margo/www/govstat/WS-MAcnstat.pdf

5 *During World War II*: J. R. Minkel, "Confirmed: The U.S. Census Bureau Gave Up Names of Japanese-Americans in WW II," *Scientific American*, March 30, 2007, https://www.scientificamerican.com/article.cfm?id=confirmed-the-us-census-b& sc=I100322.

5 *And in 2002 and 2003, the Census Bureau*: Lynette Clemetson, "Homeland Security Given Data on Arab-Americans," *New York Times*, July 30, 2004, http://www .nytimes.com/2004/07/30/us/homeland-security-given-data-on-arab-americans .html.

5 *After bad publicity, it revised its policies*: Robert C. Bonner, Commissioner, United States Customs and Border Protection, "Policy for Requesting Information of a Sensitive Nature from the Census Bureau" (memo), August 9, 2004, https://epic.org/pri vacy/census/foia/policy.pdf.

5 *The United States is not alone*: William Seltzer, "On the Use of Population Data Systems to Target Vulnerable Population Subgroups for Human Rights Abuses," *Coyuntura Social*, no. 32 (June 2005): pp. 31–44, https://pantherfile.uwm.edu/margo/www /govstat/CoyunturaSocialpaper2005.pdf.

5 *Australia used population registration*: Ellen Percy Kraly and John McQuilton, "The 'Protection' of Aborigines in Colonial and Early Federation Australia: The Role of Population Data Systems," *Population, Space and Place* 11 (2005): 225–50, http://ro .uow.edu.au/era/172/.

5 *In South Africa, the census*: A. J. Christopher, "'To Define the Indefinable': Population Classification and the Census in South Africa," *Area* 34, no. 4 (2002): 401–8.

5 *During the Rwandan genocide of 1994*: Prosecutor v. Jean-Paul Akayesu, Case No. ICTR-96-4, Judgement of 2 September 1998, http://www.humanrights.is/the-human -rights-project/humanrightscasesandmaterials/cases/internationalcases/tribunal forrawanda/.

5 *During the Holocaust*: William Seltzer, "Population Statistics, the Holocaust, and the Nuremberg Trials," *Population and Development Review* 24, no. 3 (September 1998): 511–52, https://pantherfile.uwm.edu/margo/www/govstat/seltzer.pdf.

6 *One of the most infamous cases was a program*: "Dr. Martin Luther King, Jr., Case Study," *Final Report of the Select Committee to Study Governmental Operations with*

Respect to Intelligence Activities United States Senate, April 23, 1976, http://www
.aarclibrary.org/publib/church/reports/book3/pdf/ChurchB3_2_MLK.pdf.

6 *Consider how Chinese hackers*: RSA, "Anatomy of an Attack," *Speaking of Security:
The Official RSA Blog and Podcast*, April 1, 2011, http://blogs.rsa.com/anatomy-of-an
-attack/.

7 *In 1999, a deranged man named Liam Youens*: Helen Remsburg, *Administratrix of
the Estate of Amy Lynn Boyer v. Docusearch, Inc.*, No. CV-00-211-B (N.H. 2002),
http://www.courts.state.nh.us/supreme/opinions/2003/remsb017.htm.

7 *Boyer's parents got very little*: Holly Ramer, "Mother of Slain Woman Settles Lawsuit
Against Info-Broker," *USA Today*, March 10, 2004, http://usatoday30.usatoday.com
/tech/news/internetprivacy/2004-03-10-boyer-suit-settled_x.htm?POE=TECISVA.

7 *Docusearch is still in business*: the website of Docusearch, docusearch.com.

7 *Since then, the price of buying people's addresses*: Boyer, CV-00-211-B.

7 *to as low as 95 cents for a full report*: Intelius.com.

7 *Consider just one example: In 2010*: Andy Furillo, "Wife of Slain Officer Satisfied
with Murder Verdict Against Vue," *Sacto 9-1-1* (blog), *Sacramento Bee*, September
29, 2010, http://blogs.sacbee.com/crime/archives/2010/09/chu-vue-found-g.html.

7 *During the trial it came out that Vue*: Kim Minugh, "Former Deputy Sought Data on
Slain Man, Trial Is Told," *Sacramento Bee*, August 17, 2010.

7 *had asked a colleague to look up*: Ibid.

7 *and had searched for Lo's address*: Andy Furillo, "Cell Phone Calls Place Vues near
Slaying Victim," *Sacramento Bee*, August 24, 2010.

7 *Vue was sentenced*: Andy Furillo, "Ex-Deputy Gets Life for Arranging Correctional
Officer's Murder," *Sacramento Bee*, November 29, 2010, http://blogs.sacbee.com/crime
/archives/2010/11/ex-deputy-gets.html.

7 *In 2007, a Commerce Department employee*: United States Department of Justice,
"Former Department of Commerce Agent Indicted for Making a False Statement
and Exceeding Authorized Access to a Government Database" (press release), September 19, 2007, http://www.justice.gov/criminal/cybercrime/press-releases/2007/
robinsonIndict.htm.

7 *After a breakup with a woman*: U.S. v. Benjamin Robinson, CR-07-00596 (N.D.
Cal., 2001), http://ia600500.us.archive.org/11/items/gov.uscourts.cand.195976/gov
.uscourts.cand.195976.1.0.pdf.

8 *In 2009, Robinson pleaded guilty to unlawfully*: Ibid.

8 *radio-frequency identification (RFID) chips*: "FAQ on RFID and RFID Privacy," *RSA
Laboratories*, accessed September 8, 2013, http://www.emc.com/emc-plus/rsa-labs
/research-areas/faq-on-rfid-and-rfid-privacy.htm#4.

8 *in passports*: "The U.S. Electronic Passport Frequently Asked Questions," Travel.
State.Gov, A Service of the Bureau of Consular Affairs, accessed July 21, 2013, http://
travel.state.gov/passport/passport_2788.html.

8 *In 2013, a federal judge in Texas*: Steve Hernandez v. Northside Independent School
District, SA-12-Ca-1113-OG (W.D. Tex. 2013), https://www.rutherford.org/files
_images/general/01-08-2013_Hernandez_Ruling.pdf.

8 *California to outlaw*: Mandalit Del Barco, "California Law Outlaws RFID Implant
Mandate," *National Public Radio*, January 1, 2008, http://www.npr.org/templates
/transcript/transcript.php?storyId=17762244.

8 *Cell phone tracking has already become routine*: Angwin and Thurm, "Judges Weigh
Phone Tracking."

8 *Eight agencies produced at least summary statistics*: Scott Thurm and Justin Scheck,

"Police Respond to WSJ Survey," *Wall Street Journal*, November 8, 2011, http://online.wsj.com/article/SB10001424052970203733504577024283882878896.html.

8 *It is as routine*: Angwin and Thurm, "Judges Weigh Phone Tracking."

8 *In 2013, Verizon said it would*: Anton Troianovski, "Phone Firms Sell Data on Customers," *Wall Street Journal*, May 21, 2013, http://online.wsj.com/article/SB10001424127887323463704578497153556847658.html.

8 *In 2009, fifteen-year-old high school student Blake Robbins*: William Bender, "Webcam Uproar Figure Decries 'Unjust' Rumors," *Philadelphia Inquirer*, February 25, 2010, http://articles.philly.com/2010-02-25/news/24956642_1_webcam-blake-robbins-laptops.

9 *Blake and his family said they were Mike and Ike candies*: Mary T. Moore, "Pa. School District's Webcam Surveillance Focus of Suit," *USA Today*, May 5, 2010, http://usatoday30.usatoday.com/tech/news/surveillance/2010-05-02-school-spy_N.htm?loc=interstitialskip.

9 *However, the school did not notify students*: Warren Richey, "Did School Use Laptops to Spy on Students? Feds Won't Press Charges," *Christian Science Monitor*, August 17, 2010, http://www.csmonitor.com/USA/Justice/2010/0817/Did-school-use-laptops-to-spy-on-students-Feds-won-t-press-charges.

9 *An internal investigation revealed*: John P. Martin, "Lower Merion Schools Hit with New Webcam Spying Suit," *Philadelphia Inquirer*, June 9, 2011, http://articles.philly.com/2011-06-09/news/29638824_1_blake-robbins-jalil-hasan-new-webcam.

9 *Some students were photographed thousands of times*: Ibid.

9 *A former student, Joshua Levin*: Levin v. Lower Merion School District, no. 11:3642 (E.D. Pa. 2011).

9 *Levin, Robbins, and one other student sued*: John P. Martin, "Lower Merion Settles Another Webcam Lawsuit," *Philadelphia Inquirer*, December 28, 2011, http://articles.philly.com/2011-12-28/news/30565544_1_blake-robbins-lower-merion-school-district-school-issued-laptop.

9 *The school board banned*: Minutes of the Lower Merion School Board Business Meeting, August 16, 2010, http://www.lmsd.org/data/files/gallery/BoardMeetingMinutes/BOSD_Minutes_100816.pdf.

9 *It is estimated that there are more than four thousand surveillance*: "Who's Watching: Video Camera Surveillance in New York City and the Need for Public Oversight," New York Civil Liberties Union, Fall 2006, http://www.nyclu.org/pdfs/surveillance_cams_report_121306.pdf.

9 *London is famous for*: Brian Palmer, "Big Apple Is Watching You," *Slate*, May 3, 2010, http://www.slate.com/articles/news_and_politics/explainer/2010/05/big_apple_is_watching_you.html.

9 *In May 2013, a Seattle woman complained*: CHS X-Files, "Capitol Hill Drone Pilot Spotted, Glowing Orbs, Phone Thief on Wheels," *Capitol Hill Seattle* (blog), posted by jseattle, May 8, 2013, http://www.capitolhillseattle.com/2013/05/chs-x-files-capitol-hill-drone-pilot-spotted-glowing-orbs-phone-thief-on-wheels/.

10 *In 2013, the journalist Nate Anderson*: Nate Anderson, "Meet the Men Who Spy on Women Through Their Webcams," *Ars Technica* (blog), March 10, 2013, http://arstechnica.com/tech-policy/2013/03/rat-breeders-meet-the-men-who-spy-on-women-through-their-webcams/.

10 *In 2011, a Santa Ana man named Luis Mijangos*: Federal Bureau of Investigation, "Orange County Man Who Admitted Hacking into Personal Computers Sentenced to Six Years in Federal Prison for 'Sextortion' of Women and Teenage Girls" (press

release), September 1, 2011, https://www.fbi.gov/losangeles/press-releases/2011/orange-county-man-who-admitted-hacking-into-personal-computers-sentenced-to-six-years-in-federal-prison-for-sextortion-of-women-and-teenage-girls.

10 *The* New York Times *columnist Nick Bilton*: Nick Bilton, "At Google Conference, Cameras Even in the Bathroom," *Bits* (blog), *New York Times*, May 17, 2013, http://bits.blogs.nytimes.com/2013/05/17/at-google-conference-even-cameras-in-the-bathroom/.

10 *"I will never live a day . . . without it"*: Robert Scoble, "My Two-Week Review of Google Glass," Google+ post, April 27, 2013, https://plus.google.com/+Scobleizer/posts/ZLV9GdmkRzS.

10 *Bobbi Duncan, a twenty-two-year-old lesbian student*: Geoffrey A. Fowler, "When the Most Personal Secrets Get Outed on Facebook," *Wall Street Journal*, October 13, 2012, http://online.wsj.com/article/SB10000872396390444165804578008740578200224.html.

11 *The most notable example is CIA director David Petraeus*: Scott Shane and Sheryl Gay Stolberg, "A Brilliant Career with a Meteoric Rise and an Abrupt Fall," *New York Times*, November 10, 2012, https://www.nytimes.com/2012/11/11/us/david-petraeus-seen-as-an-invincible-cia-director-self-destructs.html?ref=davidhpetraeus&_r=0.

11 *In 2012, former CIA analyst John Kiriakou*: U.S. v. John Kiriakou, 1:12-CR-127 (E.D. Virg. 2012), https://www.fas.org/sgp/jud/kiriakou/indict.pdf.

11 *He pleaded guilty*: U.S. v. John Kiriakou, 1:12-CR-127 (E.D. Virg. 2012), https://www.fas.org/sgp/jud/kiriakou/012513-judgment.pdf.

11 *People who download porn movies*: "Copyright Trolls," Electronic Frontier Foundation, https://www.eff.org/issues/copyright-trolls.

11 *In July 2012, the U.S. Court of Appeals for the Fifth Circuit*: Matt Zimmerman, "Fifth Circuit Upholds Sanctions Against Copyright Troll Attorney," *Deeplinks Blog*, Electronic Frontier Foundation, July 12, 2012, https://www.eff.org/deeplinks/2012/07/fifth-circuit-upholds-sanctions-award-against-copyright-troll-attorney.

11 *The court described the attorney's "violations"*: Mick Haig Productions v. Does 1-670 v. Evan Stone, No. 11-10977 (appeal denied) (2nd Cir. 2012).

11 *In May 2013, a California judge*: Mitch Stoltz, "Prenda Law Is the Tip of the Iceberg," *Deeplinks Blog*, Electronic Frontier Foundation, May 7, 2013, https://www.eff.org/deeplinks/2013/05/prenda-law-tip-iceberg.

12 *Jaleesa Suell was taken away from her mother*: Jaleesa Suell, *Identity Theft 911* (podcast), http://www.idt911.com/KnowledgeCenter/VideoAndAudio/VideoAndAudioDetail.aspx?a={498D6632-1D69-4FAA-8060-3BD63105D8E2}.

12 *I prefer to call the crime "impersonation"*: Julia Angwin, "The Fallacy of Identity Theft," *Decoder* (blog), *Wall Street Journal*, October 13, 2009, http://online.wsj.com/article/SB125537784669480983.html.

12 *In response to the rising problem of impersonation among foster children*: Child and Family Services Improvement and Innovation Act, Pub. L. No. 112-34, 125 Stat. 369 (2011), http://www.gpo.gov/fdsys/pkg/PLAW-112publ34/pdf/PLAW-112publ34.pdf.

12 *Complaints of identity theft increased*: Federal Trade Commission, "Consumer Sentinel Network Data Book," February 2013.

12 *Credit card fraud used to be the most common complaint*: Steve Toporoff, in discussion with author, March 18, 2013.

13 *In 2013, two Florida women were convicted of defrauding*: U.S. Attorney's Office, Southern District of Florida, "South Florida Women Sentenced in Identity Theft Tax

Refund Fraud Scheme Involving the Filing of Approximately 2,000 Fraudulent Tax Returns Seeking $11 Million Dollars in Refunds" (press release), April 25, 2013, http://www.justice.gov/usao/fls/PressReleases/130425-01.html.

13 *The hospital, Baptist Health South Florida*: Myriam Masihy, "Hospital Identity Theft Found at Some South Florida Hospitals," *NBC 6 South Florida*, March 14, 2013, http://www.nbcmiami.com/investigations/Hospital-Identity-Theft-Growing-Amid -South-Florida-Hospitals-197866811.html.

13 *Public reports of data breaches*: "Data Loss Statistics," *DataLoss DB*, Open Security Foundation, accessed June 24, 2013, http://datalossdb.org/statistics.

13 *Through that network, the hackers gained access*: Federal Trade Commission, "FTC Files Complaint Against Wyndham Hotels for Failure to Protect Consumers' Personal Information," press release, June 6, 2012, http://www.ftc.gov/opa/2012/06 /wyndham.shtm.

13 *The hackers allegedly racked up*: FTC v. Wyndham, No. CV 12-1365-PHX- PGR (2012), http://ftc.gov/os/caselist/1023142/120809wyndhamcmpt.pdf.

13 *It claimed the FTC was unfairly penalizing*: Brent Kendall, "FTC Fires Back in Cybersecurity Case," *Wall Street Journal, Law Blog*, May 24, 2013, http://blogs.wsj.com/law /2013/05/24/ftc-fires-back-in-cybersecurity-case/.

14 *I call this type of mass customization*: Internet activist Eli Pariser calls this phenomenon the "filter bubble." Eli Pariser, *The Filter Bubble: What the Internet Is Hiding from You* (New York: Penguin Press, 2011).

14 *Consider this: searching for a traditionally black-sounding name*: Latanya Sweeney, "Discrimination in Online Ad Delivery" (Working Paper Series, Harvard University, Cambridge, Massachusetts, January 28, 2013), https://papers.ssrn.com/sol3 /papers.cfm?abstract_id=2208240.

14 *In the months leading up to the November 2012 presidential election*: Julia Angwin, "On Google, a Political Mystery That's All Numbers," *Wall Street Journal*, November 4, 2012, http://online.wsj.com/article/SB10001424052970203347104578099122530080836.html.

15 *Or is Martin Abrams, a leading privacy expert*: Martin Abrams, "Guest Headnote: Boxing and Concepts of Harm," *Privacy and Data Security Law Journal* (September 2009): 674, http://theprivacyprojects.org/wp-content/uploads/2009/08/PDSLJ-arti cle.pdf.

15 *Ryan Calo, a law professor at the University of Washington*: Ryan Calo, Digital Market Manipulation (University of Washington School of Law Research Paper No. 2013–27, August 15, 2013), http://papers.ssrn.com/sol3/papers.cfm?abstract _id=2309703.

15 *In 2010, my colleagues at the* Wall Street Journal *and I*: Emily Steel and Julia Angwin, "On the Web's Cutting Edge, Anonymity in Name Only," *Wall Street Journal*, August 3, 2010, http://online.wsj.com/article/SB1000142405274870329490457538553 2109190198.html.

16 *By 2012, when my team again tested for market manipulation*: Jennifer Valentino-DeVries, Jeremy Singer-Vine, and Ashkan Soltani, "Websites Vary Prices, Deals Based on Users' Information," *Wall Street Journal*, December 24, 2012, http://online.wsj. com/article/SB10001424127887323777204578189391813881534.html.

16 *Consider the so-called sucker lists*: Karen Blumenthal, "How Banks, Marketers Aid Scams," *Wall Street Journal*, July 15, 2009, http://online.wsj.com/article/SB10001424 052970204556804574260062522686326.html.

17 *In October 2012, the Federal Trade Commission*: Federal Trade Commission, "FTC

Settlements Require Equifax to Forfeit Money Made by Allegedly Improperly Selling Information About Millions of Consumers Who Were Late on Their Mortgages" (press release), October 10, 2012, http://www.ftc.gov/opa/2012/10/equifaxdirect .shtm.

17 *The lists were marketed with names*: U.S. v. Direct Lending Source, no. 12:2441 (S.D. Cal. 2012), http://www.ftc.gov/os/caselist/1023000/121010directlendingcmpt.pdf.

17 *One of the buyers was a particularly seedy Southern California boiler room operation*: United States of America v. Direct Lending Source Inc., CV-2441DMS BLM and California Department of Justice, Office of the Attorney General, "Four Arrested, Five Wanted for Fleecing Hundreds of Homeowners Seeking Foreclosure Relief" (press release), May 20, 2010, http://oag.ca.gov/news/press-releases/four-arrested-five -wanted-fleecing-hundreds-homeowners-seeking-foreclosure.

17 *When I asked an official at the Direct Marketing Association*: "Direct Marketing Association's Guidelines for Ethical Business Practices," revised May 2011, http:// www.dmaresponsibility.org/Guidelines/.

17 *On April 5, 2011, John Gass*: John Gass, in discussion with author, February 18, 2013.

18 *John Gass luckily was given*: Ibid.

18 *"Although Gass's pique at having to defend his identity is understandable"*: John H. Gass v. Registrar of Motor Vehicles, Appeals Court of Massachusetts, No. 12-P-205, January 7, 2013.

18 *"There are no checks and balances"*: John Gass, in discussion with author, February 18, 2013.

2. A SHORT HISTORY OF TRACKING

21 *Seven weeks after the terrorist attacks*: William Binney, in discussion with author, May 24, 2012.

21 *Lower Manhattan was still smoldering*: "World Trade Center Fires Out," ABCNews .com, December 19, 2001, http://abcnews.go.com/US/story?id=92066&page=1.

21 *Letters containing anthrax*: Edward Jay Epstein, "The Anthrax Attacks Remain Unsolved," *Wall Street Journal*, January 24, 2010, http://online.wsj.com/article/SB10 0014240527487045410045750114212233515284.html.

21 *But Bill Binney, a code breaker*: Tim Shorrock, "Obama's Crackdown on Whistleblowers," *Nation*, March 26, 2013, http://www.thenation.com/article/173521/obamas -crackdown-whistleblowers?page=0,1.

21 *As he reached the bottom of the steps*: William Binney, in discussion with author, May 24, 2012.

22 *"I could not stay after the NSA"*: Jewel, Hepting, Hicks Knutzen and Walton v. National Security Agency, CV-08-04373-JSW (N.D. Cal. 2012), Declaration of William Binney, September 28, 2012.

22 *Not only was it the year of the devastating*: Jason Zweig, "When Bubble Burst: Companies Won, Investors Lost," *Wall Street Journal, The Intelligent Investor*, March 10, 2010, http://online.wsj.com/article/SB10001424052748704145904575119520826919 26.html.

22 *To combat the smuggling epidemic*: Christopher Slobogin, "Government Dragnets" (Public Law & Legal Theory Working Paper 10–37, Vanderbilt University Law School, Nashville, Tennessee, 2010).

23 *"It appears to me the worst instrument"*: James Otis, "Against Writs of Assistance," transcript of speech, Boston, February 24, 1761, http://www.constitution.org/bor /otis_against_writs.htm.

23 *Outrage over the general warrants*: U.S. Const. amend. IV.

23 *The Supreme Court has interpreted this language*: One example of the Court's line of reasoning: *Florida v. Riley*, 488 U.S. 445 (1989), http://caselaw.lp.findlaw.com/scripts /getcase.pl?navby=CASE&court=US&vol=488&page=445.

23 *The Supreme Court has established the "Third-Party Doctrine"*: *United States v. Miller*, 425 U.S. 435 (1976) and *Smith v. Maryland*, 442 U.S. 735 (1979).

23 *As a result, even sensitive information*: Jennifer Valentino-DeVries, "How Technology Is Testing the Fourth Amendment," *Wall Street Journal, Digits* (blog), September 21, 2011, http://blogs.wsj.com/digits/2011/09/21/how-technology-is-testing-the -fourth-amendment/.

23 *Metadata is data about data*: "A Guardian Guide to Your Metadata," *Guardian*, June 12, 2013, http://www.theguardian.com/technology/interactive/2013/jun/12/what-is -metadata-nsa-surveillance#meta=0000000.

23 *In the digital era, metadata*: Evan Perez and Siobhan Gorman, "Phones Leave a Telltale Trail," *Wall Street Journal*, June 15, 2013, http://online.wsj.com/article/SB100014 24127887324049504578545352803220058.html.

24 *Courts have largely supported a "border search exception" to the Fourth Amendment*: Susan Stellin, "The Border Is a Back Door for U.S. Device Searches," *New York Times*, September 9, 2013, http://www.nytimes.com/2013/09/10/business/the-bor der-is-a-back-door-for-us-device-searches.html?pagewanted=1&_r=2&hp.

24 *In 1981, when President Ronald Reagan*: Exec. Order No. 12,333, 3 C.F.R. (1981), http://www.archives.gov/federal-register/codification/executive-order/12333.html.

24 *Documents revealed by the former NSA contractor Edward Snowden*: "NSA Inspector General Report on Email and Internet Data Collection Under Stellar Wind—Full Document," *Guardian*, June 27, 2013, http://www.guardian.co.uk/world /interactive/2013/jun/27/nsa-inspector-general-report-document-data-collec tion; or ST-09-0002 (working draft), Office of the Inspector General, NSA, March 24, 2009.

25 *In 2005, the* New York Times *broke the story*: James Risen and Eric Lichtblau, "Bush Lets U.S. Spy on Callers Without Courts," *New York Times*, December 16, 2005, http://www.nytimes.com/2005/12/16/politics/16program.html?pagewanted=all& _r=0.

26 *The broad sweep of the program*: Ryan Singel, "Whistle-Blower Outs NSA Spy Room," *Wired*, April 7, 2006, http://www.wired.com/science/discoveries/news/2006/04 /70619.

26 *"This is the infrastructure for an Orwellian"*: Mark Klein, "Whistle-Blower's Evidence, Uncut," *Wired*, May 22, 2006, http://www.wired.com/science/discoveries/ news/2006/05/70944.

26 *Then in May 2006, USA Today published*: Leslie Cauley, "NSA Has Massive Database of Americans' Phone Calls," *USA Today*, May 11, 2006, http://usatoday30.usatoday .com/news/washington/2006-05-10-nsa_x.htm?csp=34.

26 *Under pressure, President Bush briefly shut*: Eric Lichtblau, "Deal Reached in Congress to Rewrite Rules on Wiretapping," *New York Times*, June 20, 2008, http://www .nytimes.com/2008/06/20/washington/20fisacnd.html?_r=0.

26 *The PRISM program, disclosed by Snowden*: "NSA Slides Explain the PRISM Data-Collection Program," *Washington Post*, June 6, 2013, last updated July 10, 2013, http://www.washingtonpost.com/wp-srv/special/politics/prism-collection-docu ments/.

26 *Yahoo! apparently fought to declare*: Kim Zetter, "Yahoo Supplied Data to PRISM

Only After Losing Scrappy FISA Fight," *Wired, Threat Level* (blog), June 14, 2013, http://www.wired.com/threatlevel/2013/06/yahoo-failed-fisa-fight/.

26 *Far more sweeping were the vast amounts*: Robert S. Litt, "Privacy, Technology and National Security: An Overview of Intelligence Collection," Remarks at Brookings Institution, Washington, D.C., July 19, 2013, http://www.dni.gov/index.php/news room/speeches-and-interviews/195-speeches-interviews-2013/896-privacy,-tech nology-and-national-security-an-overview-of-intelligence-collection.

26 *Snowden revealed a secret court order*: "Verizon Forced to Hand over Telephone Data—Full Court Ruling," *Guardian*, June 5, 2013, http://www.guardian.co.uk /world/interactive/2013/jun/06/verizon-telephone-data-court-order.

26 *Soon after, Senator Dianne Feinstein of California*: Ed O'Keefe, "Transcript: Dianne Feinstein, Saxby Chambliss Explain, Defend NSA Phone Records Program," *Washington Post, Post Politics* (blog), June 6, 2013, http://www.washingtonpost.com/blogs /post-politics/wp/2013/06/06/transcript-dianne-feinstein-saxby-chambliss-explain -defend-nsa-phone-records-program/.

27 *Snowden also revealed a 2007 memo*: Kenneth L. Wainstein, Memorandum for the Attorney General, November 20, 2007, http://s3.documentcloud.org/documents /717974/nsa-memo.pdf.

27 *The Obama administration said that the Internet*: Glenn Greenwald and Spencer Ackerman, "How the NSA Is Still Harvesting Your Online Data," *Guardian*, June 27, 2013, http://www.guardian.co.uk/world/2013/jun/27/nsa-online-metadata-collec tion.

27 *After 9/11, a massive rush of counterterrorism spending*: Intelligence Budget Data, Federation of American Scientists, https://www.fas.org/irp/budget/index.html.

27 *Since 9/11, the department has doled*: Budget-in-Brief, Department of Homeland Security, Fiscal Year 2012.

27 *and respond to terrorism*: Homeland Security Grant Program, Department of Home land Security, Fiscal Year 2012, http://www.fema.gov/fy-2012-homeland-security -grant-program.

27 *More than $50 million of DHS's grants*: Julia Angwin and Jennifer Valentino-DeVries, "New Tracking Frontier: Your License Plates," *Wall Street Journal*, September 29, 2012, http://online.wsj.com/article/SB10000872396390443995604578004723 603576296.html.

27 *The department also helped fund the creation*: "Federal Support for and Involvement in State and Local Fusion Centers," Homeland Security and Governmental Affairs Permanent Subcommittee on Investigations, October 3, 2012, www.hsgac.senate. gov/subcommittees/investigations/media/investigative-report-criticizes-counter terrorism-reporting-waste-at-state-and-local-intelligence-fusion-centers.

27 *And local police increasingly began tracking people*: Julia Angwin and Scott Thurm, "Judges Weigh Phone Tracking," *Wall Street Journal*, November 9, 2011. http:// online.wsj.com/article/SB10001424052970203733504577024092345458210.html.

27 *In 2008, the attorney general issued*: *The Attorney General's Guidelines for Domestic FBI Operations*, September 28, 2008, http://www.justice.gov/ag/readingroom/guide lines.pdf.

28 *And in 2012, the Justice Department authorized*: Julia Angwin, "U.S. Terrorism Agency to Tap a Vast Database of Citizens," *Wall Street Journal*, December 13, 2012, http://online.wsj.com/article/SB10001424127887324478304578171623040640006 .html.

28 *Its stock price shot up*: Steve Hamm, "The Education of Marc Andreessen," *Business-*

Week, April 2, 1998, http://www.businessweek.com/1998/15/topstory.htm; L. A. Lorek, "Investors Not Just Browsing: Netscape Navigator Stock Goes Public in One of Wall Street's Most Impressive Debuts," *Fort Lauderdale Sun-Sentinel*, August 10, 1995; and Kathy M. Kristof, "Why Individual Investors Lose on IPOs," *Los Angeles Times*, August 10, 1995, http://articles.latimes.com/1995-08-10/business/fi-33617_1 _individual-investors.

28 *The following year, Andreessen was pictured*: "The Golden Geeks," *Time*, February 19, 1996, http://www.time.com/time/covers/0,16641,19960219,00.html.

28 *In 1998, the Department of Justice*: *United States v. Microsoft*, 253 F.3d 34 (D.C. 2001), https://law.justia.com/cases/federal/appellate-courts/F3/253/34/576095/.

29 *But by the time that Microsoft*: "Microsoft Consent Decree Compliance Advisory," August 1, 2003, http://www.justice.gov/atr/cases/f201200/201205a.htm.

29 *In 1998, Internet Explorer surpassed Netscape*: Michael Calore, "Internet Explorer Leaves Netscape in Its Wake," *Wired, This Day in Tech* (blog), September 28, 1998, http://www.wired.com/thisdayintech/2009/09/0928ie-beats-netscape.

29 *and by 2008 Netscape's software*: Tom Drapeau, "End of Support for Netscape Web Browsers," *Netscape Blog*, December 28, 2007, http://blog.netscape.com/2007/12/28 /end-of-support-for-netscape-web-browsers/.

29 *Yahoo!, whose revenue came mostly from online advertising*: Joelle Tessler, "Tech Sector Mirrors Downfall of Silicon Valley General Economy," *San Jose Mercury News*, April 16, 2001.

29 *"Two years ago, nearly all advertisers were saying"*: Vanessa O'Connell, "The Best Way to . . . Advertise," *Wall Street Journal*, November 12, 2001.

29 *Wendy Taylor, the editor of Ziff Davis Smart Business*: Wendy Taylor, "Online Ads Need to Get a Clue," *ZDWire Small Business Advisor*, September 19, 2001.

29 *In 2000, a federal class action suit*: "In re DoubleClick Inc. Privacy Litigation," 154 F. Supp. 2d 497 (S.D. N.Y. 2001), http://cyber.law.harvard.edu/is02/readings/double click.html.

30 *Gupta, a recent immigrant from India*: Mike McIntire, "Clinton Backer's Ties to Powerful Cut Both Ways," *New York Times*, July 14, 2007, http://www.nytimes.com /2007/07/14/us/politics/14gupta.html.

30 *"Just about every list is available"*: Vinod Gupta, interview with Scott Pelley, *60 Minutes II*, CBS, April 30, 2003.

30 *In 1969, Charles Ward, a local businessman*: Robert Evatt, "Large Corporation Begins with Small-Town Staff," Associated Press Newswires, August 18, 2002.

30 *Between 1993 and 1998, Acxiom's revenue*: Robert O'Harrow Jr., "Are Data Firms Getting Too Personal?" *Washington Post*, March 8, 1998, http://www.washington post.com/wp-srv/frompost/march98/privacy8.htm.

31 *The credit card companies Capital One and Discover*: Bruce Biegel (senior managing director, Winterberry Group) and Jonathan Margulies (managing director, Winterberry Group), in discussion with author, April 17, 2013.

31 *The state of Florida alone*: Michael George, "State Made $62 Million by Selling Florida Drivers' License Information," *ABC Action News*, June 21, 2011, http://www .abcactionnews.com/dpp/news/local_news/investigations/i-team%3A-state-made -$62-million-by-selling-florida-drivers%27-license-information.

31 *The U.S. Postal Service generates $9.5 million*: Spokesperson for the Postal Regulatory Commission, in discussion with researcher Lauren Kirchner, April 30, 2013.

31 *In the 2000s, as the Internet became pervasive*: Bruce and Jonathan Margulies, in discussion with author, April 17, 2013.

31 *AOL bought the behavioral targeting firm Tacoda*: Kate Kaye, "Tacoda Buy Could Bolster AOL's Relevance in Web Ad Arena," *Clickz Marketing News*, July 24, 2007, http://www.clickz.com/clickz/news/1712324/tacoda-buy-could-bolster-aols-rele vance-web-ad-arena.

31 *Google paid $3.1 billion*: Paul R. La Monica, "Google to Buy DoubleClick for $3.1 Billion," CNNMoney.com, April 13, 2007, http://money.cnn.com/2007/04/13/technol ogy/google_doubleclick/index.htm.

31 *Microsoft paid $6 billion*: Chris Isidore, "Microsoft Buys aQuantive for $6 Billion," CNNMoney.com, May 18, 2007, http://money.cnn.com/2007/05/18/technology /microsoft_aquantive/.

31 *Acxiom, along with others, began*: Kevin J. Delaney and Emily Steel, "Firm Mines Offline Data to Target Online Ads," *Wall Street Journal*, October 17, 2007, http:// online.wsj.com/article/SB119258320189661423.html.

31 *At the same time, Acxiom started selling*: Evelyn M. Rusli, "Buy Signal: Facebook Widens Data Targeting," *Wall Street Journal*, April 9, 2013, http://online.wsj.com /article/SB10001424127887324504704578412960951909032.html.

31 *When you look at a digital camera on eBay*: Julia Angwin, "The Web's New Gold Mine: Your Secrets," *Wall Street Journal*, July 30, 2010, http://online.wsj.com/article /SB10001424052748703940904575395073512989404.html.

31 *Due in large part to tracking, online advertising*: Interactive Advertising Bureau, *Internet Advertising Revenue Report*, April 2013, https://www.iab.net/media/ file/IABInternetAdvertisingRevenueReportFY2012POSTED.pdf.

31 *Tracking is so crucial to the industry that in 2013*: Randall Rothenberg, "Has Mozilla Lost Its Values?" Interactive Advertising Bureau, *IABlog*, July 16, 2013, https://www .iab.net/iablog/2013/07/has-mozilla-lost-its-values.html.

32 *Meglena Kuneva, a member of the European Commission*: Meglena Kuneva, "Round Table on Online Data Collection, Targeting and Profiling" (keynote speech, Brussels, March 31, 2009), http://europa.eu/rapid/press-release_SPEECH-09-156_en.htm.

33 *To register to vote, citizens*: "Voter Privacy in the Digital Age," California Voter Foundation, 2002, http://www.calvoter.org/issues/votprivacy/pub/0504voterprivacy.pdf.

33 *A 2011 study found that a statewide voter list*: Ibid.

33 *For instance, the data broker Aristotle Inc.*: "Political Date: Learn More," Aristotle, accessed September 11, 2013, http://www.aristotle.com/political-data/political-data -learn-more/.

33 *such as their credit rating*: "Premium Enhancement for Your Political Data," Aristotle, accessed September 13, 2013, http://www.aristotle.com/political-data/premium -enhancements/.

33 *Aristotle crows that*: "About Us," Aristotle, accessed September 13, 2013, http://www .aristotle.com/about-us/.

33 *In fact, an intrepid 2012 thesis*: Melissa Carrie Oppenheim, "The Dark Data Cycle: How the U.S. Government Has Gone Rogue in Trading Personal Data from an Unsuspecting Public," Harvard University, March 2012.

33 *allowing them to identify their constituents*: "Premium Enhancement for Your Political Data."

33 *And thus, the data come full circle*: Oppenheim, "The Dark Data Cycle."

33 *State auto vehicle records are swept*: "Prime Award Service Data: Search Term: LEXIS-NEXIS; Department: Homeland Security," USAspending.gov, http://www .usaspending.gov/search?form_fields={%22search_term%22%3A%22LEXIS -NEXIS%22%2C%22dept%22%3A[%227000%22]}&sort_by=dollars&per_page=25.

34 *Foreclosure records are compiled in state courts*: "CoreLogic Reports 55,000 Completed Foreclosures in June," CoreLogic.com, July 30, 2013, http://www.corelogic .com/about-us/news/corelogic-reports-55,000-completed-foreclosures-in-june.aspx.

34 *which sells packages of real estate data*: "Our Company," CoreLogic, accessed September 15, 2013, http://www.corelogic.com/about-us/news/asset_upload_file856 _22101.pdf.

34 *While at the NSA, Binney had developed*: William Binney, in discussion with author, May 24, 2012.

34 *NSA's lawyers worried*: Jane Mayer, "The Secret Sharer," *New Yorker*, May 23, 2011, http://www.newyorker.com/reporting/2011/05/23/110523fa_fact_mayer.

34 *Another reason*: Siobhan Gorman, "Scuttled NSA Program Had Privacy Safeguards," *Baltimore Sun-Sentinel*, May 18, 2006, http://articles.sun-sentinel.com /2006-05-18/news/0605171528_1_warrantless-surveillance-nsa-communications -data.

34 *In 2002, Binney's colleague*: William Binney, Kirk Wiebe, and Thomas Drake, in discussion with author, May 18, 2012.

34 *The inspector general's report, issued in 2005*: Inspector General, "Audit of the Requirements for the TRAILBLAZER and THINTHREAD Systems" (memo), December 15, 2004, https://www.fas.org/irp/agency/dod/ig-thinthread.pdf.

34 *In 2006, the Baltimore Sun published an article*: Siobhan Gorman, "NSA Rejected System That Sifted Phone Data Legally," *Baltimore Sun*, May 18, 2006, http://articles .baltimoresun.com/2006-05-18/news/0605180094_1_surveillance-national-secu rity-agency-well-informed.

35 *On July 26, 2007, the FBI*: William Binney, in discussion with author, May 24, 2012.

35 *"The guy came in and pointed a gun at me"*: Laura Poitras, "Surveillance Teach-In," April 20, 2012, http://whitney.org/WatchAndListen/Exhibitions?play_id=722.

35 *Wiebe, who had retired*: William Binney, Kirk Wiebe, and Thomas Drake, in discussion with author, May 24, 2012.

35 *On November 28, 2007*: Thomas Drake, in discussion with author, May 24, 2012.

35 *Two and a half years later, Drake was indicted*: *United States v. Thomas Andrews Drake*, Cr. No 10-cr-0181-RDB (N.D. Md. 2010).

35 *Drake was financially devastated*: Thomas Drake, in discussion with author, May 24, 2012.

35 *After spending $82,000*: *USA vs. Drake*, Sentencing (transcript), July 15, 2011 (U.S. District Court District of Maryland).

35 *In 2011, after a wave of publicity about Drake's plight*: David Wise, "Leaks and the Law: The Story of Thomas Drake," *Smithsonian Magazine*, July–August 2011, http:// www.smithsonianmag.com/history-archaeology/Leaks-and-the-Law-The-Story-of -Thomas-Drake.html.

35 *During the sentencing, the U.S. District Court judge*: *USA vs. Drake*, Sentencing (transcript), July 15, 2011.

36 *When I first met Binney, the first thing*: Binney, in discussion with author, March 18, 2012.

36 *"It's a real danger when a government assembles"*: Binney, in discussion with author, May 24, 2012.

3. STATE OF SURVEILLANCE

37 *The Stasi was the largest secret police operation*: Gary Bruce, *The Firm: The Inside Story of the Stasi* (New York: Oxford University Press, 2010), 11.

37 *Famously repressive, it kept files on 4 million*: Ibid.

37 a *total population of*: *Statistisches Jahrbuch der Deutschen Demokratischen Republik*, 1998 (translated by Gary Bruce in e-mail message to author, February 27, 2013).

37 *In 1989, roughly one in fifty East Germans*: Bruce, *The Firm*, 10.

38 *Social network mapping, he told me*: Günter Bormann, in discussion with author, September 19, 2011.

39 *"Their main surveillance technology"*: Gary Bruce, in discussion with author, February 6, 2013.

39 *In this case, the Stasi watched a rather boring*: Gary Bruce, translation for author, February 6, 2013.

39 *The second file documented a surveillance operation known as an OPK*: Bruce, *The Firm*, 4.

39 *It was a medium-size operation*: Bruce, translation.

39 *Stasi officers received bonuses when they launched OPKs*: Bruce, *The Firm*, 111.

39 *Ultimately, however, the OPK of the poet was fruitless*: Bruce, translation.

40 *In one file*: David Burnett, translation for author, March 10, 2013.

40 *The second file was simply a hand-drawn*: Ibid.

40 *The Stasi would most likely have conducted surveillance of everybody*: Gary Bruce, in discussion with author, February 6, 2013.

40 *The problem was that a Stasi file*: Bruce, *The Firm*, 156.

41 *In a study of psychological effects of Stasi surveillance*: Babett Bauer, *Kontrolle und Repression: individuelle Erfahrungen in der DDR (1971–1989)*, described in Bruce, *The Firm*, 158. Original: http://nypl.bibliocommons.com/item/show /16455058052907_kontrolle_und_repression.

41 *The power of observation to be repressive*: Jeremy Bentham, *The Panopticon Writings* (Brooklyn, N.Y.: Verso, 2010).

41 *In 1975, the French philosopher Michel Foucault*: Michel Foucault, *Discipline and Punish: The Birth of the Prison* (New York: Vintage, 1995).

41 *In 2011, Finnish researchers installed*: Antti Oulasvirta et al., "Long-Term Effects of Ubiquitous Surveillance in the Home," Helsinki Institute for Information Technology, Helsinki, 2012.

42 *The lead author of the paper*: Aalto University, "Study Exposes the Negative Effects of Increasing Computerized Surveillance" (press release), April 10, 2012, http://www .aalto.fi/en/current/news/view/2012-10-04/.

42 *Another way to cope with ubiquitous surveillance*: David Brin, *The Transparent Society: Will Technology Force Us to Choose Between Privacy and Freedom?* (Cambridge, Mass.: Perseus Books, 1998).

43 *In 1958, Senator John F. Kennedy claimed*: Christopher A. Preble, "Who Ever Believed in the 'Missile Gap'? John F. Kennedy and the Politics of National Security," *Presidential Studies Quarterly* 33, no. 4 (December 2003): 805–6.

43 *the United States successfully launched photoreconnaissance*: Corona Fact Sheet, National Reconnaissance Office, accessed July 19, 2013, http://www.nro.gov/history /csnr/corona/factsheet.html.

43 *The images captured by the satellite*: Dwayne A. Day, "Of Myths and Missiles: The Truth About John F. Kennedy and the Missile Gap," *Space Review*, January 3, 2006, http://www.thespacereview.com/article/523/1.

43 *in 1961, the Soviets had just four*: John T. Correll, "Airpower and the Cuban Missile Crisis," *Air Force Magazine* 88, no. 8 (August 2005), http://www.airforcemag.com /MagazineArchive/Pages/2005/August%202005/0805u2.aspx.

43 *In 1972, the United States and the Soviet Union*: Treaty on the Limitation of Anti-Ballistic Missile Systems, U.S.-U.S.S.R., May 26, 1972, 23 U.S.T. 3435, https://www.fas.org/nuke/control/abmt/text/abm2.htm.

43 *Six years later, President Jimmy Carter*: Jimmy Carter, "Remarks at the Congressional Space Medal of Honor Awards Ceremony," Kennedy Space Center, Florida, October 1, 1978, *Weekly Compilation of Presidential Documents* 14, no. 40 (October 9, 1978): 1671–1727, http://www.gwu.edu/~nsarchiv/NSAEBB/NSAEBB231/doc32.pdf.

44 *The belief that another person is present*: Ryan Calo, "The Boundaries of Privacy Harm," Consumer Privacy Project, Center for Internet and Society, Stanford Law School, 2010.

44 *In one study, people who stared at a photo*: Vanessa Woods, "Pay Up, You Are Being Watched," *New Scientist*, March 18, 2005.

44 *In 2011, researchers at Newcastle University in Britain*: Max Ernest-Jones, Daniel Nettle, and Melissa Bateson, "Effects of Eye Images on Everyday Cooperative Behavior: A Field Experiment," *Evolution and Human Behavior* 32 (2011): 172–78, http://www.staff.ncl.ac.uk/daniel.nettle/ernestjonesnettlebateson.pdf.

44 *The following year, a similar group of researchers*: David Nettle, Kenneth Nott, and Melissa Bateson, " 'Cycle Thieves, We Are Watching You': Impact of a Simple Signage Intervention Against Bicycle Theft," *PLoS ONE* 7, no. 12 (December 12, 2012).

44 *A 2008 analysis by the California Research Bureau*: Aundreia Cameron, Elke Kolodinski, Heather May, and Nicholas Williams, *Measuring the Effects of Video Surveillance on Crime*, report prepared for the California Research Bureau, May 5, 2008, http://www.library.ca.gov/crb/08/08-007.pdf.

44 *In 2011, the Urban Institute analyzed*: Nancy G. La Vigne, Samantha S. Lowry, Joshua A. Markman, and Allison M. Dwyer, "Evaluating the Use of Public Surveillance Cameras for Crime Control and Prevention," Urban Institute, September 2011, http://www.urban.org/publications/412403.html.

45 *In 2004, Leon Hempel and Eric Töpfer*: Leon Hempel and Eric Töpfer, "On the Threshold to Urban Panopticon?: Analysing the Employment of CCTV in European Cities and Assessing Its Social and Political Implications" (Working Paper No. 1: Inception Report, Urban Eye, January 2002), 23, http://www.urbaneye.net/results/ue_wp1.pdf.

45 *Another Urban Institute study from 2011*: Nancy G. La Vigne and Samantha S. Lowry, "Evaluation of Camera Use to Prevent Crime in Commuter Parking Facilities: A Randomized Controlled Trial," Urban Institute, September 2011, http://www.urban.org/publications/412451.html.

45 *In 2004, the criminologists Brandon Welsh and David Farrington*: Brandon C. Welsh and David Farrington, "Surveillance for Crime Prevention in Public Space: Results and Policy Changes," *Criminology and Public Policy* 3, no. 3 (July 2004): 497.

46 *The authors of the Urban Institute study*: La Vigne and Lowry, "Evaluation of Camera Use."

46 *The Shoe Bomber. In 2001, Richard Colvin Reid*: Christopher Cooper, "Reid's Shoe Bomb Was Sophisticated, Like an Explosive Used by Palestinians," *Wall Street Journal*, January 9, 2002, http://online.wsj.com/article/SB1010533661808003000.html.

46 *The LAX Shooter. In 2002, Hesham Mohamed Hadayet*: Barbara Whitaker, "Immigration Unit Almost Deported Airport Gunman in 1996," *New York Times*, July 7, 2002, http://www.nytimes.com/2002/07/07/us/immigration-unit-almost-deported-airport-gunman-in-1996.html.

46 *The Fort Hood Shooter. In 2009, U.S. Army major Nidal Malik Hasan: Final Report of the William H. Webster Commission on the Federal Bureau of Investigation, Counterterrorism Intelligence, and the Events at Fort Hood, Texas, on November 5, 2009,* https://www.fbi.gov/news/pressrel/press-releases/final-report-of-the-william-h. -webster-commission.

46 *The Underwear Bomber. On Christmas Day 2009, Umar Farouk Abdulmutallab*: The White House, "White House Review Summary Regarding 12/25/2009 Attempted Terrorist Attack," January 7, 2010, http://www.whitehouse.gov/the-press-office /white-house-review-summary-regarding-12252009-attempted-terrorist-attack.

46 *The Times Square Bomber. In 2010, Faisal Shahzad*: Andrea Elliott, "Militant's Path from Pakistan to Times Square," *New York Times,* June 22, 2010, http://www.nytimes .com/2010/06/23/world/23terror.html?pagewanted=all.

46 *The Boston Marathon Bombers. In 2013, Tamerlan and Dzhokhar Tsarnaev*: Marc Arsenault, "Dead Suspect Broke Angrily with Muslim Speakers," *Boston Globe,* April 21, 2013, http://www.boston.com/news/nation/2013/04/21/bombing-suspect -tamerlan-tsarnaev-had-broken-angrily-with-muslim-speakers-mosque/XCBP dDswOKxaa4AJ0mkuVL/singlepage.html.

47 *In the wake of the Snowden leaks, General Keith Alexander*: General Keith Alexander, "Remarks at the AFCEA International Cyber Symposium," Baltimore, Maryland, June 27, 2013.

47 *In 2009, Zazi was arrested: U.S. v. Najibullah Zazi,* No. 10–60 (E.D. N.Y. 2011), http:// www.justice.gov/opa/documents/zazi-indictment.pdf.

47 *According to Alexander, Zazi was swept up*: General Keith Alexander, "Remarks at the AFCEA International Cyber Symposium."

47 *Once the FBI was alerted, its agents*: "House Permanent Select Committee on Intelligence Holds a Hearing on Surveillance Programs," Washington, D.C., June 18, 2013.

47 *A few days later, he flew back to Denver*: Newsweek, "Inside the Zazi Takedown," *Daily Beast,* September 25, 2009, http://www.thedailybeast.com/newsweek/2009/09 /26/inside-the-zazi-takedown.html.

47 *Zazi was arrested in Colorado: United States of America v. Najibullah Zazi,* 09 CR 663 (E.D. N.Y. 2010).

48 *When closely questioned by the Senate*: General Keith Alexander, testimony before the House Permanent Select Committee on Intelligence, June 18, 2013.

48 *And even President Obama was lukewarm*: President Barack Obama, interviewed by Charlie Rose, June 16, 2013, http://www.charlierose.com/watch/60230424.

48 *In their book*: Matt Apuzzo and Adam Goldman, *Enemies Within: Inside the NYPD's Secret Spying Unit and Bin Laden's Final Plot Against America* (New York: Simon and Schuster, 2013), p. 89.

48 *The father of Umar Farouk Abdulmutallab*: Eric Lipton and Scott Shane, "Questions on Why Suspect Wasn't Stopped," *New York Times,* December 27, 2009, https://www .nytimes.com/2009/12/28/us/28terror.html.

48 *A White House investigation found*: The White House, "White House Review Summary Regarding 12/25/2009 Attempted Terrorist Attack."

48 *An FBI field office had been monitoring Fort Hood: Final Report of the William H. Webster Commission.*

49 *And the future Boston Marathon bomber Tamerlan Tsarnaev*: Greg Miller and Sari Horwitz, "Boston Bombing Suspect Put on Terrorist Watch List at CIA Request," *Washington Post,* April 25, 2013, http://articles.washingtonpost.com/2013-04-24 /national/38781588_1_dagestan-u-s-embassy-paul-bresson.

49 *A 2006 paper by Jeff Jonas, an IBM research scientist*: Jeff Jonas and Jim Harper, "Effective Counterterrorism and the Limited Role of Predictive Data Mining," Cato Institute, *Policy Analysis*, no. 584, December 11, 2006, http://www.cato.org/sites /cato.org/files/pubs/pdf/pa584.pdf.

49 *Credit card companies develop "red flags"*: Siddhartha Bhattacharyya, in discussion with author, June 11, 2013.

49 *"Unlike consumers' shopping habits and financial fraud"*: Jonas and Harper, "Effective Counterterrorism."

49 *In 2008, the National Academy of Sciences*: Committee on Technical and Privacy Dimensions of Information for Terrorism Prevention and Other National Goals, National Research Council, *Protecting Individual Privacy in the Struggle Against Terrorists* (Washington, D.C.: National Academies Press, 2008).

49 *In a 2012 speech, Matthew Olsen, the director of the National Counterterrorism Center*: Matthew Olsen (Director, National Counterterrorism Center), "The National Counterterrorism Center's Role in Counterterrorism" (speech), Aspen Institute, Washington, D.C., July 26, 2012, http://www.aspeninstitute.org/video/national -counterterrorism-center-s-role-counterterrorism.

49 *And after the Boston Marathon bombings, the city's police commissioner, Ed Davis*: Michael Naughton, "Davis: Feds Didn't Tell Boston Police About Tamerlan Tsarnaev," *Metro.us*, May 13, 2013, http://www.metro.us/boston/news/local/2013/05/09 /davis-feds-didnt-tell-boston-police-about-tamerlan-tsarnaev/.

50 *Even the Stasi failed to predict*: Richard Popplewell, "The Stasi and the East German Revolution of 1989," *Contemporary European History* 1, no. 1 (March 1992): 37–63.

4. FREEDOM OF ASSOCIATION

51 *Yasir Afifi no longer*: Yasir Afifi, in discussion with author, January 17, 2013.

51 *Paranoia doesn't come naturally*: Yasir Afifi, in discussion with author, August 15, 2012.

51 *"I'm one of those guys"*: Yasir Afifi, in discussion with author, January 17, 2013.

52 *She told me, "He's"*: Yasir Afifi and Angelina Asfour, in discussion with author, June 8, 2013.

52 *The Iranians are obsessed*: Farnaz Fassihi, "Iranian Crackdown Goes Global," *Wall Street Journal*, December 3, 2009, http://online.wsj.com/article/SB 125978649644673331.html.

52 *The Chinese are obsessed*: Jenny W. Hsu and Eva Dou, "Chinese Dissident Skirts Talk of NYU," *Wall Street Journal*, June 23, 2013, http://online.wsj.com/article/SB1000142 4127887323998604578565310545277192.html.

52 *That's why freedom of association*: Article 17, The Universal Declaration of Human Rights, adopted December 10, 1948, https://www.un.org/en/documents/udhr/index .shtml#atop.

52 *In 1958, the Supreme Court*: National Association for the Advancement of Colored People v. Patterson, 357 U.S. 449 (1958).

53 *Consider people who track*: Fitbit Inc., http://www.fitbit.com.

53 *"community of interest"*: Glenn A. Fine, Inspector General, U.S. Department of Justice Statement before the House Committee on the Judiciary Subcommittee on the Constitution, Civil Rights and Civil Liberties concerning "Report by the Office of the Inspector General on the Federal Bureau of Investigation's Use of Exigent Letters and Other Informal Requests for Telephone Records," April 14, 2010, http:// www.justice.gov/oig/testimony/t1004.pdf.

53 *In their 2013 book,* Big Data: Viktor Mayer-Schönberger and Kenneth Cukier, *Big Data: A Revolution That Will Transform How We Live, Work, and Think* (New York: Houghton Mifflin Harcourt, 2013), 175–82.

54 *And no less a big data*: Eric Schmidt, *The New Digital Age: Reshaping the Future of People, Nations and Business* (New York: Alfred A. Knopf, 2013), 55.

54 *Although Schmidt and Cohen*: Ibid., 77.

54 *In the hands of a police state*: Ibid., 62.

54 *The surveillance of Yasir Afifi*: The events described on the following pages are largely based on allegations in a lawsuit subsequently filed by Mr. Afifi, *Yasir Afifi v. Eric Holder et al.*, 1:11cv460 (D.C., 2012). As of October 2013, the suit was still pending.

54 *On June 24, 2010, a user*: JayClay, "So if My Deodorant Could Be a Bomb, Why Are You Just Chucking It in the Bin?" *Reddit*, June 24, 2010, captured on January 28, 2013, http://www.reddit.com/r/AskReddit/comments/ciiag/so_if_my_deodorant _could_be_a_bomb_why_are_you/?limit=500.

54 *On June 25, a user named "Khaledthegypsy"*: khaledthegypsy, comment on Reddit, June 24, 2010, http://www.reddit.com/r/AskReddit/comments/ciiag/so_if_my _deodorant_could_be_a_bomb_why_are_you/c0sve5q.

54 *Four months later*: Yasir Afifi, in discussion with author, August 15, 2012.

55 *"That is not part of the car"*: Khaled Ibrahim, in discussion with author, August 16, 2012.

55 *When the mechanic tugged*: Yasir Afifi, in discussion with author, August 15, 2012.

55 *Yasir thought to himself*: Yasir Afifi, e-mail correspondence with author, February 2, 2013.

55 *Soon after Yasir's return*: Yasir Afifi, in discussion with author, August 15, 2012.

55 *And so at 10:15 p.m. Khaled*: Khaledthegypsy, "Does This Mean the FBI Is After Us?" *Reddit*, October 3, 2010, captured January 28, 2013, http://www.reddit.com /comments/dmh5s/does_this_mean_the_fbi_is_after_us/.

55 *Yasir recalled thinking*: Yasir Afifi, in discussion with author, August 15, 2012.

56 *Vincent played tough*: *Afifi v. Holder*.

57 *"We just want the device back"*: Yasir Afifi, in discussion with author, August 15, 2012.

57 *Yasir suggested that he could*: *Afifi v. Holder*.

57 *"Why are you doing"*: Yasir Afifi, in discussion with author, August 15, 2012.

57 *The four agents with guns*: *Afifi v. Holder*, Doc. 21.

57 *She gave him a business card*: Yasir Afifi, in discussion with author, August 15, 2012.

58 *The FBI must have been*: Yasir Afifi, e-mail correspondence with author, February 2, 2013.

58 *After the agents left*: Yasir Afifi, in discussion with author, August 15, 2012.

58 *On March 2, 2011, CAIR*: *Afifi v. Holder*, 17.

58 *The complaint alleged that Yasir*: Ibid.

59 *The FBI won the right*: *Afifi v. Holder*, Defendants' Motion for Privacy Act Protective Order and Leave to File Under Seal, June 16, 2011.

59 *In its limited public filings*: *Afifi v. Holder et al.*, Doc. 37-1, January 11, 2013.

59 *Since then, the Supreme Court*: *United States v. Jones*, (2012), accessed at http://www. law.cornell.edu/supremecourt/text/10-1259.

59 *The government also argued*: *Afifi v. Holder et al.*, Reply in Support of Defendants Holder and Mueller's Motion to Dismiss and for Summary Judgment, January 11, 2013.

59 *"Congress shall make no law"*: U.S. Const. amend. I.

59 *"First Amendment theory"*: Lee Bollinger, in discussion with author, June 19, 2013.

59 *For instance, in 1964, the Supreme Court*: New York Times v. Sullivan, 376 U.S. 254 (1964).

59 *And in 2000, the Supreme Court*: Boy Scouts of America et al. v. Dale, 530 U.S. 640 (2000).

60 *In 1972, the Court ruled 5-4*: Laird v. Tatum, 408 U.S. 1 (1972).

60 *And again in 2013, the Supreme Court*: Clapper v. Amnesty International USA et al. (2013), accessed at http://www.law.cornell.edu/supremecourt/text/11-1025.

60 *"What can you do?"*: Khaled Ibrahim, in discussion with author, August 16, 2012.

61 *When Redditers began pestering*: khaledthegypsy, comment on Reddit, April 9, 2011, http://www.reddit.com/r/AskReddit/comments/gmcw5/hey_reddit_what_hap pened_to_that_kid_who_sued_the/c1oo07i.

61 *When Khaled and I met*: Khaled Ibrahim, in discussion with author, August 16, 2012.

61 *After 9/11, the FBI set up*: Trevor Aaronson, "The Informants," *Mother Jones*, September/October 2011, http://www.motherjones.com/politics/2011/08/fbi-terrorist -informants?

61 *The investigative journalist Trevor Aaronson*: Trevor Aaronson, question and answer session, Columbia Law School, New York, January 31, 2013.

61 *One of the most aggressive efforts*: "AP's Probe into NYPD Intelligence Operations," Associated Press, http://www.ap.org/Index/AP-In-The-News/NYPD.

62 *In 2008, an undercover agent accompanied*: Chris Hawley, "NYPD Monitored Muslim Students All over Northeast," Associated Press, February 18, 2012, http://www .ap.org/Content/AP-In-The-News/2012/NYPD-monitored-Muslim-students-all -over-Northeast.

62 *Consider the story of Asad Dandia*: Asad Dandia, "My Life Under NYPD Surveillance: A Brooklyn Student and Charity Leader on Fear and Mistrust," American Civil Liberties Union, *Blog of Rights*, June 18, 2013, http://www.aclu.org/blog/national -security-religion-belief-criminal-law-reform-technology-and-liberty/my-life -under-nypd.

62 *On October 2, 2012, Rahman posted*: Adam Goldman and Matt Apuzzo, "Informant: NYPD Paid Me to 'Bait' Muslims," Associated Press, October 23, 2012, http://www .ap.org/Content/AP-In-The-News/2012/Informant-NYPD-paid-me-to-bait-Mus lims.

62 *"When I learned the news"*: Dandia, "My Life."

62 *Dandia has joined in a lawsuit*: Raza et al. v. City of New York et al., CV 13-2448 (E.D. N.Y. 2013).

63 *Yasir Afifi has also withdrawn*: Yasir Afifi, in discussion with author, January 17, 2013.

63 *"Would I like some policy"*: Yasir Afifi, in discussion with author, August 15, 2012.

63 *One hot day, I came to visit*: Afifi, author visit, June 8, 2013.

5. THREAT MODELS

66 *In the computer security industry*: Larry Osterman, "Threat Modeling Again, Threat Modeling Rules of Thumb," *Larry Osterman's WebLog*, September 21, 2007, retrieved April 22, 2013, http://blogs.msdn.com/b/larryosterman/archive/2007/09/21/threat -modeling-again-threat-modeling-rules-of-thumb.aspx.

66 *Bruce Schneier calls this*: Bruce Schneier, *Schneier on Security* (Indianapolis: Wiley Publishing, 2008), viii.

66 *In 2012, the FBI uncovered*: Jeff Stein, "Draft Dodgers," *Foreign Policy*, November 14, 2012, retrieved April 22, 2013, http://www.foreignpolicy.com/articles/2012/11/14/draft_dodgers.

67 *FBI agents traced*: Kim Zetter, "Email Location Data Led FBI to Uncover Top Spy's Affair," *Wired*, November 12, 2012, retrieved April 23, 2013, http://www.wired.com/threatlevel/2012/11/gmail-location-data-petraeus/.

67 *Even then, there's no guarantee*: Nicole Perlroth, "Trying to Keep Your E-Mails Secret When the C.I.A. Chief Couldn't," *New York Times*, November 16, 2012, retrieved April 23, 2013, http://www.nytimes.com/2012/11/17/technology/trying-to-keep-your-e-mails-secret-when-the-cia-chief-couldnt.html.

67 *Consider another case*: Theodore J. Kaczynski: Robert D. McFadden, "Prisoner of Rage," *New York Times*, May 26, 1996, retrieved April 23, 2013, http://www.nytimes.com/1996/05/26/us/prisoner-of-rage-a-special-report-from-a-child-of-promise-to-the-unabom-suspect.html.

67 *The FBI eventually tracked him*: David Johnston, "17-year Search, an Emotional Discovery and Terror Ends," *New York Times*, May 5, 1998, retrieved April 23, 2013, http://www.nytimes.com/1998/05/05/us/17-year-search-an-emotional-discovery-and-terror-ends.html.

68 *Since 2009, the administration*: Daniel Politi, "Obama Has Charged More Under Espionage Act Than All Other Presidents Combined," Slate.com, June 22, 2013, http://www.slate.com/blogs/the_slatest/2013/06/22/edward_snowden_is_eighth_person_obama_has_pursued_under_espionage_act.html.

68 *providing classified information to journalists*: David Carr, "Blurred Line Between Espionage and Truth," *New York Times*, February 26, 2012, http://www.nytimes.com/2012/02/27/business/media/white-house-uses-espionage-act-to-pursue-leak-cases-media-equation.html.

69 *When my husband and I bought*: Julia Angwin, "The Mess We're In," *Wall Street Journal*, Brownstone Diary, February 19, 2010, retrieved April 23, 2013, http://online.wsj.com/article/SB10001424052748704041504575045241309357722.html.

69 *Although I never published*: Ulysses, "Revive: The West 123rd Street Brownstone," *Harlem + Bespoke* (blog), February 17, 2010, retrieved April 23, 2013, http://harlembespoke.blogspot.com/2010/02/revive-west-123rd-street-brownstone.html.

70 *In* How to Be Invisible: J. J. Luna, *How to Be Invisible: Protect Your Home, Your Children, Your Assets, and Your Life* (New York: Thomas Dunne Books, 2004).

70 *In* One Nation, Under Surveillance: Kenneth W. Royce, *One Nation, Under Surveillance* (Gillette, Wyo.: Javelin Press, 2009).

71 *But in New York, where I live*: N.Y. VAT. Law § 402: NY Code—Section 402: Distinctive Number; Form of Number Plates; Trailers, http://codes.lp.findlaw.com/nycode/VAT/IV/14/402.

72 *I asked Mark Eckenwiler*: Mark Eckenwiler, in discussion with author, March 6, 2013.

72 *Mark pointed me*: 18 USC § 1028—Fraud and Related Activity in Connection with Identification Documents, Authentication Features, and Information, http://www.law.cornell.edu/uscode/text/18/1028.

72 *But he also pointed me*: Flores-Figueroa v. United States (No. 08-108) 274 Fed. Appx. 501, reversed and remanded, http://www.law.cornell.edu/supct/html/08-108.ZO.html.

72 *But then he pointed me*: 18 USC § 1343—Fraud by Wire, Radio, or Television, http://www.law.cornell.edu/uscode/text/18/1343.

72 *John J. Strauchs, a former CIA*: John Strauchs, in discussion with author, March 5, 2013.

73 *In his delightful book*: Michael Pollan, *The Omnivore's Dilemma: A Natural History of Four Meals* (New York: Penguin Books, 2006), 392.

75 *The Wiretap Act requires police officers*: The Surveillance Self-Defense Project, "Wiretapping Law Protections," Electronic Frontier Foundation, accessed July 26, 2013, https://ssd.eff.org/wire/govt/wiretapping-protections.

75 *Considering that in the last half*: Google, Inc., "Transparency Report: User Data Requests," https://www.google.com/transparencyreport/userdatarequests/.

77 *Federal prosecutors have argued*: Jennifer Valentino-Devries, "'Stingray' Phone Tracker Fuels Constitutional Clash," *Wall Street Journal*, September 22, 2011, retrieved May 2, 2013, http://online.wsj.com/article/SB1000142405311190419460457658311272 3197574.html.

77 *And NSA documents revealed*: Eric Holder, "Minimization Procedures Used by the National Security Agency in Connection with Acquisitions of Foreign Intelligence Information Pursuant to Section 702 of the Foreign Intelligence Surveillance Act of 1978, as Amended," July 28, 2004.

77 *After 9/11, Perry was outraged*: Mike Perry, in discussion with author, June 5, 2013.

78 *Public places are apparently*: John Strauchs, in discussion with author, March 5, 2013.

6. THE AUDIT

80 *"You should know your data"*: Michael Sussmann, in discussion with author, October 24, 2012.

81 *To find my Google data*: The Data Liberation Front, http://www.dataliberation.org/.

82 *A Google spokesman*: Rob Shilkin, e-mail to the author, July 30, 2013.

82 *My Facebook data were a pale shadow*: Nicole Lundeen and Kerry Skrying, "Student Group Challenges Facebook on Privacy," *Wall Street Journal*, *Tech Europe* (blog), February 2, 2012, http://blogs.wsj.com/tech-europe/2012/02/08/student -group-challenges-facebook-on-privacy/.

82 *Schrems, a law student in Vienna*: "Facebook's Data Pool," europe-v-facebook.org, http://www.europe-v-facebook.org/EN/Data_Pool/data_pool.html.

82 *The European Union requires*: Directive 95/46/EC of the European Parliament and of the Council of October 24, 1995. http://eur-lex.europa.eu/LexUriServ/LexUriServ .do?uri=CELEX:31995L0046:EN:HTML.

83 *As a result, the Irish commission*: Data Protection Commissioner, "Facebook Ireland Ltd, Report of Audit," December 21, 2011, http://europe-v-facebook.org/Facebook _Ireland_Audit_Report_Final.pdf.

83 *A year later, Facebook changed*: Facebook, Data Use Policy, Date of Last Revision: December 11, 2012, https://www.facebook.com/full_data_use_policy.

83 *In 2012, the Irish commission*: Data Protection Commission, "Facebook Ireland Ltd, Report of Re-Audit," September 21, 2012, http://europe-v-facebook.org/ODPC _Review.pdf.

83 *Twitter didn't give users*: Mollie Vandor, "Your Twitter Archive," *Twitter Blog*, December 19, 2012, https://blog.twitter.com/2012/your-twitter-archive.

83 *even though since 2010*: Jud Valeski, "New Gnip & Twitter Partnership," *Company Blog, Gnip*, November 17, 2010, http://blog.gnip.com/gnip-twitter-partnership/.

84 *This happened when I was sitting*: Mike Griffin, in discussion with author, September 21, 2012.

84 *Mike is a "repo" man who stumbled*: Julia Angwin and Jennifer Valentino-DeVries, "New Tracking Frontier: Your License Plates," *Wall Street Journal*, September 29, 2012, http://online.wsj.com/article/SB10000872396390443995604578004723603576 296.html.

84 *He mused about one possible*: Mike Griffin, in discussion with author, September 21, 2012.

84 *Asher made millions*: Michael Shnayerson, "The Net's Master Data-Miner," *Vanity Fair*, December 2004.

85 *In 2009*: Bloomberg Businessweek, "Company Overview of TLO, LLC," accessed April 25, 2013, http://investing.businessweek.com/research/stocks/private/snapshot .asp?privcapId=128678962.

85 *founding a database company called*: Ann Woolner, "Hank Asher's Startup TLO Knows All About You," *Bloomberg Businessweek Magazine*, September 15, 2011, http://www.businessweek.com/magazine/hank-ashers-startup-tlo-knows-all-about -you-09152011.html.

85 *He turned out to be right*: TLO, LLC, "Press Release Honoring Frank," January 12, 2013, http://www.tlo.com/hank_press_release.html.

85 *Mike said TLO's data*: Mike Griffin, in discussion with author, September 21, 2012.

85 *which years earlier had*: Ellen Nakashima and Robert O'Harrow Jr., "LexisNexis Parent Set to Buy ChoicePoint," *Washington Post*, February 22, 2008, http://articles. washingtonpost.com/2008-02-22/business/36857083_1_choicepoint-data-broker -lexisnexis-group; and Robert O'Harrow Jr., "LexisNexis to Buy Seisint for $775 Million," *Washington Post*, July 15, 2004, http://www.washingtonpost.com/wp-dyn /articles/A50577-2004Jul14.html.

85 *TLO charged only 25 cents*: Woolner, "Hank Asher's Startup."

85 *By comparison, LexisNexis's*: PeopleWise, https://www.peoplewise.com/people /report.

86 *In 2007, Josh Levy and Ross Cohen*: Dean Takahashi, "BeenVerified Hopes to Make Background Checks Easier and Cheaper," *VentureBeat*, October 21, 2008, http:// venturebeat.com/2008/10/21/beenverified-hopes-to-make-background-checks-eas ier-and-cheaper/.

86 *By 2011, the company said*: Julia Angwin, "Sites Are Accused of Privacy Failings," *Wall Street Journal*, February 13, 2012, http://online.wsj.com/article/SB10001424052 9702041364045772071 83258570186.html.

86 *Those countries require*: Directive 95/46/EC of the European Parliament and of the Council, October 24, 1995.

87 *I was shocked that Acxiom*: Acxiom Corp. 10-K annual report, http://www.sec.gov /Archives/edgar/data/733269/000073326913000012/financials.htm.

87 *One of its main products*: Acxiom Corp., "My Cluster," https://isapps.acxiom.com /personicx/personicx.aspx.

87 *Thanks to the journalist Dan Tynan*: Dan Tynan, "Further Adventures in Data Mining, or Welcome to My Lear Jet Lifestyle," ITworld.com, April 11, 2013, http://www .itworld.com/it-management/352177/adventures-data-mining-or-welcome-my-lear -jet-lifestyle.

87 *Acxiom later introduced an online*: AboutTheData.com, https://AboutTheData.com/.

88 *Datalogix, which claims to have data*: datalogix, http://www.datalogix.com/about/.

89 *Intelius, one of the largest*: Xu Wang, "Intelius May Revisit IPO After Shelving It in 2010, CEO Says," *Bloomberg*, October 25, 2011, http://www.bloomberg.com/news /2011-10-25/intelius-may-revisit-ipo-after-shelving-it-in-2010-ceo-says.html.

89 *The Fair Credit Reporting Act*: "A Summary of Your Rights Under the Fair Credit Reporting Act," FTC Consumer Response Center, http://www.consumer.ftc.gov /articles/pdf-0096-fair-credit-reporting-act.pdf.

89 *In 2003, Congress passed a law*: The White House, "Fact Sheet: President Bush Signs the Fair and Accurate Credit Transactions Act of 2003," December 4, 2003, http:// georgewbush-whitehouse.archives.gov/news/releases/2003/12/20031204-3.html.

90 *In March 2013, it was revealed*: Jordan Robertson, "Top Credit Agencies Say Hackers Stole Celebrity Reports," *Bloomberg*, March 12, 2013, http://www.bloomberg.com /news/2013-03-12/equifax-transunion-say-hackers-stole-celebrity-reports.html.

90 *The latest review of credit report*: Federal Trade Commission, *Report to Congress Under Section 319 of the Fair and Accurate Credit Transactions Act of 2003*, December 2012, http://ftc.gov/os/2013/02/130211factareport.pdf.

90 *Based in Chicago and founded in 2004*: eBureau, "About Us," accessed May 5, 2013, http://www.ebureau.com/about.

91 *The company says it analyzes*: eBureau, "Using Third Party Data and Analytics to Help You Manage Lead Quality: Part 2," *eBureau Industry Blog*, May 11, 2012, http:// www.ebureau.com/blog/using-third-party-data-and-analytics-help-you-manage -online-lead-quality-part-2.

91 *eBureau promotes its scores*: eBureau, "Credit Risk Management," http://www .ebureau.com/credit-risk-management.

91 *and allowing debt collectors*: eBureau, "Collections & Recovery," http://www.ebureau .com/collections-recovery.

91 *In a marketing sheet*: eBureau, "Income Estimator," http://www.ebureau.com/sites /default/files/file/datasheets/ebureau_income_estimator_datasheet.pdf.

91 *When I contacted eBureau*: eBureau e-mail to author dated July 31, 2013.

91 *Even creepier was a company called PYCO*: V12 Group, "The PYCO Personality Score: The Science of Motivating Consumers to Respond," March 2012, http://www .v12groupinc.com/wp-content/uploads/2012/03/PYCO_Personality_Score_White-Paper.pdf.

91 *For example, getting married*: Yen Lee, in discussion with author's assistant Lauren Kirchner, May 30, 2013.

91 *PYCO says it has built profiles*: Yen Lee, e-mail to author's assistant Lauren Kirchner, June 4, 2013.

91 *Obviously, the National Security Agency*: Bob Sullivan, "Lawyers Eye NSA Data as Treasure Trove for Evidence," *NBC News*, June 21, 2013, http://www.cnbc.com/id /100834242.

91 *Consider the story of an Ohio resident*: Shearson v. U.S. Department of Homeland Security et al., No. 08-4582 (6th cir. 2011), http://papersplease.org/wp/wp-content /uploads/2011/04/shearson-opinion-21apr2011.pdf.

92 *Shearson, who is a convert to Islam*: Julia Shearson, in discussion with Lauren Kirchner, September 3, 2013.

92 *the U.S. Court of Appeals for the Sixth Circuit*: Shearson v. U.S. Department of Homeland Security et al., No. 08-4582 (6th cir. 2011).

92 *Shearson settled for damages*: Julia Shearson, in discussion with Lauren Kirchner, September 3, 2013.

92 *I requested my FBI files*: Federal Bureau of Investigations, correspondence to author, May 17, 2013.

92 *For help interpreting the files*: Edward Hasbrouck, in discussion with author, May 2, 2013.

92 *He lost when a federal court*: Hasbrouck v. U.S. *Customs and Border Protection*, Order Re Cross-Motions for Summary Judgment, no. 10-3793 (N.D. Cal. 2012).

93 *The first eight pages*: Edward Hasbrouck, in discussion with author, May 2, 2013.

93 *But after the 9/11 terrorist attacks*: Aviation and Transportation Security Act, H.R. 107-71 (2001), http://www.gpo.gov/fdsys/pkg/PLAW-107publ71/html/PLAW -107publ71.htm.

93 *In typical fashion, "upon request"*: 19 C.F.R. 122.49d—Passenger Name Record (PNR) Information, http://www.law.cornell.edu/cfr/text/19/122.49d.

93 *Now, airlines routinely contribute*: U.S. Department of Homeland Security, *Privacy Impact Assessment for the Automated Targeting System*, June 1, 2012, http://www .dhs.gov/xlibrary/assets/privacy/privacy_pia_cbp_ats006b.pdf.

93 *After a protracted legal*: "EU Court Annuls Data Deal with US," *BBC News*, May 30, 2006, http://news.bbc.co.uk/2/hi/europe/5028918.stm.

93 *After all, they didn't want their citizens*: "MEPs Back Deal to Give Air Passenger Data to US," *BBC News*, April 19, 2012, http://www.bbc.co.uk/news/world-europe -17764365.

95 *"We are working closely with our"*: Colleen Schwartz (Dow Jones spokesperson), in discussion with author, July 30, 2013.

7. THE FIRST LINE OF DEFENSE

97 *I had also considered*: Michael Tiffany, in discussion with author, February 2, 2013.

97 *"We have a saying in this business"*: Lawrence Wright, "The Spymaster," *New Yorker*, January 21, 2008, http://www.newyorker.com/reporting/2008/01/21/080121fa_fact _wright.

97 *"We have to cast aside"*: Janet Napolitano, "Achieving Security and Privacy," May 2, 2012, Australian National University, Canberra, http://www.dhs.gov/news/2012/05 /02/remarks-secretary-homeland-security-janet-napolitano-achieving-security -and-privacy.

98 *The advice being peddled*: "Comcast Partners with AG Blumenthal to Keep Kids Safe Online," *Red Orbit*, June 15, 2009, http://www.redorbit.com/news/entertainment /1705787/comcast_partners_with_ag_blumenthal_to_keep_kids_safe_online/.

99 *In 2010, computer security researchers*: Ashlee Vance, "If Your Password Is 123456, Just Make It HackMe," *New York Times*, January 20, 2010, https://www.nytimes.com /2010/01/21/technology/21password.html?_r=1&.

99 *The researchers, at the computer security firm Imperva*: The Imperva Application Defense Center, "Consumer Password Worst Practices," 2010, http://www.imperva .com/docs/WP_Consumer_Password_Worst_Practices.pdf.

99 *The British telecom regulator*: Ofcom, "UK Adults Taking Online Password Security Risks," April 23, 2013, http://media.ofcom.org.uk/2013/04/23/uk-adults-taking -online-password-security-risks/.

100 *In his well-regarded textbook*: Ross Anderson, *Security Engineering* (Hoboken, N.J.: Wiley, 2008), 33, http://www.cl.cam.ac.uk/~rja14/Papers/SEv2-c02.pdf.

100 *In 2004, the Institute of Electrical and Electronics Engineers*: Jeff Yan, Alan Blackwell, Ross Anderson, and Alasdair Grant, "Password Memorability and Security: Empirical Results," *IEEE Security & Privacy*, September/October 2004, http://homepages.cs .ncl.ac.uk/jeff.yan/jyan_ieee_pwd.pdf.

100 *In 2010, computer scientists*: Philip Inglesant and M. Angela Sasse, "The True Cost of Unusable Password Policies: Password Use in the Wild," April 15, 2010, https://www .cl.cam.ac.uk/~rja14/shb10/angela2.pdf.

101 *And by the way, many*: Per Thorsheim (password security expert), in discussion with Lauren Kirchner, June 28, 2013.

101 *In 2005, Jesper Johansson*: Munir Kotadia, "Microsoft Security Guru: Jot Down Your Passwords," *CNET*, May 23, 2005, http://news.cnet.com/Microsoft-security-guru-Jot -down-your-passwords/2100-7355_3-5716590.html?tag=nefd.pop.

101 *I was reminded of a study*: "Online Americans Fatigued by Password Overload Janrain Study Finds," Janrain press release, August 23, 2012, http://janrain.com/about /newsroom/press-releases/online-americans-fatigued-by-password-overload-jan rain-study-finds/.

103 *And I bought a wallet*: Spencer Michels, "Radio Frequency Identification Tags: Identity Theft Danger or Modern Aid?," August 16, 2010, http://www.pbs.org/newshour /rundown/2010/08/radio-frequency-identification-a-danger-or-a-help-1.html.

103 *To combat hackers*: "HTTPS Everywhere," Electric Frontier Foundation, https:// www.eff.org/https-everywhere.

103 *On Gmail, that meant installing*: Google, Inc., "Google Authenticator," iTunes App Store, Updated September 7, 2013, https://itunes.apple.com/us/app/google-authenti cator/id388497605?mt=8.

104 *I also tried using a system*: Little Snitch, Objective Development Software GmbH, http://www.obdev.at/products/littlesnitch/index.html.

104 *I liked that it didn't look*: SpiderOak, https://spideroak.com/.

105 *Over coffee, he told me his story*: Ethan Oberman, in discussion with author, August 15, 2012.

105 *He was, as I had guessed*: Meredith M. Bagley, "M. Lax Blows Lead, Loses to Dartmouth," *Harvard Crimson*, May 10, 1999, http://www.thecrimson.com/article/1999 /5/10/m-lax-blows-lead-loses-to/.

105 *After graduation in 2000*: Ethan Oberman, in discussion with author, August 15, 2012.

105 *Two weeks later I spoke by phone*: Alan Fairless, in discussion with author, August 28, 2012.

106 *Increased computing power*: Jeremi Gosney (PasswordsCon, co-organizer and CEO of Stricture Group), in discussion with Lauren Kirchner, July 12, 2013.

106 *To show how easy it has become*: Nate Anderson, "How I Became a Password Cracker," *Ars Technica* (blog), March 24, 2013, http://arstechnica.com/security/2013/03/how-i -became-a-password-cracker/.

107 *Brute force attacks*: Robert Graham, "LinkedIn vs. Password Cracking," Errata Security, June 6, 2012, http://erratasec.blogspot.com/2012/06/linkedin-vs-password -cracking.html.

107 *For that reason, Anderson*: Anderson, "How I Became a Password Cracker."

107 *One lesson from the world*: Dan Goodin, "Why Passwords Have Never Been Weaker— and Crackers Have Never Been Stronger," *Ars Technica* (blog), August 20, 2012, http://arstechnica.com/security/2012/08/passwords-under-assault/.

107 *Sadly, salting is not*: Paul Wagenseil, "LinkedIn, eHarmony Don't Take Your Security Seriously," *TechNewsDaily*, NBC News, June 8, 2012, http://www.nbcnews.com /technology/linkedin-eharmony-dont-take-your-security-seriously-819858.

107 *Jeffrey Goldberg, a password expert at AgileBits*: Jeffrey Goldberg, in discussion with author, May 14, 2013.

107 *Julian Assange knew this*: "Row Between Wikileaks and Guardian over Security Breach," *BBC News*, September 1, 2011, http://www.bbc.co.uk/news/uk-14743410.

108 *One day I was sitting outside*: Dan Wheeler, "Open Source Password Strength

Estimator," April 2012, https://dl.dropboxusercontent.com/u/209/zxcvbn/test/index .html.

109 *In 2012, researchers at the University of Cambridge*: Joseph Bonneau and Ekaterina Shutova, "Linguistic Properties of Multi-Word Passphrases," USEC '12: Workshop on Usable Security, Kralendijk, Bonaire, Netherlands, March 2, 2012, http://www.jbonneau.com/doc/BS12-USEC-passphrase_linguistics.pdf.

109 *I found what I needed*: Arnold Reinhold, "The Diceware Passphrase FAQ," last updated April 18, 2012, http://world.std.com/~reinhold/dicewarefaq.html.

110 *But even the simple Diceware*: Bruce Marshall, in discussion with author's assistant Lauren Kirchner, July 3, 2013.

110 *the NSA had authored*: Nicole Perlroth, "Government Announces Steps to Restore Confidence in Encryption Standards," *New York Times, Bits Blog*, September 10, 2013, http://bits.blogs.nytimes.com/2013/09/10/government-announces-steps-to -restore-confidence-on-encryption-standards/?src=twrhp&_r=0.

8. LEAVING GOOGLE

112 *On June 8, 2004*: Joan Airoldi, "Privacy and Library Records, a Case Study in Whatcom County," *Journal of Educational Controversy* 5, no. 2 (Summer 2010), http://www.wce.wwu.edu/Resources/CEP/eJournal/v005n002/a007.shtml.

112 *Nothing like that had ever*: Deming, Washington, Population: Census 2010 and 2000 Interactive Map, Demographics, Statistics, Quick Facts, http://censusviewer.com /city/WA/Deming.

112 *Even so, the librarians*: Joan Airoldi (director, Whatcom County Library System, Washington), in discussion with author, March 29, 2013.

112 *A year earlier, the Whatcom*: Deborra Garrett, in discussion with Lauren Kirchner, May 30, 2013.

112 *Subsequently, forty-eight states*: American Library Association, "State Privacy Laws Regarding Library Records," http://www.ala.org/offices/oif/ifgroups/stateifcchairs /stateifcinaction/stateprivacy.

112 *So when the FBI agent*: Amory Peck (former board of trustees chair, Whatcom County Library System), in discussion with Lauren Kirchner, June 7, 2013.

112 *the librarian on duty*: Deborra Garrett, in discussion with Lauren Kirchner, May 30, 2013.

113 *But a few weeks later*: Amory Peck, in discussion with Lauren Kirchner, June 7, 2013.

113 *Garrett suggested that it could*: Phillip Taylor, "Kramerbooks Declares Victory in Subpoena Battle," Freedom Forum, First Amendment Center, June 22, 1998, http:// www.freedomforum.org/templates/document.asp?documentID=9736.

113 *"It was a frightening stand"*: Amory Peck, "Remarks Made by Amory Peck, Board of Trustees Chair, Whatcom County Library System" (Robert B. Downs Intellectual Freedom Reception, University of Illinois at Urbana-Champaign, January 15, 2005), http://www.lis.illinois.edu/articles/2005/01/remarks-made-amory-peck-board -trustees-chair-whatcom-county-library-system.

113 *"In my view, this case"*: Deborra Garrett, in discussion with Lauren Kirchner, May 30, 2013.

114 *In 2006, Google challenged*: Nicole Wong, "Judge Tells DoJ 'No' on Search Queries," *Google Official Blog*, March 17, 2006, http://googleblog.blogspot.com/2006/03/judge -tells-doj-no-on-search-queries.html.

114 *In 2007, Amazon successfully*: Order in re Grand Jury Subpoena to Amazon.com

Dated August 7, 2006 (W.D. Wis. 2007), http://dig.csail.mit.edu/2007/12/In-re -grand-jury-subpoena-amazon.PDF.

114 *The relevant law governing most*: Julia Angwin, "Secret Orders Target Email," *Wall Street Journal*, October 9, 2011, http://online.wsj.com/article/SB10001424052970203 476804576613284007315072.html.

114 *Not only that, courts often*: Stephen W. Smith, "Gagged, Sealed & Delivered: Reforming ECPA's Secret Docket," *Harvard Law & Policy Review* 6 (May 21, 2012): forthcoming, https://papers.ssrn.com/sol3/papers.cfm?abstract_id=2071399.

114 *In 2012, Microsoft produced*: Microsoft 2012 Law Enforcement Requests Report, https://www.microsoft.com/about/corporatecitizenship/en-us/reporting/transparency/#FAQs1.

114 *That same year, Google handed*: "Google Transparency Report," accessed August 15, 2013, https://www.google.com/transparencyreport/userdatarequests/countries /?t=table&p=2012-06.

114 *The leading Internet companies*: Digital Due Process Coalition, http://www.digital dueprocess.org/.

115 *In 2011, Sonic.net*: Angwin, "Secret Orders Target Email."

115 *By speaking to me, Jasper*: Dane Jasper, correspondence with Lauren Kirchner, September 2, 2013.

115 *As for Yahoo!, in 2008*: Claire Cain Miller, "Secret Court Ruling Put Tech Companies in Data Bind," *New York Times*, June 13, 2013, http://www.nytimes.com/2013/06/14 /technology/secret-court-ruling-put-tech-companies-in-data-bind.html.

115 *Yahoo! argued that the government's*: United States Foreign Intelligence Surveillance Court of Review Case No. 08-01 In Re Directives [redacted text] Pursuant to Section 105B of the Foreign Intelligence Surveillance Act (FISA Ct. Rv. August 22, 2008), http://www.fas.org/irp/agency/doj/fisa/fiscr082208.pdf.

115 *It was the first big Internet*: David Drummond, "Greater Transparency Around Government Requests," *Google Official Blog*, April 20, 2010, http://googleblog.blogspot. com/2010/04/greater-transparency-around-government.html.

115 *And Google is appealing*: Motion for Declaratory Judgment of Google Inc.'s First Amendment Right to Publish Aggregate Information About FISA Orders (FISA Ct. June 18, 2013), http://www.wired.com/images_blogs/threatlevel/2013/06/Foreign -Intelligence-Surveillance-Court-Motion-for-Declaratory-Judgment.pdf.

115 *In 2010, Google launched*: Federal Trade Commission, "FTC Charges Deceptive Privacy Practices in Google's Rollout of its Buzz Social Network," press release, March 30, 2011, http://www.ftc.gov/opa/2011/03/google.shtm.

116 *paid $8.5 million*: Chloe Albanesius, "Google Settles Buzz Class-Action Suit for $8.5M," *PC Magazine*, September 3, 2010, http://www.pcmag.com/article2/0,2817 ,2368714,00.asp.

116 *In 2012, my colleagues*: Julia Angwin and Jennifer Valentino-DeVries, "Google's iPhone Tracking," *Wall Street Journal*, February 17, 2012, http://online.wsj.com/news /articles/SB10001424052970204880404577225380456599176.

116 *Later that year*: Federal Trade Commission, "Google Will Pay $22.5 Million to Settle FTC Charges It Misrepresented Privacy Assurances to Users of Apple's Safari Internet Browser," press release, August 9, 2012, http://ftc.gov/opa/2012/08/google.shtm.

116 *Google agreed to pay $7 million*: Connecticut Attorney General George Jepsen, "Attorney General Announces $7 Million Multistate Settlement with Google Over Street View Collection of WiFi Data," press release, March 12, 2013, http://www.ct .gov/ag/cwp/view.asp?Q=520518&A=2341.

116 *I'd been annoyed*: Alma Whitten, "Updating Our Privacy Policy and Terms of Service," *Google Official Blog*, January 24, 2012, http://googleblog.blogspot.com/2012/01/updating-our-privacy-policies-and-terms.html.

116 *that allowed Google to combine*: Jennifer Valentino-Devries, "What Do Google's Privacy Changes Mean for You?," *Wall Street Journal, Digits* (blog), January 25, 2012, http://blogs.wsj.com/digits/2012/01/25/what-do-googles-privacy-changes-mean-for-you/.

116 *Google also doesn't delete*: Rob Shilkin (Google spokesman), in correspondence with author, July 30, 2013.

117 *It doesn't store any of the information*: DuckDuckGo, Inc., "DuckDuckGo Privacy," accessed August 20, 2013, https://duckduckgo.com/privacy.

118 *"The spread of computers"*: Tim Mullaney, "Jobs Fight: Haves vs. the Have-Nots," *USA Today*, September 16, 2012, http://usatoday30.usatoday.com/money/business/story/2012/09/16/jobs-fight-haves-vs-the-have-nots/57778406/1.

119 *It had principles but few*: Miguel Helft and David Barboza, "Google Shuts Down Site in Dispute over Censorship," *New York Times*, March 22, 2010, http://www.nytimes.com/2010/03/23/technology/23google.html?_r=0.

119 *He told me that*: Gabriel Weinberg (CEO, DuckDuckGo, Inc.), in discussion with author, October 24, 2012.

119 *After selling a social networking*: "United Online, Inc., Acquires Opobox, Inc." (press release), *Houston Chronicle*, March 20, 2006, http://www.chron.com/news/article/PZ-United-Online-Inc-Acquires-Opobox-Inc-1654933.php.

121 *Of course, Google says*: Google, Inc., "Ads in Gmail," accessed September 29, 2013, https://support.google.com/mail/answer/6603?hl=en.

121 *Yes, its computers are*: Glenn Greenwald and James Ball, "The Top Secret Rules That Allow NSA to Use US Data Without a Warrant," *Guardian*, June 20, 2013, http://www.theguardian.com/world/2013/jun/20/fisa-court-nsa-without-warrant.

121 *In 2010, Google fired*: Adrian Chen, "GCreep: Google Engineer Stalked Teens, Spied on Chats," Gawker, September 14, 2010, http://gawker.com/5637234/gcreep-google-engineer-stalked-teens-spied-on-chats.

121 *and said it was the second*: Jason Kincaid, "This Is the Second Time a Google Engineer Has Been Fired for Accessing User Data," TechCrunch, September 14, 2010, http://techcrunch.com/2010/09/14/google-engineer-fired-security/.

121 *In 2008, two former NSA*: Brian Ross, Vic Walter, and Anna Schecter, "Inside Account of U.S. Eavesdropping on Americans," *ABC News*, October 9, 2008, http://abcnews.go.com/Blotter/exclusive-inside-account-us-eavesdropping-americans/story?id=5987804.

121 *Finally, it was a project*: MIT Media Lab, "Immersion: A People-centric View of Your Email Life," accessed August 20, 2013, https://immersion.media.mit.edu/.

122 *I briefly considered running*: Drew Crawford, "NSA-Proof Your E-Mail in 2 Hours," *Sealed Abstract* (blog), June 25, 2013, http://sealedabstract.com/code/nsa-proof-your-e-mail-in-2-hours/.

122 *That left only a few*: Lavabit LLC, https://lavabit.com/, accessed July 2, 2013 (website has since been shut down).

122 *a Texas service that*: Michael Phillips, "How the Government Killed a Secure E-Mail Company," *New Yorker, Elements* (blog), August 8, 2013, http://www.newyorker.com/online/blogs/elements/2013/08/the-government-versus-your-secrets.html.

123 *and Riseup, a service run by*: Riseup.net, "About Us," accessed August 20, 2013, https://help.riseup.net/en/about-us.

123 *But Riseup also stripped out*: "When you send email with riseup.net, your internet address (IP address) is not embedded in the email." Riseup.net, "Riseup Email Help," accessed August 20, 2013, https://help.riseup.net/en/email.

123 *while Lavabit said it*: "The Lavabit e-mail servers do record the IP address used to send an outgoing message in the header of an outgoing e-mail. Because of this, it is possible for the recipient of a message to identify what IP was used to send a message. We record this information in the message header so that law enforcement officials in possession of a message that violates the law can identify the original sender. Lavabit does not retain this information." Accessed July 2, 2013, https://lavabit.com/privacy_policy.html (website has since been shut down).

123 *"We ask that you do not"*: Riseup.net, "Social Contract," https://help.riseup.net/en/social-contract.

123 *Riseup lets users store*: Riseup.net, "Email Storage Quota," https://www.riseup.net/en/quota.

124 *Riseup promises*: Riseup.net, "Privacy Policy," accessed August 20, 2013, https://help.riseup.net/en/privacy-policy.

124 *The 1986 Electronic Communications Privacy Act*: Electronic Communications Privacy Act, 18 USC § 2510–22, https://it.ojp.gov/default.aspx?area=privacy&page=1285.

124 *But Thunderbird's biggest backer, Mozilla*: Mitchell Baker, "Thunderbird: Stability and Community Innovation," *Lizard Wrangling* (blog), July 6, 2012, http://blog.lizardwrangler.com/2012/07/06/thunderbird-stability-and-community-innovation/.

124 *Hewing to my guiding principle*: Postbox, Inc. "Postbox," accessed August 20, 2013, http://www.postbox-inc.com/index.php.

124 *It is worth noting that*: In Re Google Inc. Gmail Litigation, 5:13-md-02430 (N.D. Cal. 2013).

124 *Google argues that there*: Defendant Google Inc.'s Motion to Dismiss Plaintiffs' Consolidated Individual and Class Action Complaint; Memorandum of Points and Authorities in Support Thereof at 19, in re Google Inc. Gmail Litigation, 5:13-md-02430 (N.D. Cal. 2013).

125 *The founder, Ladar Levison*: "Lavabit," https://lavabit.com/, accessed July 2, 2013 (website has since been shut down).

125 *But after some documents*: Nicole Perloth and Scott Shane, "As F.B.I. Pursued Snowden, an E-Mail Service Stood Firm," *New York Times*, October 3, 2013, http://www.nytimes.com/2013/10/03/us/snowdens-e-mail-provider-discusses-pressure-from-fbi-to-disclose-data.html?pagewanted=all&_r=0.

125 *In 2007, Hushmail, a privacy-oriented*: Ryan Singel, "Encrypted E-Mail Company Hushmail Spills to Feds," *Wired*, November 7, 2007, http://www.wired.com/threatlevel/2007/11/encrypted-e-mai/.

126 *But I couldn't help*: Somini Sengupta, "Lavabit Founder Says He Had 'Obligation' to Shut Service," *New York Times*, Bits (blog), August 12, 2013, http://bits.blogs.nytimes.com/2013/08/12/lavabit-founder-says-he-had-obligation-to-shut-service/?_r=0.

126 *"Years of email accounts"*: Ladar Levinson, "My Fellow Users . . . ," Lavabit LLC's Facebook page, August 8, 2013, https://www.facebook.com/permalink.php?story_fbid=529849123730760&id=432285083487165.

126 *After Lavabit shut down*: Jon Callas, "To Our Customers," *Silent Circle Blog*, August 9, 2013, http://silentcircle.wordpress.com/2013/08/09/to-our-customers/.

126 *The Riseup collective posted*: Riseup.net, "Riseup and Government FAQ," accessed August 20, 2013, https://www.riseup.net/en/riseup-and-government-faq.

9. INTRODUCING IDA

127 *Ida Tarbell was*: Kathleen Brady, *Ida Tarbell: Portrait of a Muckraker* (New York: Seaview/Putnam, 1984).

129 *Some studies show that avoiding*: Jeffrey T. Hancock, Michael T. Woodworth, and Saurabh Goorha, "See No Evil: The Effect of Communication Medium and Motivation on Deception Detection," *Group Decision and Negotiation* 19, no. 4 (July 2009): 327–43.

129 *In a 2012 study, Hancock asked 119 college*: Jamie Guillory and Jeffrey T. Hancock, "The Effect of LinkedIn on Deception in Resumes," *Cyberpsychology, Behavior, and Social Networking* 15, no. 3 (February 2012): 135–40.

129 *On the whole, Hancock said*: Jeffrey T. Hancock, "The Future of Lying," lecture, TEDx, Winnipeg, Canada, September 13, 2012, http://www.ted.com/talks/jeff_hancock_3_types_of_digital_lies.html#63003.

129 *In an earlier study, Hancock*: Jeffrey T. Hancock, Catalina Toma, and Nicole Ellison, "The Truth About Lying in Online Dating Profiles," *Proceedings of the SIGCHI Conference on Human Factors in Computing Systems* (New York: ACM, 2007), 449–52, http://dl.acm.org/citation.cfm?doid=1240624.1240697.

129 *Most of the men lied*: Hancock, "The Future of Lying."

129 *In other studies, he found that lies*: Darcy Warkentin, Michael Woodworth, Jeffrey T. Hancock, and Nicole Cormier, "Warrants and Deception in Computer Mediated Communication," *Proceedings of the 2010 ACM Conference on Computer Supported Cooperative Work* (New York: ACM, 2010), 9–12, https://dl.acm.org/citation.cfm?id=1718922.

129 *One of the strongest views on lying*: Immanuel Kant, "On a Supposed Right to Lie from Altruistic Motives (1797)," in *Critique of Practical Reason and Other Writings in Moral Philosophy*, ed. and trans. Lewis Black (Chicago: University of Chicago Press, 1949), 346–50, http://www.mesacc.edu/~davpy35701/text/kant-sup-right-to-lie.pdf.

130 *I found myself attracted*: Sissela Bok, *Lying: Moral Choice in Private and Public Life* (New York: Vintage, 1999), 93.

130 *In 2012, the International Air Transport Association*: International Air Transport Association, "Industry Group Adopts Foundation Standard for New Distribution Capability" (press release), October 19, 2012, http://www.iata.org/pressroom/pr/pages/2012-10-19-02.aspx.

130 *the* New York Times *editorial*: "Frequent Fliers, Prepare to Pay More," *New York Times*, March 3, 2013, http://www.nytimes.com/2013/03/04/opinion/frequent-fliers-prepare-to-pay-more.html.

131 *In 2013, Blue Cross and Blue Shield of North Carolina*: Jen Weiczner, "How the Insurer Knows You Just Stocked Up on Ice Cream and Beer," *Wall Street Journal*, February 25, 2013, http://online.wsj.com/article/SB10001424127887323384604578326151014237898.html.

131 *Maybe it was even the kind*: Paul Myerberg, "Dr. Phil: Tuiasosopo 'romantically in love' with Te'o," *USA Today*, January 30, 2013, http://www.usatoday.com/story/gameon/2013/01/30/dr-phil-ronaiah-tuiasosopo-confused-sexual-identity/1876995/.

132 *He had come to my office*: Jon Callas, in discussion with author, September 5, 2012.

133 *I consulted with Michael Sussmann*: Michael Sussmann, in discussion with author, January 23, 2013.

133 *I sat down, ordered*: "Tor: Overview," Tor Project, accessed October 2, 2013, https://www.torproject.org/about/overview.html.en.

134 *I declined Amazon's offer*: Amazon.com, Inc., "Amazon Betterizer," accessed August 21, 2013, http://www.amazon.com/gp/betterizer.

134 *The first book I ordered*: Herbert N. Foerstel, *Surveillance in the Stacks: The FBI's Library Awareness Program* (Westport, Conn.: Greenwood Press, 1991).

134 *the program that prompted*: American Library Association, "State Privacy Laws Regarding Library Records," http://www.ala.org/offices/oif/ifgroups/stateifcchairs/stateifcinaction/stateprivacy.

135 *American Express says*: Marina Hoffmann Norville (vice president, corporate, financial, and risk public relations at American Express), discussion with Lauren Kirchner, October 4, 2013.

135 *For instance, if I created*: "How Spamgourmet Works," https://spamgourmet.com/.

135 *So I started using*: MaskMe, Abine, Inc., https://www.abine.com/maskme/.

137 *I hoped to buy bitcoins*: "FAQ—Bitcoin," accessed August 21, 2013, https://en.bitcoin.it/wiki/FAQ#How_can_I_get_bitcoins.3F.

137 *Bitcoins can be used on*: Adrian Chen, "The Underground Website Where You Can Buy Any Drug Imaginable," Kotaku.com, June 1, 2011, http://kotaku.com/5805928/the-underground-website-where-you-can-buy-any-drug-imaginable.

137 *In May 2013, Kashmir Hill*: Kashmir Hill, "Living on Bitcoin for a Week: The Journey Begins," Forbes.com, May 1, 2013, http://www.forbes.com/sites/kashmirhill/2013/05/01/living-on-bitcoin-for-a-week-the-journey-begins/.

137 *A digital cash start-up, E-gold*: United States Department of Justice, "Digital Currency E-Gold Indicted for Money Laundering and Illegal Money Transmitting," press release, April 27, 2007, http://www.justice.gov/opa/pr/2007/April/07_crm_301.html.

137 *The following year*: United States Department of Justice, "Digital Currency Business E-Gold Pleads Guilty to Money Laundering and Illegal Money Transmitting Charges," press realease, July 21, 2008, http://justice.gov/opa/pr/2008/July/08_crm_635.html.

137 *And in 2013, federal prosecutors*: Marc Santora, William K. Rashbaum, and Nicole Perlroth, "Online Currency Exchange Accused of Laundering $6 Billion," *New York Times*, May 28, 2013, http://www.nytimes.com/2013/05/29/nyregion/liberty-reserve-operators-accused-of-money-laundering.html?ref=technology.

138 *In 1996, self-proclaimed Internet anarchist*: Declan McCullagh, "Crypto-Convict Won't Recant," Wired.com, April 14, 2000, http://www.wired.com/politics/law/news/2000/04/35620.

138 *Jim Bell posted on an Internet forum*: Jim Bell, "Assassination Politics," Google Groups posting, January 23, 1996, https://groups.google.com/forum/?hl=en#!search/assasination$20politics$20jim$20bell|sort:date/list.libernet/Mo2RIiViYDE/Pp7BMppVDBYJ.

138 *In 1997, IRS agents raided Bell's home*: Associated Press, "Bell Gets 11 Months in Prison, 3 Years Supervised Release, Fine," December 12, 1997, http://cryptome.org/jdb/jimbell7.htm.

139 *They are debts between*: David Graeber, *Debt: The First 5,000 Years* (Brooklyn, N.Y.: Melville House, 2010), 120.

10. POCKET LITTER

140 *I had just arrived in the city*: Julia Angwin, "Secret Orders Target Email," *Wall Street Journal*, October 9, 2011, http://online.wsj.com/article/SB10001424052970203476804576613284007315072.html.

141 *About a year after our meeting*: Ira Hunt, "The CIA's 'Grand Challenges' with Big Data," GigaOM Structure: Data Conference 2013, http://new.livestream.com/accounts/74987/events/1927733/videos/14306067.

141 *But in 2006, the FBI sought*: Declan McCullagh and Anne Broache, "FBI Taps Cell Phone Mic as Eavesdropping Tool," *CNET News*, December 1, 2006, http://news.cnet.com/2100-1029-6140191.html.

142 *The most outrageous example*: "Verizon Forced to Hand Over Telephone Data—Full Court Ruling," *Guardian*, June 5, 2013, http://www.guardian.co.uk/world/interactive/2013/jun/06/verizon-telephone-data-court-order.

142 *President Obama described the program*: Barack Obama, interviewed by Charlie Rose, June 16, 2013, http://www.charlierose.com/watch/60230424.

142 *In 2011, the top U.S. wireless carriers*: Eric Lichtblau, "Wireless Firms Are Flooded by Requests to Aid Surveillance," *New York Times*, July 8, 2013, http://www.nytimes.com/2012/07/09/us/cell-carriers-see-uptick-in-requests-to-aid-surveillance.html?pagewanted=all&_r=0.

142 *As warrantless cell phone tracking*: Julia Angwin and Scott Thurm, "Judges Weigh Phone Tracking," *Wall Street Journal*, November 9, 2011, http://online.wsj.com/article/SB10001424052970203733504577024092345458210.html.

143 *In 2010, the Third Circuit Court of Appeals*: No. 08-4227, "In the Matter of the Application of the United States of America for an Order Directing a Provider of Electronic Communication Service to Disclose Records to the Government," United States Court of Appeals for the Third Circuit, September 7, 2010, https://www.eff.org/files/3d%20Circuit%20Opinion%20%28Cell%20Site%29.pdf.

143 *But in 2013, the Fifth Circuit Court of Appeals*: No. 11-20884, "In Re: Application of the United States of America for Historical Cell Site Data," United States Court of Appeals for the Fifth Circuit, July 30, 2013, http://legaltimes.typepad.com/files/cell-site-5th.pdf.

143 *During World War I*: "The Origination and Evolution of Radio Traffic Analysis: The World War I Era," *Cryptologic Quarterly* (date unknown): 21–40, http://www.nsa.gov/public_info/_files/cryptologic_quarterly/trafficanalysis.pdf.

143 *Prior to the attack on Pearl Harbor*: George Danezis and Richard Clayton, "Introducing Traffic Analysis," January 26, 2007, https://research.microsoft.com/en-us/um/people/gdane/papers/TAIntro-book.pdf.

143 *In 1942, it set up a traffic analysis group*: "The Origination and Evolution of Radio Traffic Analysis."

144 *The goal of a traffic analyst*: Author Redacted, "Computerizing Traffic Analysis," in *A Collection of Writings on Traffic Analysis, Vol. 4: Sources in Cryptologic History*, Center for Cryptologic History, National Security Agency, 1993, 204, http://www.governmentattic.org/8docs/NSA-TrafficAnalysisMonograph_1993.pdf.

144 *In 2004, Hezbollah in Lebanon*: Matt Apuzzo, "Hezbollah Unravels CIA Spy Network in Lebanon," Associated Press, November 21, 2011, http://www.guardian.co.uk/world/feedarticle/9958834.

144 *According to a law enforcement document*: "Retention Periods for Major Cellular Service Providers," U.S. Department of Justice, August 2010, http://www.aclu.org/files/pdfs/freespeech/retention_periods_of_major_cellular_service_providers.pdf.

145 *In 2010, President Obama signed*: S. 30 (111th), "Truth in Caller ID Act of 2009," December 22, 2010, http://www.govtrack.us/congress/bills/111/s30/text.

146 *Harlo Holmes, head of metadata at the Guardian Project*: Harlo Holmes, e-mail correspondence with author, May 19, 2013.

147 *Depressed, I called Moxie Marlinspike*: Moxie Marlinspike, in discussion with author, March 20, 2013.

148 *In 2003, a Boston company called Skyhook*: Julia Angwin and Jennifer Valentino-Devries, "Apple, Google Collect User Data," *Wall Street Journal*, April 20, 2011, http://online.wsj.com/article/SB10001424052748703983704576277101723453610.html.

148 *In 2010, the privacy investigative*: Scott Thurm and Yukari Iwatani Kane, "Your Apps Are Watching You," *Wall Street Journal*, December 17, 2010, http://online.wsj.com/article/SB10001424052748704694004576020083703574602.html.

149 *Some companies placed the equipment in*: Anton Troianovski, "New Wi-Fi Pitch: Tracker," *Wall Street Journal*, June 18, 2012, http://online.wsj.com/article/SB10001424052702303379204577474961075248008.html.

149 *One London marketing company*: Siraj Datoo, "This Recycling Bin Is Following You," *Quartz*, August 8, 2013, http://qz.com/112873/this-recycling-bin-is-following-you/.

149 *(The company stopped)*: Zachary M. Seward and Siraj Datoo, "City of London Halts Recycling Bins Tracking Phones of Passers-by," *Quartz*, August 12, 2013, http://qz.com/114174/city-of-london-halts-recycling-bins-tracking-phones-of-passers-by/.

149 *Kaveh Memari, the CEO of Renew*: Datoo, "This Recycling Bin Is Following You."

149 *In 2012, Verizon launched*: Verizon Wireless, "Our Measurement Solutions," http://business.verizonwireless.com/content/b2b/en/precision/our-measurement-solutions.html.

149 *In 2013, AT&T said it would also*: AT&T, "Our Updated Privacy Policy," June 28, 2013, http://www.attpublicpolicy.com/privacy/our-updated-privacy-policy-2/.

149 *spawning conferences such as Location Intelligence*: Location Intelligence Conference, http://www.locationintelligence.net/.

149 *the Geoweb Summit*: Geoweb Summit, http://geowebsummit.com/.

149 *Location Business Summit USA*: Location Business Summit USA, http://www.mformobile.com/location-business-summit-usa/.

149 *the Signal conference in Chicago in 2012*: Signal: Chicago, http://www.federatedmedia.net/events/11/.

149 *a location analysis company*: JiWire, http://jiwire.com/audience.

149 *"Where you are says"*: David Staas (CEO, JiWire), "Using Location Patterns to Power Big Data on Mobile," Signal Conference, September 11, 2012, Chicago, Illinois, http://link.brightcove.com/services/player/bcpid1450672650001?bckey=AQ~~,AAAAFktgNgk~,QKA7V92zyumLLIZb3v45LGr2NPanaTlq&bclid=1826428698001&bctid=1843067500001.

149 *"We cannot and never will receive"*: Will Smith, correspondence to Al Franken, March 28, 2013, http://www.franken.senate.gov/files/docs/130328_Euclid.pdf.

150 *to Senator Al Franken of Minnesota*: "Sens. Franken, Blumenthal Introduce Bill to Protect Consumer Privacy on Mobile Devices" (press release), June 15, 2011, http://www.franken.senate.gov/?p=press_release&id=1587.

150 *Euclid helps retailers to identify shoppers*: Will Smith, correspondence to Al Franken, March 28, 2013.

150 *But the truth is that location*: Yves-Alexandre de Montjoye, César A. Hidalgo, Michel Verelysen, and Vincent D. Blondel, "Unique in the Crowd: The Privacy Bounds of Human Mobility," *Scientific Reports* 3, no. 1376 (March 2013).

150 *Researchers at Microsoft found*: Adam Sadilek and John Krumm, "Far Out: Predict-
    ing Long-Term Human Mobility," Association for the Advancement of Artificial
    Intelligence, 2012, https://research.microsoft.com/en-us/um/people/jckrumm/Pub
    lications%202012/Sadilek-Krumm_Far-Out_AAAI-2012.pdf.

150 *adding _nomap to the end of the name*: "Greater Choice for Wireless Access Point
    Owners," Google, Inc., *Official Blog*, November 14, 2011, http://googleblog.blogspot
    .com/2011/11/greater-choice-for-wireless-access.html.

151 *Such bags are called "Faraday cages"*: Geeta Dayal, "QuickStudy: Faraday Cages,"
    Computerworld, August 23, 2006, http://www.computerworld.com/s/article
    /9002661/Faraday_cages?pageNumber=1.

151 *Since then, Faraday cages*: "Faraday Cages in Health Care," TNO Prevention and
    Health, http://web.archive.org/web/20060324100513/http://www.tno.nl/kwaliteit
    _van_leven/preventie_en_zorg/kwaliteit_in_de_zorg/faraday_cages_in_health_c
    /046.pdf.

151 *When I told John Strauchs*: John Strauchs, in discussion with author, March 5, 2013.

152 *Tall and lanky, Adam*: Adam Harvey, in discussion with author, April 19, 2013.

152 *It would reduce the signal*: Adam Harvey, in correspondence with author, August 12,
    2013.

11. OPTING OUT

153 *its privacy policy states*: LinkedIn Corp., "Privacy Policy: LinkedIn," accessed May
    21, 2013, http://www.linkedin.com/legal/privacy-policy. Language has since
    changed.

153 *LinkedIn says*: Doug Madey (corporate communications associate for LinkedIn
    Corp.), in e-mail correspondence with Lauren Kirchner, September 12, 2013.

154 *"They still could not stand to see"*: Dan Ariely, *Predictably Irrational: The Hidden
    Forces That Shape Our Decisions* (New York: Harper Perennial, 2009), 150.

154 *"They still had the same irrational"*: Ibid., 147.

154 *I consulted two experts*: Author in discussion with Alex Bennert on February 26,
    2013, and Rhea Drysdale on March 11, 2013.

154 *A website whose passwords had been hacked*: Elinor Mills, "LinkedIn Confirms Pass-
    words Were 'Compromised,'" *CNET*, June 6, 2012, http://news.cnet.com/8301-1009
    _3-57448465-83/linkedin-confirms-passwords-were-compromised/.

154 *LinkedIn said that after*: LinkedIn Corp., "Privacy Policy: LinkedIn."

155 *"A public display of connections"*: Judith Donath and Danah Boyd, "Public Displays
    of Connection," *BT Technology Journal* 22, no. 4 (October 2004): 73, http://www.
    danah.org/papers/PublicDisplays.pdf.

155 *Scientists have found that people*: Nalini Ambady and Robert Rosenthal, "Thin Slices
    of Expressive Behavior as Predictors of Interpersonal Consequences: A Meta-
    Analysis," *Psychological Bulletin* 111, no. 2 (1992): 256, http://ambadylab.stanford
    .edu/pubs/1992Ambady.pdf.

155 *Online photos are notoriously misleading*: Lauren F. Sessions, "'You Looked Better
    on MySpace': Deception and Authenticity on Web 2.0," *First Monday* 14, no. 7 (July
    6, 2009), http://firstmonday.org/ojs/index.php/fm/article/view/2539/2242#4a.

155 *Donath . . . has done fascinating work*: Judith S. Donath, "Identity and Deception
    in the Virtual Community," in *Communities in Cyberspace* (New York: Routledge,
    1999), 27.

155 *For example, consider the "femme fatale"*: Ibid., 54.

155 *"Potential rivals or mates need not"*: Ibid., 30.

155 *If an unknown person is a friend of my friend*: Donath and Boyd, "Public Displays of Connection," 72.

155 *But the pressure to create*: Judith Donath, in discussion with author, April 4, 2013.

156 *Todesco deleted her Facebook account during*: Gaebriella Todesco, in discussion with author, December 7, 2011.

156 *"There was nothing to do but go on"*: Gaebriella Todesco, in discussion with author, January 23, 2013.

156 *Before a breakup*: Gaebriella Todesco, e-mail to author, March 21, 2013.

156 *In the fall of her senior year*: Todesco, in discussion with author, December 7, 2011.

157 *"I realized that if I had been on Facebook"*: Todesco, in discussion with author, January 23, 2013.

158 *when Sean Lane bought*: Ellen Nakashima, "Feeling Betrayed, Facebook Users Force Site to Honor Their Privacy," *Washington Post*, November 30, 2007, http://www.washingtonpost.com/wp-dyn/content/article/2007/11/29/AR2007112902503.html.

158 *In 2009, Facebook agreed*: Juan Carlos Perez, "Facebook Will Shut Down Beacon to Settle Lawsuit," IDG News Service, September 18, 2009, http://www.pcworld.com/article/172272/facebook_will_shut_down_beacon_to_settle_lawsuit.html.

158 *Facebook revived it in 2011*: Rob Pegoraro, "Facebook 'Sponsored Stories' Turn You into the Ad," *Washington Post*, January 27, 2011, http://voices.washingtonpost.com/fasterforward/2011/01/facebook_sponsored_stories_tur.html.

158 *Facebook agreed to pay $20 million*: Dan Levine, "U.S. Judge Approves Facebook Privacy Settlement over Ads," Reuters, August 26, 2013, http://www.reuters.com/article/2013/08/26/net-us-facebook-privacy-settlement-idUS BRE97P0VG20130826.

158 *Facebook simply added new language*: Jessica Guynn, "Facebook under Fire from Privacy Watchdogs over 'Sponsored Stories' Ads," *Los Angeles Times*, September 4, 2013.

158 *Google has since joined the fray*: Alexei Oreskovic, "Google Unveils Plans for User Names, Comments to Appear in Ads," Reuters, October 14, 2013, http://www.reuters.com/article/2013/10/14/net-us-google-ads-idUSBRE99A0S720131014.

158 *Facebook suddenly made changes to its privacy policy*: Ruchi Sanghvi, "New Tools to Control Your Experience," *Facebook Blog*, December 9, 2009, http://blog.facebook.com/blog.php?post=196629387130.

158 *Outraged, I wrote a column*: Julia Angwin, "How Facebook Is Making Friending Obsolete," *Wall Street Journal*, December 15, 2009, http://online.wsj.com/article/SB126084637203791583.html.

158 *Facebook later agreed to settle charges*: Federal Trade Commission, "Facebook Settles FTC Charges That It Deceived Consumers by Failing to Keep Privacy Promises," November 29, 2011, http://www.ftc.gov/opa/2011/11/privacysettlement.shtm.

159 *I dug around in Facebook's privacy settings*: "Data Use Policy," Facebook, last revised December 11, 2012, https://www.facebook.com/full_data_use_policy.

160 *I learned that lesson the hard way*: Julia Angwin, "How Are You? No, How Are You Really?" *Wall Street Journal*, June 16, 2009, http://online.wsj.com/article/SB1 24510254756316521.html.

161 *For the big data brokers*: Catalog Choice, TrustedID, https://www.catalogchoice.org/.

162 *For the lookup sites, I signed up for*: Abine Inc., "DeleteMe—Protect Your Personal Data and Reputation Online," accessed May 21, 2013, http://www.abine.com/deleteme/landing.php.

162   *I called Jim Adler*: Jim Adler, in discussion with author, April 10, 2013.

162   *When I contacted Abine*: Sarah Downey, in discussion with author, April 12, 2013.

162   *USA People Search doesn't accept*: USA People Search, "Privacy Policy Highlights," May 7, 2013, http://www.usa-people-search.com/privacy.aspx.

162   *"That's one of the reasons why I've"*: Sarah Downey, e-mail to author, May 13, 2013.

163   *A spokeswoman for Catalog Choice said*: Lyn Chitow Oakes (TrustedID Catalog Choice spokeswoman), e-mails with author, July 29, 2013.

163   *I didn't feel comfortable*: Free Phone Tracer, http://www.freephonetracer.com/.

163   *It stated*: MyLife.com, Inc., "Public Profile FAQ's," accessed May 21, 2013, http://www.mylife.com/faq.pub.

164   *It seemed particularly underhanded*: PeopleSmart.com, "How We're Different," accessed October 4, 2013, http://www.peoplesmart.com/difference.

164   *Its website describes the company as*: Inflection LLC, "Careers," accessed May 21, 2013, http://inflection.com/careers/.

164   *To his credit, the company's*: Matthew Monahan, e-mail to author, May 6, 2013.

164   *One day later, he sent a detailed*: Matthew Monahan, e-mail to author, May 7, 2013.

164   *"There's no mal-intent here"*: Matthew Monahan, in discussion with author, May 14, 2013.

165   *Intelius claimed to include ninety million cell phone numbers*: M. Alex Johnson, "Cell Phone Directory Rings Alarm Bells," *NBC News*, January 30, 2008, http://www.nbcnews.com/id/22902400/.

165   *A few months later, Intelius shut down*: Suzanne Choney, "Company Shuts Down Cell Phone Directory," *NBC News*, February 1, 2008, http://www.nbcnews.com/id/22956815/.

165   *In 2012, Ancestry.com bought Archives.com*: Inflection LLC, "Inflection Sells Archives.com to Ancestry.com Inc.," PR Newswire, April 25, 2012, http://www.prnewswire.com/news-releases/inflection-sells-archivescom-to-ancestrycom-inc-148969015.html.

165   *"I just feel like our work is not done"*: Matthew Monahan, in discussion with author, May 14, 2013.

12. THE HALL OF MIRRORS

167   *When Rayne Puertos started a new job*: Rayne Puertos, in discussion with author, February 12, 2013.

167   *In 2013, there were 328*: "The State of Data Collection on the Web," 2013 Krux Cross Industry Study.

168   *Ashley Hayes-Beaty was shocked*: Julia Angwin, "The Web's New Gold Mine: Your Secrets," *Wall Street Journal*, July 30, 2010, http://online.wsj.com/article/SB10001424052748703940904575395073512989404.html.

168   *And Google accurately identified a dozen*: Steve Stecklow, "On the Web, Children Face Intensive Tracking," *Wall Street Journal*, September 17, 2010, http://online.wsj.com/article/SB10001424052748703904304575497903523187146.html.

168   *In 2006, the New York Times*: Michael Barbaro and Tom Zeller Jr., "A Face Is Exposed for AOL Searcher No. 4417749," *New York Times*, August 9, 2006, http://www.nytimes.com/2006/08/09/technology/09aol.html?_r=0&gwh=2CACC912D19D87BDFD3A39B96C429022.

168   *In 2008, researchers at the University of Texas*: Arvind Narayanan and Vitaly Shma-

tikov, "Robust De-anonymization of Large Sparse Datasets," *Security and Privacy* (2008): 111–25, http://www.cs.utexas.edu/~shmat/shmat_oak08netflix.pdf.

168 *In 2012, my* Wall Street Journal *team*: Jennifer Valentino-Devries and Jeremy Singer-Vine, "They Know What You're Shopping For," *Wall Street Journal*, December 7, 2012, http://online.wsj.com/article/SB10001424127887324784404578143144132736214.html.

169 *But Professor Ryan Calo of the University of Washington*: M. Ryan Calo, "Digital Market Manipulation," Research Paper No. 2013–27, University of Washington School of Law, August 15, 2013, http://papers.ssrn.com/sol3/papers.cfm?abstract_id=2309703.

170 *In one experiment, researchers at Carnegie Mellon*: Laura Brandimarte, Alessandro Acquisti, and George Loewenstein, "Misplaced Confidences: Privacy and the Control Paradox," Social Psychological and Personality Science, August 9, 2012. http://spp.sagepub.com/content/early/2012/08/08/1948550612455931.abstract.

170 *Calo says that market*: Calo, "Digital Market Manipulation."

170 *Benjamin Reed Shiller, an economics*: Benjamin Reed Shiller, "First Degree Price Discrimination Using Big Data" (Working Paper Series, Brandeis University, August 20, 2013), http://www.brandeis.edu/departments/economics/RePEc/brd/doc/Brandeis_WP58R.pdf.

170 *Incognito mode is privacy protection*: Google, Inc., "Incognito Mode (Browse in Private)," google.com, accessed August 22, 2013, https://support.google.com/chrome/answer/95464?hl=en.

171 *My next stop was the advertising industry's*: "Consumer Opt-Out," Network Advertising Initiative, http://www.networkadvertising.org/choices/.

171 *Even then, the industry's list*: 2013 Krux Cross Industry Study.

171 *The first, Adblock Plus*: Adblock Plus, https://adblockplus.org/.

171 *The second, NoScript*: NoScript Firefox extension, Inform Action, Open Source Software, noscript.net.

172 *Google's online advertising*: DoubleClick by Google, accessed March 28, 2013, http://www.google.com/doubleclick/.

172 *a company that boasts*: "Data Drives Everything," AddThis, accessed March 28, 2013, http://www.addthis.com/data.

172 *ConvergeTrack, which describes*: ConvergeDirect, accessed March 28, 2013, http://www.convergedirect.com/technology/convergetrack/.

172 *Bazaarvoice, which says it*: "Join the Bazaarvoice Network," accessed March 28, 2013, http://www.bazaarvoice.com/.

172 *Coremetrics*: "IBM Product Recommendations," accessed March 28, 2013, http://www-03.ibm.com/software/products/us/en/personalized-product-recommendations/.

172 *I asked FreshDirect*: Sarah Promisloff, e-mail to author, June 27, 2013.

173 *Reading FreshDirect's privacy policy*: "Privacy Policy," FreshDirect, LLC, accessed August 22, 2013, https://www.freshdirect.com/help/privacy_policy.jsp.

173 *In 1995, Daniel Jaye*: Dan Jaye, in discussion with author, May 6, 2010.

174 *Engage was part of a conglomerate*: Paul C. Judge, "David Wetherell: Internet Evangelist," *BusinessWeek*, October 25, 1999, http://www.businessweek.com/1999/99_43/b3652001.htm.

174 *CMGI's losses had reached $1 billion*: Keith Regan, "Fallen Dot-Com Star CMGI Drops Stadium Deal," *E-Commerce Times*, August 6, 2002, http://www.ecommercetimes.com/story/commerce/18904.html.

174 *Meanwhile, Dan figured that*: Dan Jaye, in discussion with author, May 6, 2010.

175 *Soon, online tracking was*: Kate Kaye, "Tacoda Buy Could Bolster AOL Relevance in Web Ad Arena," *Clickz*, July 24, 2007, http://www.clickz.com/clickz/news/1712324 /tacoda-buy-could-bolster-aols-relevance-web-ad-arena.

175 *Google paid $3.1 billion*: Paul R. La Monica, "Google to Buy DoubleClick for $3.1 Billion," *CNN Money*, April 13, 2007, http://money.cnn.com/2007/04/13/technology /google_doubleclick/index.htm.

175 *Microsoft paid $6 billion*: Chris Isidore, "Microsoft Buys aQuantive for $6 Billion, Pays 85% Premium," *CNN Money*, May 18, 2007, http://money.cnn.com/2007/05/18 /technology/microsoft_aquantive/.

175 *Online auction houses such*: Lauren Bell, "New Online Data Company BlueKai Strives for Quality, Privacy," *Direct Marketing News*, September 15, 2008, http:// www.dmnews.com/new-online-data-company-bluekai-strives-for-quality-privacy /article/116668/.

175 *Each day, BlueKai sells eighteen million*: AdAge, "Custom Programs: BlueKai," accessed October 5, 2013, http://brandedcontent.adage.com/adnetworkguide10/network.php ?id=20.

175 *for as little as a tenth of a cent apiece*: Julia Angwin, "The Web's New Gold Mine: Your Secrets," *Wall Street Journal*, July 30, 2010, http://online.wsj.com/article/SB100 01424052748703940094575395073512989404.html.

175 *Online–off-line matching is why Linda Twombly*: Emily Steel, "A Web Pioneer Profiles Users by Name" *Wall Street Journal*, October 25, 2010, http://online.wsj.com /article/SB10001424052702304410504575560243259416072.html.

176 *Dan worried that this development*: Dan Jaye, in discussion with author, May 6, 2010.

176 *"When you're in the business of slinging"*: Ibid.

176 *Google is said to be developing*: Alistair Barr, "Google May Ditch 'Cookies' as Online Ad Tracker," *USA Today*, September 17, 2013, http://www.usatoday.com/story/tech /2013/09/17/google-cookies-advertising/2823183/.

176 *"If you don't want anybody"*: Adam Tanner, "The Web Cookie Is Dying. Here's the Creepier Technology That Comes Next," *Forbes*, June 17, 2013, http://www.forbes .com/sites/adamtanner/2013/06/17/the-web-cookie-is-dying-heres-the-creepier -technology-that-comes-next/.

176 *A company called FaceFirst*: FaceFirst Retail Brochure, FaceFirst, LLC.

177 *A retail executive who requested anonymity*: Chris Trlica, "Facial Recognition: A Game-Changing Technology for Retailers," *LP Magazine*, May–June 2013, http:// www.lpportal.com/feature-articles/item/2482-facial-recognition-a-game-changing -technology-for-retailers.html.

177 *"Build a database of good customers"*: FaceFirst Retail Brochure.

177 *I wasn't going to wear a baseball cap*: "How to Make an Infrared Mask to Hide Your Face from Cameras," WonderHowTo, posted by Amie, http://mods-n-hacks.won derhowto.com/how-to/make-infrared-mask-hide-your-face-from-cameras-201280/.

178 *or an anti-drone hoodie*: Adam Harvey, "Exhibition: Stealth Wear: New Designs for Counter Surveillance," *Primitive London*, January 4, 2013, http://www.primitivelon don.co.uk/exhibition-adam-harvey-stealth-wear-new-designs-for-counter-surveil lance-presented-by-primitive-london-and-tank-magazine/.

178 *So I called Ashkan Soltani*: Ashkan Soltani, in discussion with author, March 29, 2013.

179 *Ashkan showed me the setting*: For the nerds: Ashkan also showed me two small tweaks to make in my browser that involved bypassing a warning that said, "Chang-

ing these advanced settings can be harmful to the stability, security, and performance of this application." Those tricks were: I enabled "Click_to_play," which disables plugins until I choose to play them, and I set "network.http.sendReferer-Header = 0," which strips referer headers when browsing the Internet, so that websites I visit don't know which website I just arrived from.

179 *In 2009, an entrepreneur named*: David Cancel, "The Future of Ghostery," *David Cancel* (blog), January 19, 2010, http://davidcancel.com/the-future-of-ghostery/.

179 *In 2010, he sold it to an advertising services*: Adam DeMartino, "Better Advertising Acquires Ghostery," *The Evidon Blog*, January 19, 2010, http://www.evidon.com/blog/better-advertising-acquires-ghostery.

180 *one of the most comprehensive lists*: There are some other crowd-sourced comprehensive lists—such as the EasyPrivacy list that can be added to AdblockPlus—https://easylist-downloads.adblockplus.org/easyprivacy.txt. (As of October 5, 2013, the list included 8,376 items.)

180 *of tracking technologies*: Andy Kahl, in discussion with author, May 30, 2013.

180 *Brian Kennish, an engineer at Google*: Julia Angwin, "Wall Street Journal Privacy Series Inspires One Start-Up," *Wall Street Journal, Digits* (blog), February 27, 2011, http://blogs.wsj.com/digits/2011/02/27/wall-street-journal-privacy-series-inspires-one-start-up/.

181 *So that evening, Kennish went home*: Alexia Tsotsis, "Google Engineer Builds Facebook Disconnect," *TechCrunch*, October 20, 2010, http://techcrunch.com/2010/10/20/google-facebook-disconnec/.

181 *Within two weeks, his free software*: Angwin, "One Start-Up."

181 *In December, he launched a free program*: Alexia Tsotsis, "Former Googler Launches Disconnect, Browser Extension That Disables Third Party Data Tracking," *TechCrunch*, December 13, 2010, http://techcrunch.com/2010/12/13/former-googler-launches-disconnect-browser-extension-that-disables-third-party-data-tracking/.

181 *In October 2011, he raised $600,000*: Rip Empson, "Disconnect: Ex-Googlers Raise Funding to Stop Google, Facebook & More from Tracking Your Data," *TechCrunch*, March 22, 2012, http://techcrunch.com/2012/03/22/disconnect-me-raise/.

181 *And they had a dashboard of statistics*: Brian Kennish, in discussion with author, August 16, 2012.

182 *"I think that might be why I'm into data"*: Ibid.

13. LONELY CODES

185 *First, I downloaded free encryption software*: "The GNU Privacy Guard," Free Software Foundation, Inc., http://gnupg.org/.

185 *a program called Enigmail*: "A Simple Interface to OpenPGP Email Security," The Enigmail Project, https://www.enigmail.net/home/index.php.

185 *designed to run with*: GnuPG, "GnuPG Frequently Asked Questions," http://www.gnupg.org/faq/GnuPG-FAQ.html.

185 *The Postbox support page said*: Postbox, Inc., "Extending Postbox," http://www.postbox-inc.com/extensions.

185 *The Enigmail support forums said*: SourceForge, Inc., "PostBox 3.0.7 and Enigmail 1.2.3 Freezing Problem" (forum), http://sourceforge.net/p/enigmail/forum/support/thread/bfd56f75/?limit=25#1d58.

185 *I had eagerly downloaded*: "The CrytpoParty handbook," Version: 2013-08-21, http://www.cryptoparty.in/documentation/handbook.

186 *Snowden apparently used the Lavabit address*: Danny Yadron, "Snowden's Email Service Shuts," *Wall Street Journal, Digits* (blog), August 8, 2013, http://blogs.wsj .com/digits/2013/08/08/snowdens-email-service-shuts/; and "Snowden to Meet with Human Rights Groups in Moscow," Novinvite.com, July 12, 2013, http://www .novinite.com/view_news.php?id=151966.

186 *I posted my key "fingerprint"*: Author's website "Angwin GPG Key," posted July 11, 2013, http://juliaangwin.com/contact/ed06b6f6/.

187 *"I really dislike using GPG"*: Christopher Soghoian, in discussion with author, June 5, 2013.

187 *Robinson showed me*: David Robinson, in discussion with author, June 6, 2013.

187 *"I don't trust my ability to use"*: Karl Fogel, "Karl Fogel's GPG Public Key," November 22, 2010, http://www.red-bean.com/kfogel/public-key.html.

187 *In 2010, Immigration and Customs Enforcement investigators*: Susan Stellin, "The Border Is a Back Door for U.S. Device Searches," *New York Times*, September 9, 2013, http://www.nytimes.com/2013/09/10/business/the-border-is-a-back-door-for-us -device-searches.html.

188 *House sued the Department of Homeland Security*: "U.S. Settles Lawsuit with Bradley Manning Supporter Who Had Laptop Seized at Airport," ACLU.org (press release), https://www.aclu.org/free-speech/us-settles-lawsuit-bradley-manning-supporter -who-had-laptop-seized-airport.

188 *Consider the story of Husain Abdulla*: Vernon Silver, "Cyber Attacks on Activists Traced to FinFisher Spyware of Gamma," Bloomberg.com, July 25, 2012, http://www .bloomberg.com/news/2012-07-25/cyber-attacks-on-activists-traced-to-finfisher- spyware-of-gamma.html.

189 *After months of painstaking examination*: Nicole Perlroth, "Software Meant to Fight Crime Is Used to Spy on Dissidents," *New York Times*, August 20, 2012, http://www .nytimes.com/2012/08/31/technology/finspy-software-is-tracking-political-dissi dents.html?ref=technology&_r=0.

189 *Gamma told Bloomberg that*: Vernon Silver, "Gamma Says No Spyware Sold to Bahrain; May Be Stolen Copy," Bloomberg, July 27, 2012, http://www.bloomberg.com /news/2012-07-27/gamma-says-no-spyware-sold-to-bahrain-may-be-stolen-copy .html.

189 *In October 2011, my colleague*: Jennifer Valentino-DeVries, Julia Angwin, and Steve Stecklow, "Document Trove Exposes Surveillance Methods," *Wall Street Journal*, November 19, 2011, http://online.wsj.com/article/SB1000142405297020361140457704 4192607407780.html.

189 *We published much of the literature online*: "The Surveillance Catalog," *Wall Street Journal*, updated February 7, 2012, http://projects.wsj.com/surveillance-catalog/.

189 *The brochure for Gamma Group's FinSpy*: *Remote Monitoring and Infection Solutions*, FinSpy (brochure), FinFisher, Gamma Group, *The Surveillance Catalog*, *Wall Street Journal*, http://projects.wsj.com/surveillance-catalog/documents/267841 -merged-finspy/.

189 *"FinSpy is a field-proven Remote Monitoring Solution"*: "Remote Control System: Cyber Intelligence Made Easy," HackingTeam, *The Surveillance Catalog*, *Wall Street Journal*, http://projects.wsj.com/surveillance-catalog/documents/267005-hacking-team -remote-control-system/#document/p3/a38816.

190 *Jerry Lucas, the organizer of the Wiretapper's Ball, told us*: Valentino-Devries, Angwin, and Stecklow, "Document Trove Exposes Surveillance Methods."

190 *In June 2007, for instance, the FBI obtained*: Declan McCullagh, "FBI Remotely

Installs Spyware to Trace Bomb Threat," *CNET*, July 18, 2007, http://news.cnet.com /8301-10784_3-9746451-7.html#!.

190 *Judge Stephen Smith, the Texas magistrate*: "In Re Warrant to Search a Target Computer at Premises Unknown," Case no. H-13-234M (S.D. Tex. 2013), http://files .cloudprivacy.net/Order%20denying%20warrant.MJ%20Smith.042213.pdf.

190 *that have the capacity to pull in roughly 75 percent*: Siobhan Gorman and Jennifer Valentino-Devries, "New Details Show Broader NSA Surveillance Reach," *Wall Street Journal*, August 20, 2013, http://online.wsj.com/article/SB1000142412788732410820 4579022874091732470.html.

190 *In a 2009 memo revealed by Edward Snowden*: Eric Holder, "Minimization Procedures Used by the National Security Agency in Connection with Acquisitions of Foreign Intelligence Information Pursuant to Section 702 of the Foreign Intelligence Surveillance Act of 1978, as Amended," July 28, 2004, https://s3.amazonaws.com/s3 .documentcloud.org/documents/716634/exhibit-b.pdf.

191 *"I don't trust any crypto in the public realm"*: William Binney, in discussion with author, March 18, 2012.

191 *One night I met the three*: William Binney, Thomas Drake, and Kirk Wiebe, in discussion with author, May 24, 2012.

191 *Off-the-Record was created in 2004*: Nikita Borisov, Ian Goldberg, and Eric Brewer, "Off-the-Record Communication, or, Why Not to Use PGP," 2004, http://www .cypherpunks.ca/otr/otr-wpes.pdf; and Brian Whitley, "Students Develop Encryption for Instant Messaging," *Daily Californian*, February 22, 2005, http://www.cypher punks.ca/otr/press/www.dailycal.org/article.php%3fid=17720.html.

191 *Off-the-Record helps solve the problem*: Borisov, Goldberg, and Brewer, "Off-the-Record Communication, or, Why Not to Use PGP."

192 *(Tails) operating system*: "Documentation," Tails, https://tails.boum.org/doc/index .en.html.

192 *At his military court proceedings*: Bradley Manning, "Bradley Manning's Statement Taking Responsibility for Releasing Documents to WikiLeaks," February 28, 2013, http://www.bradleymanning.org/news/bradley-mannings-statement-taking -responsibility-for-releasing-documents-to-wikileaks.

192 *He was betrayed by a friend*: Kevin Poulsen and Kim Zetter, "U.S. Intelligence Analyst Arrested in Wikileaks Video Probe," *Wired, Threat Level* (blog), June 6, 2010, http://www.wired.com/threatlevel/2010/06/leak/.

192 *Government investigators later found traces*: Eva Blum-Dumontet, "Bradley Manning Legal Proceedings: Fact Sheet," *WikiLeaks Press*, March 31, 2012, http:// wikileaks-press.org/bradley-manning-legal-procedures-fact-sheet/.

192 *that has any paid staff*: "Core Tor People," The Tor Project, https://www.torproject .org/about/corepeople.html.en.

192 *Jabber is run by volunteers*: "Notices," Jabber, Inc., http://www.jabber.org/notices .html.

193 *Off-the-Record is a volunteer project*: Off-the-Record Messaging, "The OTR Development Team," http://www.cypherpunks.ca/otr/people.php.

193 *It turned out he was*: Evan Schoenberg, in discussion with author, November 25, 2012.

193 *When the antinuclear activist Phil Zimmermann*: Phil Zimmermann, "Creator of PGP and Zfone: Background," Philzimmermann.com (personal blog), http://www .philzimmermann.com/EN/background/index.html.

193 *The software I was using*: "The GNU Privacy Guard," GnuPG, http://gnupg.org/.

193 *On March 9, 1993, Eric Hughes published*: Eric Hughes, "A Cypherpunk's Manifesto," March 9, 1993, http://www.activism.net/cypherpunk/manifesto.html.

194 *The U.S. Customs Service began investigating whether*: Phil Zimmermann, "Testimony of Philip R. Zimmermann to the Subcommittee on Science, Technology, and Space of the US Senate Committee on Commerce, Science, and Transportation," philzimmermann.com (personal blog), June 26, 1996, http://www.philzimmermann.com/EN/testimony/.

194 *In 1996, however, the government dropped*: Phil Zimmermann, "Significant Moments in PGP's History: Zimmermann Case Dropped" philzimmermann.com (personal blog), January 12, 1996, http://www.philzimmermann.com/EN/news/PRZ_case_dropped.html.

194 *And in 1999, the United States dropped*: Jeri Clausing, "White House Eases Export Controls on Encryption," *New York Times*, September 17, 1999, http://www.nytimes.com/library/tech/99/09/biztech/articles/17encrypt.html.

194 *It developed the "Clipper chip" to encrypt*: John Markoff, "Technology; Wrestling over the Key to the Codes," *New York Times*, May 9, 1993, http://www.nytimes.com/1993/05/09/business/technology-wrestling-over-the-key-to-the-codes.html.

194 *copies of the encryption keys*: Steven Levy, "Battle of the Clipper Chip," *New York Times*, June 12, 1994, http://www.nytimes.com/1994/06/12/magazine/battle-of-the-clipper-chip.html?pagewanted=all&src=pm.

194 *In 1994, Matt Blaze at AT&T Bell Labs*: Matt Blaze, in discussion with author, May 8, 2013.

194 *"It is insufficient to protect ourselves"*: Bruce Schneier, *Applied Cryptology: Protocols, Algorithms, and Source Code in C* (New York: Wiley, 1996).

194 *The Cypherpunks built "remailers"*: Steve Lohr, "Technology; Privacy on Internet Poses Legal Puzzle," *New York Times*, April 19, 1999, http://www.nytimes.com/1999/04/19/business/technology-privacy-on-internet-poses-legal-puzzle.html.

194 *the largest remailer*: Peter H. Lewis, "Computer Jokes and Threats Ignite Debate on Anonymity," *New York Times*, December 31, 1994, http://www.nytimes.com/1994/12/31/us/computer-jokes-and-threats-ignite-debate-on-anonymity.html?pagewanted=all&src=pm.

194 *shut down rather than comply with a court order*: Dave Mandl, "Life After Penet: The Remailer Is Dead, Long Live the Remailer," *Village Voice*, October 8, 1996, http://wfmu.org/~davem/docs/penet.html; and Peter H. Lewis, "Behind an Internet Message Service's Close," *New York Times*, September 6, 1996, http://www.nytimes.com/1996/09/06/business/behind-an-internet-message-service-s-close.html.

194 *By 2000, Bruce Schneier issued a correction*: Bruce Schneier, *Secrets & Lies: Digital Security in a Networked World* (New York: Wiley, 2000).

195 *"aggressive, multipronged effort to break"*: Nicole Perlroth, Jeff Larson, and Scott Shane, "N.S.A. Able to Foil Basic Safeguards of Privacy on Web," *New York Times*, September 5, 2013, http://www.nytimes.com/2013/09/06/us/nsa-foils-much-internet-encryption.html.

195 *"Trust the math"*: Bruce Schneier, "NSA Surveillance: A Guide to Staying Secure," *Guardian*, September 6, 2013, https://www.schneier.com/essay-450.html.

195 *Julian Assange, a longtime Cypherpunk, transformed*: Raffi Khatchadourian, "No Secrets: Julian Assange's Mission for Total Transparency," *New Yorker*, June 7, 2010, http://www.newyorker.com/reporting/2010/06/07/100607fa_fact_khatchadourian?currentPage=all.

195 *Moxie Marlinspike in San Francisco built encryption apps*: Moxie Marlinspike, in discussion with author, March 20, 2013.

195 *Nathan Freitas and the Guardian Project*: Nancy Scola, "The Guardian Project: Building Mobile Security for a Dangerous World," *Personal Democracy Plus, Tech President* (blog), March 31, 2011, http://techpresident.com/blog-entry/guardian -project-building-mobile-security-dangerous-world.

195 *The U.S. government funded some projects*: Moody, Famiglietti & Andronico, *The TOR Project, Inc. and Affiliate, Consolidated Financial Statements and Reports Required for Audits in Accordance with Government Auditing Standards and OMB Circular A-133*, December 31, 2011, and 2010, https://www.torproject.org/about /findoc/2011-TorProject-Amended-Final-Report.pdf.

195 *while at the same time the Justice Department*: Julia Angwin, "Secret Orders Target Email," *Wall Street Journal*, October 9, 2011, http://online.wsj.com/article/SB100014 24052970203476804576613284007315072.html?mod=WSJ_whattheyknow2011_ LeftTopNews.

195 *He sold PGP to Network Associates*: Jamie Beckett, "New Company's Fast Start / Network Associates Buys Software Firm for $36 Million," *San Francisco Chronicle*, December 2, 1997, http://www.sfgate.com/business/article/New-Company-s-Fast -Start-Network-Associates-2792220.php.

195 *And in 2012, he joined with*: Nicole Perlroth, "Security Pioneer Creates Service to Encrypt Phone Calls and Text Messages," *New York Times, Bits* (blog), February 5, 2013, http://bits.blogs.nytimes.com/2013/02/05/security-pioneer-creates-service-to -encrypt-phone-calls-and-text-messages/.

196 *cofounder Mike Janke told me*: Mike Janke, in discussion with author, November 5, 2012.

196 *This meant passing key information*: Jon Callas, in discussion with author, April 5, 2013.

14. FIGHTING FEAR

199 *The American Academy of Pediatrics recommends*: Daniel D. Broughton, "Keeping Kids Safe in Cyberspace," *AAP News*, August 1, 2005, http://aapnews.aappublica tions.org/content/26/8/11.full.

199 *The FBI recommends that parents use*: "A Parent's Guide to Internet Safety," *Federal Bureau of Investigation Publications*, http://www.fbi.gov/stats-services/publications /parent-guide.

200 *The Department of Homeland Security suggests*: Stop.Think.Connect. (pamphlet), Department of Homeland Security, http://www.dhs.gov/xlibrary/assets/stc/stc-chat ting-with-kids-printable.pdf.

200 *The rate of violent crime declined*: "Table 1: Crime in the United States by Volume and Rate per 100,000 Inhabitants, 1990–2009," Federal Bureau of Investigation, http://www2.fbi.gov/ucr/cius2009/data/table_01.html.

200 *Murders are down 83 percent*: *CompStat Report Covering the Week 9/16/2013 Through 9/22/2013*, Police Department of the City of New York, http://www.nyc.gov/html /nypd/downloads/pdf/crime_statistics/cscity.pdf.

200 *The city had the second-lowest*: Anthony M. Destefano, "FBI Crime Stats Mixed for NYC," *Newsday*, June 13, 2013, http://www.newsday.com/news/new-york/fbi-crime -stats-mixed-for-nyc-1.5479442; and *Crime in the United States 2012*, Federal Bureau of Investigation, http://www.fbi.gov/about-us/cjis/ucr/crime-in-the-u.s/2012/crime -in-the-u.s.-2012.

200 *Sexual abuse of children plummeted*: David Finkelhor and Lisa Jones, "Have Sexual Abuse and Physical Abuse Declined Since the 1990s?," Crimes Against Children Research Center, November 2012, http://www.unh.edu/ccrc/pdf/CV267_Have %20SA%20%20PA%20Decline_FACT%20SHEET_11-7-12.pdf.

200 *Other studies show that bullying*: David Finkelhor, "Trends in Bullying and Peer Victimization," Crimes Against Children Research Center, January 2013, http://cola .unh.edu/sites/cola.unh.edu/files/CV280_Bullying_Peer_Victimization_Bulletin _1-23-13_with_toby_edits.pdf.

200 *Teen suicide*: "Teen Homicide, Suicide and Firearm Deaths," Child Trends Data Bank, http://www.childtrends.org/?indicators=teen-homicide-suicide-and-firearm -deaths.

200 *and teen pregnancy*: "Teen Births," Child Trends DataBank, http://childtrends.org /?indicators=teen-births.

201 *"juvenoia"*: David Finkelhor, "The Internet, Youth Safety and the Problem of 'Juvenoia,'" Crimes Against Children Research Center, January 2011, http://www .unh.edu/ccrc/pdf/Juvenoia%20paper.pdf.

201 *A landmark 1975 study*: Mark R. Lepper and David Greene, "Turning Play into Work: Effects of Adult Surveillance and Extrinsic Rewards on Children's Intrinsic Motivation," *Journal of Personality and Social Psychology* 31, no. 3 (1975): 479–86, http://www.jwalkonline.org/docs/Grad%20Classes/Fall%2007/Org%20Psy/Cases /motivation%20articles/PERUSED/effects%20of%20surveillance.pdf.

202 *it began threatening to delete our photos*: David Lazarus, "Precious Photos Disappear," *San Francisco Chronicle*, February 2, 2005, http://www.sfgate.com/business /article/Precious-photos-disappear-2734149.php.

203 *The law required websites to get parental permission*: "Title XIII—Children's Online Privacy Protection Act of 1998," Federal Trade Commission, http://www.ftc.gov/ogc /coppa1.htm.

203 *In 2013, the law was updated*: Anton Troianovski and Danny Yadron, "U.S. Expands Child Online Privacy Law to Cover Apps, Social Networks," *Wall Street Journal*, December 19, 2012, http://online.wsj.com/article/SB1000142412788732377204578189430101877770.html.

203 *In 2011, researchers led by Microsoft's Danah Boyd*: Danah Boyd, "Why Parents Help Children Violate Facebook's 13+ Rule," *Apophenia* (blog), November 1, 2011, http:// www.zephoria.org/thoughts/archives/2011/11/01/parents-survey-coppa.html.

204 *The researchers concluded*: Danah Boyd, Eszter Hargittai, Jason Schultz, and John Palfrey, "Why Parents Help Their Children Lie to Facebook About Age: Unintended Consequences of the 'Children's Online Privacy Protection Act,'" *First Monday* 16, no. 11 (November 7, 2011), http://journals.uic.edu/ojs/index.php/fm /article/view/3850/3075.

204 *The Family Educational Rights and Privacy Act of 1974*: "FERPA General Guidance for Parents," U.S. Department of Education, http://www2.ed.gov/policy/gen/guid /fpco/ferpa/parents.html.

204 *send student data to an outside data storage center*: Corrinne Lestch and Ben Chapman, "New York Parents Furious at Program, inBloom, That Compiles Private Student Information for Companies That Contract with It to Create Teaching Tools," *New York Daily News*, March 13, 2013, http://www.nydailynews.com/new -york/student-data-compiling-system-outrages-article-1.1287990; and "Our Vision: Personal Path, Common Ground," inBloom, https://www.inbloom.org /our-vision.

204 *"teachers take on the role of coaches"*: Darrell M. West, "Using Technology to Personalize Learning and Assess Students in Real-Time," Brookings Institution, October 6, 2011, http://www.brookings.edu/~/media/research/files/papers/2011/10/06%20personalize%20learning%20west/1006_personalize_learning_west.pdf.

204 *could start paying $2 to $5 per kid*: Leonie Haimson, "NYC Parent Sounds Alarm on Student Privacy," WNYC.org, July 23, 2013, http://www.wnyc.org/story/307074-what-you-need-know-about-inbloom-student-database/; and Adam Gaber (inBloom spokesman), in correspondence with Lauren Kirchner, August 29, 2013.

204 *"organizations conducting studies"*: "FERPA General Guidance for Parents," U.S. Department of Education, http://www2.ed.gov/policy/gen/guid/fpco/ferpa/parents.html.

204 *InBloom, which is a nonprofit*: Natasha Singer, "Deciding Who Sees Students' Data," *New York Times*, October 5, 2013, http://www.nytimes.com/2013/10/06/business/deciding-who-sees-students-data.html?pagewanted=all&_r=0.

205 *eighteen-year-old Justin Carter of Texas, who was arrested*: Doug Gross, "Teen in Jail for Months over 'Sarcastic' Facebook Threat," CNN.com, July 3, 2013, http://edition.cnn.com/2013/07/02/tech/social-media/facebook-threat-carter/index.html; and Jennifer Carter, "Release My Son Justin Carter—Being Prosecuted for a Facebook Comment," Change.org, https://www.change.org/petitions/release-my-son-justin-carter-being-prosecuted-for-a-facebook-comment.

205 *He was arrested and charged*: Brandon Griggs, "Teen Jailed for Facebook 'Joke' Is Released," CNN.com, July 12, 2013, http://www.cnn.com/2013/07/12/tech/social-media/facebook-jailed-teen/index.html.

205 *an anonymous donor posted the $500,000 bail*: Pulin Modi, "Statement from Justin's Lawyer," Change.org, July 12, 2013, https://www.change.org/petitions/release-my-son-justin-carter-being-prosecuted-for-a-facebook-comment.

205 *In January 2012, two British tourists were detained*: Richard Hartley-Parkinson, "'I'm Going to Destroy America and Dig Up Marilyn Monroe': British Pair Arrested in U.S. on Terror Charges over Twitter Jokes," *Daily Mail*, January 31, 2012, http://www.dailymail.co.uk/news/article-2093796/Emily-Bunting-Leigh-Van-Bryan-UK-tourists-arrested-destroy-America-Twitter-jokes.html.

205 *On September 9, 2009, Joe Lipari had*: Julius Motal, "Charges Dropped over Facebook Apple Rant," *PC Magazine*, June 28, 2011, http://www.pcmag.com/article2/0,2817,2387730,00.asp.

205 *They searched his house for explosives*: Joe Lipari, in discussion with author, July 23, 2013.

205 *A 2012 survey of teens*: Mary Madden, Amanda Lenhart, Sandra Cortesi, and Urs Gasser, "Teens and Mobile Apps Privacy," Pew Research Center's Internet & American Life Project, August 22, 2013, http://pewinternet.org/Reports/2013/Teens-and-Mobile-Apps-Privacy.aspx.

205 *The study also found that 70 percent*: Amanda Lenhart, Mary Madden, Sandra Cortesi, Urs Gasser, and Aaron Smith, "Where Teens Seek Online Privacy Advice," Pew Research Center's Internet & American Life Project, August 15, 2013, http://pewinternet.org/Reports/2013/Where-Teens-Seek-Privacy-Advice.aspx.

206 *according to interviews with 163 teens*: Danah Boyd and Alice Marwick, "Social Privacy in Networked Publics: Teens' Attitudes, Practices, and Strategies" (paper presented at Oxford Internet Institute's "A Decade in Internet Time: Symposium on the Dynamics of the Internet and Society"), September 22, 2011, http://www.danah.org/papers/2011/SocialPrivacyPLSC-Draft.pdf.

209 *the Ghostery app*: Ghostery, Evidon, Inc., https://itunes.apple.com/us/app/ghostery /id472789016?mt=8.

209 *Disconnect Kids*: "Introducing Disconnect Kids!," Disconnect, https://www.discon nect.me/kids.

15. AN UNFAIRNESS DOCTRINE

211 *when black students in Greensboro, North Carolina*: "The Greensboro Chronology," International Civil Rights Center & Museum, http://www.sitinmovement.org/his tory/greensboro-chronology.asp.

212 *In 1969, a chocolate-brown oil slick*: "American's Sewage System and the Price of Optimism," *Time*, August 1, 1969, http://content.time.com/time/magazine/article /0,9171,901182,00.html.

212 *It was not the first time that debris*: Jonathan H. Adler, "Fables of the Cuyahoga: Reconstructing a History of Environmental Protection," *Fordham Environmental Law Journal* 14 (2003): 89–146.

212 *The air is cleaner*: "Highlights from the Clean Air Act 40th Anniversary Celebration," United States Environmental Protection Agency, http://www.epa.gov/air/caa /40th_highlights.html.

212 *The water is cleaner*: Nancy Stoner, "Celebrate the 40th Anniversary of the Clean Water Act," *It's Our Environment* (blog), U.S. EPA, October 18, 2012, http://blog.epa .gov/blog/2012/10/cwa40/.

212 *Endangered species have been saved*: John R. Platt, "The Endangered Species Act at 40: Forty Things Journalists Should Know," *Society of Environmental Journalists*, July 15, 2013, http://www.sej.org/publications/sejournal-su13/endangered-species -act-40.

212 *Now there are more than forty*: Michael Scott and James Owens, "2009 Year of the River," *Cleveland Plain Dealer*, January 4, 2009, http://blog.cleveland.com/metro /2009/01/04CGRIVER.pdf.

212 *even a few freshwater mussels*: Michael Scott, "Freshwater Mussels Found in Cuyahoga River, Indicating Improved Water Quality," *Cleveland Plain Dealer*, August 22, 2009, http://www.cleveland.com/science/index.ssf/2009/08/freshwater _mussels_found_in_cu.html.

213 *To understand the links*: Dennis Hirsch, in discussion with author, July 26, 2011.

213 *as portrayed in Garrett Hardin's*: Garrett Hardin, "The Tragedy of the Commons," *Science* 162, no. 3859 (December 13, 1968): 1423–48, http://www.sciencemag.org/ content/162/3859/1243.full.

213 *"The risk here is that eventually"*: Dennis Hirsch, in discussion with author, July 26, 2011.

214 *This is the argument put forth*: David Brin, *The Transparent Society* (New York: Basic Books, 1999).

214 *Brin argues that*: David Brin and Ben Goertzel, "David Brin on the Path to Positive Sousveillance," *h+*, May 23, 2011, http://hplusmagazine.com/2011/05/23/david-brin -on-the-path-to-positive-sousveillance/.

214 *a police officer who pepper-sprayed nonviolent*: "Cop Who Pepper-Sprayed Students at Occupy Protest Wants Worker's Compensation for 'Psychiatric Injury,'" Associated Press, July 26, 2013, http://talkingpointsmemo.com/news/pepper-spray-cop -occupy-protest-wants-workers-compensation-for-psychiatric-injury.php.

214 *In 2010, the actor George Clooney*: "Our Story," Satellite Sentinel Project, http://www .satsentinel.org/our-story.

214 *In May 2013, Clooney*: "Broken Agreement: Violations in the Demilitarized Border Zone by Sudan and South Sudan," Satellite Sentinel Project, May 2013, http://www .satsentinel.org/sites/default/files/Broken_Agreement.pdf.

214 *Snowden's revelations of the intelligence agencies'*: Barton Gellman and Greg Miller, "U.S. Spy Network's Successes, Failures and Objectives Detailed in 'Black Budget' Summary," *Washington Post*, August 29, 2013, http://www.washingtonpost.com /world/national-security/black-budget-summary-details-us-spy-networks-successes-failures-and-objectives/2013/08/29/7e57bb78-10ab-11e3-8cdd-bcdc09410972 _story.html.

214 *an accurate count of the civilians killed in the Iraq*: David Leigh, "Iraq War Logs Reveal 15,000 Previously Unlisted Civilian Deaths," *Guardian*, October 22, 2010, http://www.theguardian.com/world/2010/oct/22/true-civilian-body -count-iraq.

214 *and Afghanistan wars*: David Leigh, "Afghanistan War Logs: Secret CIA Paramilitaries' Role in Civilian Deaths," *Guardian*, July 25, 2010, http://www.theguardian .com/world/2010/jul/25/afghanistan-civilian-deaths-rules-engagement.

215 *In 2013, Manning was sentenced to*: Paul Lewis, "Bradley Manning Given 35-Year Prison Term for Passing Files to WikiLeaks," *Guardian*, August 21, 2013, http:// www.theguardian.com/world/2013/aug/21/bradley-manning-35-years-prison -wikileaks-sentence.

215 *Snowden obtained temporary political asylum*: Alec Luhn, Luke Harding, and Paul Lewis, "Edward Snowden Asylum: US 'Disappointed' by Russian Decision," *Guardian*, August 1, 2013, http://www.theguardian.com/world/2013/aug/01/edward -snowden-asylum-us-disappointed.

215 *In 2013, the Justice Department informed*: Devlin Barrett, "U.S. Seized Phone Records of AP Staff," *Wall Street Journal*, May 13, 2013, http://online.wsj.com/article /SB10001424127887324715704578481461374133612.html.

215 *"We regard this action"*: Gary Pruitt (president and CEO of the Associated Press), "Updated: AP Responds to Latest DOJ Letter," May 14, 2013, http://blog.ap.org/2013 /05/13/ap-responds-to-intrusive-doj-seizure-of-journalists-phone-records/.

215 *And the Department of Justice is pushing for*: Scott Shane, "Prosecutors Press Subpoena for Times Reporter in Leak Case," *New York Times*, August 26, 2013, http:// www.nytimes.com/2013/08/27/us/prosecutors-press-subpoena-for-times-reporter -in-leak-case.html?_r=0.

215 *Risen has said that he will go*: Charlie Savage, "Court Tells Reporter to Testify in Case of Leaked C.I.A. Data," *New York Times*, July 19, 2013, http://www.nytimes .com/2013/07/20/us/in-major-ruling-court-orders-times-reporter-to-testify.html ?pagewanted=all.

215 *A few start-ups have popped up*: Julia Angwin and Emily Steel, "Web's Hot New Commodity: Privacy," *Wall Street Journal*, February 28, 2011, http://online.wsj.com/ article/SB10001424052748703529004576160764037920274.html.

215 *the World Economic Forum declared*: World Economic Forum, *Personal Data: The Emergence of a New Asset Class* (report), January 2011, http://www3.weforum.org /docs/WEF_ITTC_PersonalDataNewAsset_Report_2011.pdf.

216 *An analysis by the* Financial Times: Emily Steel, "Financial Worth of Data Comes In at Under a Penny a Piece," *Financial Times*, June 12, 2013, http://www.ft.com/intl /cms/s/0/3cb056c6-d343-11e2-b3ff-00144feab7de.html?siteedition=intl#axzz 2dglKkHpd.

216 *In one experiment, Acquisti*: Alessandro Acquisti, Leslie K. John, and George

Loewenstein, "What Is Privacy Worth?" *Journal of Legal Studies* 42, no. 2 (June 2013): 249–74, http://www.jstor.org/stable/10.1086/671754.

216 *"What this tells us"*: Alessandro Acquisti, in discussion with author, March 11, 2011.

217 *health*: "Health Information Privacy," U.S. Department of Health and Human Services, http://www.hhs.gov/ocr/privacy/hipaa/understanding/index.html.

217 *finance*: "Privacy Act Issues Under Gramm-Leach-Bliley," Federal Deposit Insurance Corporation, http://www.fdic.gov/consumers/consumer/alerts/glba.html.

217 *children*: Title XIII—Children's Online Privacy Protection, http://www.ftc.gov/ogc/coppa1.pdf.

217 *government records*: The Privacy Act of 1974, http://www.justice.gov/opcl/privstat.htm

217 *The Children's Online Privacy Protection Act*: Title XIII.

217 *Or consider the Health Insurance*: "Health Information Privacy," US DHHS.

217 *It also prohibits the sale of*: "Memo on *Sorrell v. IMS Health Inc.*" (memo), Center for Democracy & Technology, March 22, 2011, https://www.cdt.org/files/pdfs/20110324_SorrellvIMS.pdf.

217 *Vermont tried to ban the sale of*: Sorrell v. IMS Health Inc., 131 S. Ct. 2653, 180 L. Ed. 2d 544 (June 23, 2011), http://www2.bloomberglaw.com/public/desktop/document/Sorrell_v_IMS_Health_Inc_131_S_Ct_2653_180_L_Ed_2d_544_2011_Court.

217 *Or consider the Federal Privacy Act*: Julia Angwin, "U.S. Terrorism Agency to Tap a Vast Database of Citizens," *Wall Street Journal*, December 13, 2012, http://online.wsj.com/article/SB10001424127887324478304578171623040640006.html.

217 *But, instead of seeking consent*: "Privacy: Congress Should Consider Alternatives for Strengthening Protection of Personally Identifiable Information," Government Accountability Office, June 18, 2008, http://www.gao.gov/assets/130/120411.html.

217 *failed to prevent*: Angwin, "U.S. Terrorism Agency to Tap a Vast Database of Citizens."

218 *In 2009, Gulet Mohamed, a U.S. citizen*: Gulet Mohamed v. Eric Holder, Robert Mueller, Timothy Healy et al., Third Amended Complaint, August 29, 2013 (E.D. Va.); and Mark Mazzetti, "Detained American Says He Was Beaten in Kuwait," *New York Times*, January 5, 2011, http://www.nytimes.com/2011/01/06/world/middleeast/06detain.html?_r=3&hp&.

218 *Instead, the government argues that*: Gulet Mohamed v. Eric Holder Jr. and Janet Napolitano, No. 11-1924, Consolidated Reply in Support of Motion to Dismiss and Opposition to Cross-Motion for Remand, January 2013.

218 *Travelers who are denied boarding can*: "DHS Traveler Redress Inquiry Program (DHS TRIP)," U.S. Department of Homeland Security, http://www.dhs.gov/dhs-trip.

218 *However, the department is not required to offer*: Latif et al. v. Holder et al., No. 11-35407, D.C. No. 3:10-cv-00750-BR, Opinion, http://aclu-or.org/sites/default/files/ACLU_OR_No_Fly_9th_Circuit.pdf.

218 *Mohamed claims that by denying*: Gulet Mohamed v. Eric Holder, Robert Mueller, Timothy Healy et al., Third Amended Complaint.

219 *The European Union requires companies to provide*: European Parliament, Council, "Directive 95/46/EC of the European Parliament and of the Council of 24 October 1995 on the Protection of Individuals with Regard to the Processing of Personal Data and on the Free Movement of Such Data," http://eur-lex.europa.eu/LexUriServ/LexUriServ.do?uri=CELEX:31995L0046:en:NOT.

219 *In 2011, Senators John McCain and John Kerry proposed*: "S. 779—Commercial Privacy Bill of Rights Acts of 2011," 112th Cong., April 12, 2011, http://www.opencon gress.org/bill/112-s799/text.

219 *by both privacy advocates*: "Consumer Groups Welcome Bipartisan Privacy Effort, But Warn Kerry-McCain Bill Insufficient to Protect Consumers' Online Privacy," Center for Digital Democracy, April 18, 2011, http://www.democraticmedia.org /consumer-groups-welcome-bipartisan-privacy-effort-warn-kerry-mccain-bill -insufficient-protect-consum.

219 *and data brokers*: "Senators Kerry and McCain Introduce Privacy Bill; Legislation Could Undercut Information Economy," Direct Marketing Association, April 12, 2011, http://www.the-dma.org/cgi/disppressrelease?article=1479+++++.

219 *and failed to make progress*: "S. 779—Commercial Privacy Bill of Rights Acts of 2011, Actions & Votes," 112th Cong., April 12, 2011, http://www.opencongress.org /bill/112-s799/actions_votes.

219 *In 2012, the Obama administration declared*: "We Can't Wait: Obama Administration Unveils Blueprint for a 'Privacy Bill of Rights' to Protect Consumers Online" (press release), White House Office of the Press Secretary, February 23, 2012, http:// www.whitehouse.gov/the-press-office/2012/02/23/we-can-t-wait-obama-adminis tration-unveils-blueprint-privacy-bill-rights.

219 *One of the most successful methods*: Fair Credit Reporting Act, http://www.ftc.gov/os /statutes/031224fcra.pdf.

219 *says its scores are used to "evaluate"*: Natasha Singer, "Secret E-Scores Chart Consumers' Buying Power," *New York Times*, August 18, 2012, http://www.nytimes.com /2012/08/19/business/electronic-scores-rank-consumers-by-potential-value.html ?pagewanted=all.

220 *Federal Trade commissioner Julie Brill has advocated*: Julie Brill, "Reclaim Your Name" (keynote address, 23rd Computers Freedom and Privacy Conference, Washington, D.C., June 26, 2013), http://www.ftc.gov/speeches/brill/130626computers freedom.pdf.

220 *"whether we are too risky"*: Julie Brill, "Demanding Transparency from Data Brokers," *Washington Post*, August 15, 2013, http://www.washingtonpost.com/opinions /demanding-transparency-from-data-brokers/2013/08/15/00609680-0382-11e3 -9259-e2aafe5a5f84_story_1.html.

220 *When it comes to government surveillance*: A good analysis of government dragnets comes from Christopher Slobogin: Christopher Slobogin, "Government Dragnets" (Vanderbilt Public Law research paper number 10–37, July 14, 2010), http://ssrn.com /abstract=1640108.

220 *We rejected airport body scanners*: Mike M. Ahlers, "TSA Removing 'Virtual Strip Search' Body Scanners," CNN.com, January 19, 2013, http://www.cnn.com/2013/01 /18/travel/tsa-body-scanners/index.html.

220 *We do not embed tracking microchips*: "California Bans Forced RFID Tagging of Humans," *Government Technology*, October 17, 2007, http://www.govtech.com/secu rity/California-Bans-Forced-RFID-Tagging-of.html?topic=117688.

220 *In 2013, Judge Shira Scheindlin*: *David Floyd, Lalit Clarkson, Deon Dennis, and David Ourlicht v. the City of New York*, 08 Civ. 1034 (SAS) (S.D. N.Y. 2013), http:// www.nyclu.org/files/releases/Floyd%20opinion.pdf.

221 *In 1944, the Supreme Court ruled*: *Korematsu v. United States*, 323 U.S. 214 (1944), http://supreme.justia.com/cases/federal/us/323/214/case.html.

221 *Every year, the Environmental Protection Agency publishes*: Toxics Release Inventory

(TRI) Program, United States Environmental Protection Agency, http://www2.epa .gov/toxics-release-inventory-tri-program.

221 *"Everybody wants to avoid being high"*: Lisa Heinzerling, in discussion with author, March 15, 2013.

221 *This is the essence of an argument raised*: Slobogin, "Government Dragnets."

ACKNOWLEDGMENTS

Nonfiction books are group projects that are marketed as the work of an individual. This book, in particular, owes its existence to a veritable village of collaborators and coconspirators.

The village, of course, starts with my family. My husband and children were gracious enough to participate in my privacy experiments and patiently tolerated my round-the-clock work on this project. My parents, my brother, and his fiancée swept in with crucial support at key moments in the writing process. My in-laws provided unending love and support. My definition of family also includes the women who have held my hand through every part of this journey, and without whom I would be lost. They would like to be known as Hedy Lamarr, Hildy Johnson, and George Eliot. Blessings and love to all of my family.

I also relied heavily on my family of coconspirators at the *Wall Street Journal*, past and present, who joined me on this lengthy and improbable reporting journey—of which the book is only one piece. Without Jennifer Valentino-DeVries, Ashkan Soltani, Emily Steel, Jesse Pesta, Jeremy Singer-Vine, and Scott Thurm, none of this would have been possible. Special thanks to Kevin Delaney, Rebecca Blumenstein, Mike Williams, and Alix Freedman, who nourished my vision from the beginning.

One of the most pleasant surprises of this journey was discovering a welcoming community of academic researchers who had been working for years to navigate this emerging digital terrain and who eagerly shared their findings with me. I owe a lot to their collective body of work. In particular, my deepest gratitude and thanks to Ryan Calo, Danielle Citron, and Daniel Weitzner, who were my first readers and provided indispensable insights on my drafts. I am also in debt to Julie Brill, Paul Ohm, Alessandro Acquisti, Susan Freiwald, Katherine Strandburg, Chris Hoofnagle, Rachel Levinson-Waldman, Christopher Slobogin, Gary Bruce, and Lisa Sotto, whose work and guidance particularly influenced my thinking.

I also received a warm welcome from the far-flung community of hackers around the world. Without their work, we would not know where our data was going, nor would we have any tools to protect it. Among the many who have guided my work and thinking are Ashkan Soltani, Dave Campbell, Jacob Appelbaum, Brian Kennish, Jon Callas, Michael J. J. Tiffany, Mike Perry, Christopher Soghoian, Dan Kaminsky, and Jonathan Mayer. Special thanks to John Gilmore, who offered my first window into this world so many years ago and whose story I still hope to tell in the fullness that it deserves.

I also was lucky that my publishing village was run by excellent leaders. My agent, Todd Shuster, was my savior on many fronts—but most importantly by urging me to make the book more personal. The team at Holt—Stephen Rubin, Paul Golob, Emi Ikkanda, Patricia Eisemann, Maggie Richards, and Leslie Brandon—were insightful and encouraging. I cannot sing the praises highly enough of my research assistants, Lauren Kirchner, Courtney Schley, Neena Lall, and my fact-checker Ben Kalin. They burned the midnight oil on far too many occasions and shared my passion for accuracy.

Finally, I would like to thank everybody who trusted me with their life stories—most especially Bilal Ahmed, Sharon Gill, Yasir Afifi, and Bill Binney. It is no small thing to entrust your narrative to another, and I hope that I managed to paint honest and sensitive portraits.

INDEX

ABOUT THE AUTHOR

JULIA ANGWIN is the author of *Stealing MySpace* and an award-winning investigative journalist for the independent news organization ProPublica. From 2000 to 2013 she was a staff reporter for *The Wall Street Journal*, where she was on the team of reporters awarded the 2003 Pulitzer Prize for coverage of corporate corruption and led a team covering online privacy that was a finalist for a 2012 Pulitzer Prize. She lives in New York City with her husband and two children.